T0191982

Lecture Notes in Computer Science   **13419**

More information about this series at https://link.springer.com/bookseries/558

Jérôme Durand-Lose · György Vaszil (Eds.)

Machines, Computations, and Universality

9th International Conference, MCU 2022
Debrecen, Hungary, August 31 – September 2, 2022
Proceedings

 Springer

Editors
Jérôme Durand-Lose 🄳
Université d'Orléans
Orléans, France

György Vaszil 🄳
University of Debrecen
Debrecen, Hungary

ISSN 0302-9743   ISSN 1611-3349 (electronic)
Lecture Notes in Computer Science
ISBN 978-3-031-13501-9   ISBN 978-3-031-13502-6 (eBook)
https://doi.org/10.1007/978-3-031-13502-6

This Springer imprint is published by the registered company Springer Nature Switzerland AG
The registered company address is: Gewerbestrasse 11, 6330 Cham, Switzerland

Preface

This volume contains the papers presented at MCU 2022, the 9th Conference on Machines, Computations and Universality, held during August 31 – September 2, 2022, at the Faculty of Informatics of the University of Debrecen, Hungary. This edition was co-located with the 24th International Conference on Descriptional Complexity of Formal systems (DCFS 2022) and the 12th International Workshop on Non-Classical Models of Automata and Applications (NCMA 2022).

The MCU series of international conferences traces its roots back to the mid-1990s, and has since been concerned with gaining a deeper understanding of computation through the study of models of general purpose computation. MCU explores computation in the setting of various discrete models (Turing machines, register machines, cellular automata, tile assembly systems, rewriting systems, molecular computing models, neural models, concurrent systems, etc.) and analog and hybrid models (BSS machines, infinite time cellular automata, real machines, quantum computing, etc.). There is a particular (but not exclusive) emphasis given to the following:

- The search for frontiers between decidability and undecidability in the various models. (For example, what is the smallest number of pairs of words for which the Post correspondence problem is undecidable, or what is the largest state-symbol product for which the halting problem is decidable for Turing machines?)
- The search for the simplest universal models (such as small universal Turing machines, universal rewriting systems with few rules, universal cellular automata with small neighborhoods and a small number of states, etc.).
- The computational complexity of predicting the evolution of computations in the various models. (For example, is it possible to predict an arbitrary number of time steps for a model more efficiently than explicit step by step simulation of the model?)
- Universality and undecidability in continuous models of computation.

Previous MCU conferences took place in Fontainebleau, France (2018), Famagusta, North Cyprus (2015), Zürich, Switzerland (2013), Orléans, France (2007), Saint Petersburg, Russia (2004), Chisinău, Moldova (2001), Metz, France (1998), and Paris, France (1995).

There were 18 papers submitted to this edition of MCU, all in the scope of the conference, and each submission was reviewed by three Program Committee members. The committee decided to accept 10 papers for presentation and publication in these proceedings.

The program included four invited talks.

- **Enrico Formenti** from the University of Côte d'Azur, France, presented in "Complexity of local, global and universality properties in finite dynamical systems" some complexity bounds for the case when such systems are presented as their evolution graph. Some results of universality for simulation on some classes were provided.

- **Mika Hirvensalo** from the University of Turku, Finland, presented how quantum computation can be improved by taking advantage of wave-particle dualism in "Using Interference to Boost Computing".
- **Hava T. Siegelmann** from the University of Massachusetts at Amherst, USA, explained how to handle and benefit from ever learning AI in "Super Turing Computing Enables Lifelong Learning AI".
- **Bianca Truthe** from the University of Gießen, Germany, provided "A Survey on Computationally Complete Accepting and Generating Networks of Evolutionary Processors". In this model, each processor is assigned the fixed task to add, remove, or change a single symbol on strings which move from one processor to another according to filters.

The conference was held in hybrid mode with the possibility of in-person and online presentation. More information on MCU 2022 can be found at https://konferencia.uni deb.hu/en/mcu-2022.

We would like to thank everybody in the organizing committee who worked hard to make this edition successful.

Partial financial support for the conference was provided by the Department of Computer Science and by the Faculty of Informatics of the University of Debrecen.

The editors warmly thank the Program Committee, the organizers, the invited speakers, the authors of the papers, the external reviewers, and all the participants for their contribution to the success of the conference.

June 2022   Jérôme Durand-Lose
                                                                          György Vaszil

Organization

Program Committee

Artiom Alhazov	Academy of Sciences of Moldova, Moldova
Pablo Arrighi	University of Paris-Saclay, France
Nathalie Aubrun	CNRS and University of Paris-Saclay, France
Péter Battyányi	University of Debrecen, Hungary
Erzsébet Csuhaj-Varjú	Eötvös Loránd University, Hungary
Jérôme Durand-Lose (Co-chair)	University of Orléans, France
Henning Fernau	University of Trier, Germany
Rudolf Freund	Technical University of Vienna, Austria
Kaoru Fujioka	Fukuoka Women's University, Japan
Christine Gaßner	University of Greifswald, Germany
Daniela Genova	University of North Florida, USA
Peter Leupold	University of Bremen, Germany
Maurice Margenstern	University of Lorraine, France
Kenichi Morita	Hiroshima University, Japan
Benedek Nagy	Eastern Mediterranean University, North Cyprus
Agustín Riscos-Núñez	University of Seville, Spain
Shinnosuke Seki	University of Electro-Communications, Japan
Petr Sosík	Silesian University in Opava, Czech Republic
Kumbakonam Govindarajan Subramanian	University of Science Malaysia, Malaysia
György Vaszil (Co-chair)	University of Debrecen, Hungary
Sergey Verlan	University of Paris-Est Créteil, France

Steering Committee

Jérôme Durand-Lose (Chair)	University of Orléans, France
Erzsébet Csuhaj-Varjú	Eötvös Loránd University, Hungary
Nataša Jonoska	University of South Florida, USA
Maurice Margenstern	University of Metz, France
Kenichi Morita	Hiroshima University, Japan
Benedek Nagy	Eastern Mediterranean University, Cyprus
Kumbakonam Govindarajan Subramanian	University of Science Malaysia, Malaysia
Sergey Verlan	University of Paris-Est Créteil, France

Additional Reviewers

Giovanni Pighizzini   University of Milan, Italy
Sang-Ki Ko   Kangwon National University, South Korea
Antonio E. Porreca   University of Aix-Marseille, France
Zornitza Prodanoff   University of North Florida, USA
Kostia Chardonnet   University of Paris-Saclay, France

Organizing Committee

Péter Battyányi   University of Debrecen, Hungary
Bence Hegedűs   University of Debrecen, Hungary
Arnold Pintér   University of Debrecen, Hungary
György Vaszil   University of Debrecen, Hungary

Invited Abstracts

Using Interference to Boost Computing

Mika Hirvensalo

Department of Mathematics and Statistics, University of Turku, Finland
mikhirve@utu.fi

Abstract. In the nature, interference [4] occurs almost everywhere in the presence of undulating motion. Water waves, sonic waves, as well as electromagnetic waves may interfere, meaning that sometimes the wave crests amplify each other, but sometimes the wave crest and trough annul each other. This mechanism may create patterns which a single wave propagation can never form [3].

In the smallest level, the physical world is depicted by using quantum mechanics, which involves so-called *wave-particle dualism* [1]. This principle signifies that the physical objects can be described as particles, but as waves, as well. It is possible, not only in principle, but also in practice, to regard physical systems carrying information as quantum waves and design algorithms that utilize interference as a computational resource [2]. This is actually rather generally regarded as the source of the efficiency of quantum computing [3].

We will underline some notable interference patterns used to implement famous quantum algorithms, but also to point out that interference-like effect has been used to design computational procedures already long before quantum computing [5, 6].

References

1. de Broglie, L.: Recherches sur la théorie des quanta. Ann. Phys. **10**(3), 22–128 (1925)
2. Hirvensalo, M.: Quantum Computing, 2nd edn. Springer, Berlin, Heidelberg (2004). 10.1007/978-3-662-09636-9
3. Hirvensalo, M.: Interference as a computational resource: a tutorial. Nat. Comput. (2018)
4. Kipnis, N.: History of the Principle of Interference of Light. Birkhauser Verlag, Basel, Boston and Berlin (1991)
5. Turakainen, P.: On probabilistic automata and their generalizations. Annales Academiae Scientiarum Fennicae. Series A **429** (1969).
6. Turakainen, P.: On languages representable in rational probabilistic automata. Annales Academiae Scientiarum Fennicae. Series A **439** (1969).

Super Turing Computing Enables Lifelong Learning AI

Hava Siegelmann

University of Massachusetts Amherst, USA
hava@cs.umass.edu

Abstract. State of the art AI systems demonstrate great capabilities in playing computer games and classifying images, as long as these operate on a computer screen. But once AI systems are embedded in autonomous technology and require to classify on the go and act efficiently and safely in the real world, they show a significant reduction in capabilities. This difference may be explained by the way state of the art AI is prepared, being trained in advance, typically on large datasets (and great amount of energy waste). Once fielded, the AI is frozen: It is unable to use its real-world experience to improve expertise, neither to note that situations move away from what it was originally trained on; and worse, since datasets cannot cover all possible real-world situations, systems with such frozen intelligent control are likely to fail.

A main reason that the field has developed an AI which is frozen once it is fielded, is that it was designed on the Turing machine foundations, where a fixed program is loaded to the universal machine which then follows the program's instructions. But—another theory of computation—the Super Turing computation enables more advanced type AI, one that can lifelong learn from its environment and experience, is not dependent solely on its training set, and interleave computing and learning to increase expertise.

Lifelong Learning is the cutting edge of artificial intelligence - encompassing computational methods that allow systems to learn in runtime and incorporate learning for application in new, unanticipated situations. Our presentation will introduce Super-Turing Computation from the point of view of AI, and follow with a number of state-of-the-art approaches that achieve lifelong learning intelligent systems.

Contents

Complexity of Local, Global and Universality Properties in Finite
Dynamical Systems 1
  Enrico Formenti

A Survey on Computationally Complete Accepting and Generating
Networks of Evolutionary Processors 12
  Bianca Truthe

Prescribed Teams of Rules Working on Several Objects 27
  Artiom Alhazov, Rudolf Freund, Sergiu Ivanov, and Sergey Verlan

From Networks of Reaction Systems to Communicating Reaction Systems
and Back 42
  Bogdan Aman

A Characterization of Polynomial Time Computable Functions
from the Integers to the Reals Using Discrete Ordinary Differential
Equations 58
  Manon Blanc and Olivier Bournez

Languages of Distributed Reaction Systems 75
  Lucie Ciencialová, Luděk Cienciala, and Erzsébet Csuhaj-Varjú

PSPACE-Completeness of Reversible Deterministic Systems 91
  Erik D. Demaine, Robert A. Hearn, Dylan Hendrickson, and Jayson Lynch

From Finite Automata to Fractal Automata – The Power of Recursion 109
  Benedek Nagy

Closure Properties of Subregular Languages Under Operations 126
  Viktor Olejár and Alexander Szabari

P Systems with Evolutional Communication and Separation Rules 143
  *David Orellana-Martín, Luis Valencia-Cabrera,
  and Mario J. Pérez-Jiménez*

Computational Universality and Efficiency in Morphogenetic Systems 158
  Petr Sosík and Jan Drastík

Adaptive Experiments for State Identification in Finite State Machines
with Timeouts 172
   Aleksandr Tvardovskii and Nina Yevtushenko

Author Index 189

Complexity of Local, Global and Universality Properties in Finite Dynamical Systems

Enrico Formenti[✉][ID]

Université Côte d'Azur, CNRS, I3S, Sophia Antipolis, France
enrico.formenti@unice.fr

Abstract. In this paper we study the complexity of the decision problems about generic properties on the dynamics of finite discrete dynamical systems (fDDS). Properties are grouped into two main classes : local and global. Local properties are at most in $\mathsf{NP} \cup \mathsf{coNP}$, while global ones are at most in PSPACE. We also investigate universality (w.r.t. simulation) and we provide a constructive example of universal fDDS for the family of additive fDDS having a unique global attractor. The question of the complexity of deciding universality for a given family of fDDS is left open.

Keywords: (Finite) Discrete dynamical systems · Computational Complexity · Universality

1   Introduction

Finite discrete dynamical systems (fDDS for short) are a convenient formalism used to model phenomena evolving in discrete time units which run through a finite number of states. Applications of the theory of fDDS range from biology, chemistry, up to computer science, mathematics and physics. They are particularly useful for studying complex systems [1,2,5,12,14]. The literature about the formal theory of fDDS is really huge and dozens of papers on the subject appear each year. Most of them focus on specific classes (reaction systems, cellular automata, Boolean automata networks, *etc.*) with many deep and interesting results. A long streamline of results focus on the computational complexity of deciding properties on the dynamics of such systems; without any claim of exhaustiveness one can list [3,4,6,7], for instance. However, in this paper we would like to take a more *generic* approach. We would like to study the complexity of deciding properties for the whole class of fDDS. In this way, we provide an upper bound for all classes seen so far. In order to achieve this, we adopt a descriptive complexity point of view and characterize the questions using adapted logics and signatures [11]. All dynamical properties are divided into three groups: local, global and local&global. Among local properties one can list: having a periodic point of a prescribed period; having an attractor; *etc.*

J. Durand-Lose and G. Vaszil (Eds.): MCU 2022, LNCS 13419, pp. 1–11, 2022.
https://doi.org/10.1007/978-3-031-13502-6_1

Global properties include: having a unique attractor; having at least k distinct attractors; being indecomposable; *etc.* Finally, among the local&global properties one finds, for example: having a single fixed point or having a global attracting cycle of prescribed size.

We prove that the problem of deciding a generic local (resp., global or local&global) property of a fDDS is at most in NP(resp., PSPACE).

An other property that is investigated is universality that here is intended with respect to the notion of strict simulation between fDDS. The problem of deciding if a fDDS simulates another one is NP-complete but in order to have universality one has to consider families of fDDS characterized by some sort of uniformity. At this point, we lost the initial purpose of genericity. We considered the family of additive fDDS having a unique global attractor and we showed how to build universal fDDS for this family (using size of the simulated fDDS as a uniformity criterion). The question of establishing the complexity of deciding universality for a family of fDDS is left open.

This paper is structured as follows. The next section introduces all basic notions about fDDS used in the paper. Section 3 precisely defines what we mean by property and provides the complexity results about the connected decision problems. Section 4 introduces the notion of strict simulation between fDDS and discusses about universality. An example of universal fDDS for a family of fDDS is given in Sect. 5. In the last section we draw our conclusions and provide some perspectives.

2   Basic Notions

A **finite discrete dynamical system** is a structure $\langle X, f \rangle$ where X is a finite set called the **set of states** and $f \subseteq X \times X$ is the **update relation** (or **next state relation**) and provides the new state/s $f(\{x\}) \in \mathcal{P}(X)$ when the system is started on $\{x\} \subseteq X$. For the sake of readability, when no confusion is possible, we will often confuse a fDDS $\langle X, f \rangle$ with its next state function f.

Any fDDS f can be identified with its **transitions graph** $\mathcal{T}_f$ which is a digraph $\langle V, E \rangle$ where $V = X$ and $\forall a, b \in V$, $(a, b) \in E$ iff $b \in f(a)$. In other words, $\mathcal{T}_f$ is the graph of the relation f.

Important. In all this work, when it is not differently specified, we consider that two fDDS having isomorphic TGs are the same fDDS.

We stress that $\mathcal{T}_f$ contains all the information about the dynamics of the system, however, this information is rarely given as in the for of TG in practice. Indeed, in practical applications one has a short description of the system and in most cases the size of the transitions graph is exponential in the size of that description. We leave this issue for a forthcoming paper.

We are interested in investigating the complexity of various properties on the dynamics when f is a function. In this case we will use x in place of $\{x\}$ for the states and $f(x)$ in place of $f(\{x\})$.

We briefly recall here the main properties on the dynamics of a SDD that we are going to explore in the sequel. A point $x \in X$ is a **periodic** point of f if there exists an integer p such that $f^p(x) = x$, the smallest p with the previous property is the **period** of x. A **fix** point of f is a periodic point with period $p = 1$; f^k is the k-fold composition of f with itself. A sequence of points $x_0, x_1, \ldots, x_n$ is a **cycle** of size n if $f^{i+1}(x_i) = x_{i+1 \mod n}$ and $x_0 = x_n$. A cycle $x_0, x_1, \ldots, x_n$ is an **attractor** iff there exists $y \in X$ such that $\forall k \in [0, n-1], y \neq x_k$ and $\exists i \in [0, n-1]$ such that $f(y) = x_i$. An attractor $x_0, x_1, \ldots, x_n$ is **global** if for all $x \in X$, there exists $k \in \mathbb{N}$ and $i \in [0, n-1]$ such that $f^k(x) = x_i$. In other words, an attractor is global whenever all iterations eventually terminate in the attractor. A SDD f is **decomposable** if it has not a unique attractor.

3   fDDS Properties and Their Complexity

A fDDS **property** is a (finite) graph $P = \langle V_P, E_P \rangle$. A fDDS $\langle X, f \rangle$ **has the local property** P iff $\tilde{\exists}\phi \colon P \to \mathcal{T}_f$ such that ϕ is injective and $\forall a, b \in V_p$, $(a, b) \in E_P$ implies that $(\phi(a), \phi(b))$ is an edge of $\mathcal{T}_f$. Here, the notation $\tilde{\exists}\phi$ stands for either $\exists\phi$ or $\neg\exists\phi$. In other words, a local property P is a kind of mask and a fDDS has P if the mask is a subgraph of its transition graph. In the tables below, when $\tilde{\exists}\phi$ when it is interpreted as $\neg\exists\phi$, the corresponding property is surrounded by parenthesis and prefixed by the symbol $\neg$. A fDDS $\langle X, f \rangle$ **has the global property** P iff $\tilde{\exists}\phi \colon \mathcal{T}_f \to P$ such that ϕ is surjective and $\forall a, b \in V_P$, $(a, b) \in E_P$ implies that $(\phi^{-1}(a), \phi^{-1}(b))$ is an edge of $\mathcal{T}_f$. A pair $\langle P_1, P_2 \rangle$ where P_1 is a local property and P_2 is a global one for the same fDDS $\langle X, f \rangle$ is said to be a **local&global** property iff $\langle X, f \rangle$ possesses both.

Proposition 1. *The problem of deciding a local property of a fDDS is at most in* NP $\cup$ coNP.

Proof. The problem takes in input the TG of a fDDS $\langle X, f \rangle$, while the local property $P = \langle V_P, E_P \rangle$ is part of the problem. Hence, testing if $\langle X, f \rangle$ has P can be rewritten using the following formulas (where $a \to b$ means that (a, b) is an edge of the corresponding graph) (Table 1):

$$\texttt{AllDiff}[x_1, x_2, \ldots, x_k] \equiv \neg Eq(x_1, x_2) \wedge \neg Eq(x_1, x_2) \wedge \ldots \wedge \neg Eq(x_{k-1}, x_k)$$

$$\texttt{AllCons}[g_1, g_2, \ldots, g_k, x_1, x_2, \ldots, x_k] \equiv \forall g_i \in V_P \forall g_j \in V_P \ (g_i \to g_j) \Rightarrow (x_i \to x_j)$$

$$\Psi[g_1, g_2, \ldots, g_k, x_1, x_2, \ldots, x_k] \equiv \texttt{AllCons}[g_1, g_2, \ldots, g_k, x_1, x_2, \ldots, x_k] \wedge$$
$$\wedge \texttt{AllDiff}[x_1, x_2, \ldots, x_k]$$

The idea behind the formula is that one need to non-deterministically guess the targets in $\mathcal{T}_f$ of the monomorphism; then verify that all these points are distinct i.e. we can build an injection—this is the $\texttt{AllDiff}$ part; finally we have to verify that edges in P correspond to edges in $\mathcal{T}_f$—this is the role of $\texttt{AllCons}$.

Therefore the question of the problem is logically equivalent to the formula $\exists x_1, \exists x_2, \ldots, \exists x_k \Psi[g_1, g_2, \ldots, g_k, x_1, x_2, \ldots, x_k]$ and hence by Fagin's theorem the problem in NP [15, Th. 8.3, pag. 173]. We proceed similarly for proving that the problem is in coNP when existential quantifiers are replaced by $\neg\exists$ in the previous formula.   □

Proposition 2. *The problem of deciding a global property of a fDDS is at most in* PSPACE.

Table 1. Examples of local properties.

Description	Property
There exists a fixed point	
There exists a fixed point local attractor	
There exists a cycle of period 6	
There exists an attracting cycle of per. 6	

Proof. First of all, remark that $\mathsf{NSPACE}(s(n)) = \text{co-}\mathsf{NSPACE}(s(n))$ by Immerman-Szelepcsényi theorem [15, Cor. to Th. 7.6, pag. 153]. Moreover, by Savitch's theorem [15, Cor. to Th. 7.5, pag. 150], we have $\mathsf{PSPACE}{=}\mathsf{NPSPACE}$. Hence, we can focus in proving just the existential form of the definition of global property (Table 2). Similarly to what done for local properties, the problem takes in input the TG of a DDS $\langle X, f \rangle$ and a property $P = \langle V_P, E_P \rangle$. Testing if $\langle X, f \rangle$ has P can be rewritten using the following formulas (`AllCons` has been defined in the proof of Proposition 1):

$$\texttt{AllCons}^\star[x_1, x_2, \ldots, x_k, g_1, g_2, \ldots, g_k] \equiv \text{transitive closure of } \texttt{AllCons}$$
$$\Phi[i, j, x, y, g_i, g_j] \equiv (i \neq j) \Rightarrow \texttt{AllCons}^\star[x, y, g_i, g_j]$$
$$\texttt{Part}[U_1, \ldots, U_k] \equiv \forall x \in X \exists j \in \{1, \ldots, k\}\, x \in U_j$$

Therefore the question of the problem is logically equivalent to the formula

$$\exists U_1 \subseteq X \ldots \exists U_k \subseteq X \forall i \in \{1, \ldots, k\}\, \forall j \in \{1, \ldots, k\}\, \forall x \in U_i \forall y \in U_j$$
$$\Phi[i, j, x, y, g_i, g_j] \wedge \texttt{Part}[U_1, \ldots, U_k]$$

which belongs to $\mathsf{SO}(\mathsf{TC}) = \mathsf{PSPACE}$ [11]. Let us spend a few words to explain the formula. The idea is that first of all, one has to non-deterministically extract from X a certain number (as many as the set of vertices of P in fact) of subsets $U_1, \ldots, U_k$ and verify that they form a partition of X—this is the role of `Part`. Each U_i targets a single vertex g_i of P (recall that we want an epimorphism) so if we have two vertices x, y in $\mathcal{T}_f$ (coming from distinct U_i and U_j) and these vertices are connected by a path, then it must hold the same for g_i and g_j in P—and this is checked by Φ. $\qquad\square$

Table 2. Examples of global properties. Recall that when a property is prefixed with the symbol ¬, it means that $\tilde{\exists}$ is interpreted as $\neg\exists\phi$ in the definition of the property.

Description	Property
The fDDS is undecomposable	$\neg(\,\mathcal{D}\ \ \mathcal{D}\,)$
There exists a unique attractor	$\neg(\,\mathcal{D}\ \ \mathcal{D}\,)$
There are at least three attractors	$\mathcal{D}\ \ \mathcal{D}\ \ \mathcal{D}$

Proposition 3. *The problem of deciding a local&global property of a fDDS is at most in PSPACE.*

Proof. In this case, one just can verify the two properties separately and hence the upperbound is PSPACE (Table 3). □

Table 3. Examples of local&global properties. Recall that when a property is prefixed with the symbol ¬, it means that $\tilde{\exists}$ is interpreted as $\neg\exists\phi$ in the definition of the property.

Description	Property
There exists a single fixed point	$\mathcal{D}$ and $\neg(\,\mathcal{D}\ \ \mathcal{D}\,)$
There exists a global attracting cycle of per. 6	and $\neg(\,\mathcal{D}\ \ \mathcal{D}\,)$

4   Universality

Similarly to what we have done for properties of fDDS, we want to provide a *generic* view of the property of universality in fDDS. Here universality is intended with respect to simulation. Therefore the first thing to define is the notion of simulation between fDDS.

We say that $B = \langle Z, g \rangle$ **strictly simulates** $A = \langle Y, f \rangle$ if there exists a monomorphism $\phi \colon Y \to Z$ such that $\phi \circ f = g \circ \phi$. In other words, B strictly simulates A if $\mathcal{T}_f$ is a subgraph of $\mathcal{T}_g$. Remark that here we speak about strict simulation since the simulation is one-to-one in the sense that a step in the simulated system corresponds to one step in the simulating system. The term of non-strict simulation or simply simulation is reserved to the situation in which the simulator is allowed to perform several steps for producing a single step of the simulated system.

Proposition 4. *Given two fDDS $A = \langle Y, f \rangle$ and $B = \langle Z, g \rangle$, the problem of deciding if B strictly simulates A is NP-complete if $|Y| < |Z|$. It is GI-complete if $|Y| = |Z|$ and $|f(Y)| = |g(Z)|$.*

Proof. When $|Y| < |Z|$, this is the classical subgraph isomorphism problem between $\mathcal{T}_f$ and $\mathcal{T}_g$ which is known to be NP-complete [9, Problem GT48]. If $|Y| = |Z|$ and $|f(Y)| = |g(Z)|$, this is the isomorphism problem for directed graphs which is known to be GI-complete [13].   □

It is not difficult to see that the relation of strict simulation is a pre-order on fDDS. Given a family of fDDS $\mathcal{F}$, it is therefore natural to define a fDDS $A = \langle Y, f \rangle$ **strictly universal** for $\mathcal{F}$ if A simulates all the fDDS in $\mathcal{F}$. Without bounds on $\mathcal{F}$, it is clear that strictly universal are not likely to exist. One constraint that we may impose on $\mathcal{F}$ is finiteness. If $\mathcal{F}$ is finite, then a strictly universal system trivially always exists, one has just to take the TG consisting of disjoint copies of all TGs in $\mathcal{F}$. In order to avoid trivial cases and to have tighter bounds we consider strict universality up to some bound. Let $\mathcal{F}_n$ denote the subset of fDDS in the family $\mathcal{F}$ which have exactly n states. Then, we are interested to find a strictly universal fDDS for $\mathcal{F}_n$ which shares the same dynamical properties at the fDDS in $\mathcal{F}$. The following section provide an example of universal fDDS for the family of additive fDDS with a unique global attractor.

5   Additive fDDS

An **intree** is a directed tree in which the orientation of the edges has been reversed *i.e.* edges are oriented towards the root. A *p*-**adic** intree is an intree in which all nodes have indegree p except for the leaves (which have indegree 0). Intrees are typical subgraphs of TGs of additive fDDS. Let us briefly recall some facts about additive fDDS.

A fDDS $\langle Y, f \rangle$ is **additive** when Y is a group and f a group homomorphism. Here only, cyclic groups like $\mathbb{Z}_p$ for p prime are considered. In [8], the following particular notation is adopted for additive fDDS when Y is $(\mathbb{F}_p)^n$ with p prime and $n > 0$: X_p^n denotes the dynamical system $\langle \mathbb{F}_p[x]/x^n, \sigma \rangle$, where σ is the shift map on $\mathbb{F}_p[x]/x^n$ (*i.e.* the multiplication by $x \mod x^n$). The same symbol X_p^n will also denote the TG of $\langle \mathbb{F}_p[x]/x^n, \sigma \rangle$, when no confusion is possible.

We also denote by X_p^0 or **1** the TG made by a single loop. According to [8], the TG of X_p^n ($n > 0$) is a complete p-adic intree of height $n - 1$ with a loop at the root. We also recall here an important operation between fDDS. The **Kronecker product** between a fDDS $A = \langle Y, f \rangle$ and $B = \langle Z, g \rangle$, denoted

$A \odot B$, is a new fDDS $\langle Y \times Z, h \rangle$ where $\forall (y, z) \in Y \times Z$, $h(y, z) = (f(y), g(z))$. Practically speaking, the Kronecker product of $A \odot B$ is the parallel evolution of A and B. From the point of view of TGs, the Kronecker product is the classical Kronecker product of graphs. In the sequel we are going to use the following result.

Lemma 1. *The Kronecker product of fDDS preserves additivity.*

Proof. Consider two additive fDDS $A = \langle Y, f \rangle$ and $B = \langle Z, g \rangle$. Let $H = A \odot B = \langle Y \times Z, h \rangle$ and denote $\langle Y, + \rangle$ and $\langle Z, + \rangle$ the groups on the states of A and B, respectively. Then, we can equip $Y \times Z$ with the group structure induced by $\langle Y, + \rangle$ and $\langle Z, + \rangle$ that is to say for any $y_1, y_2 \in Y$ and $z_1, z_2 \in Z$, $(y_1, z_1) + (y_2, z_2)$ in $Y \times Z$ is given by $(y_1 + y_2, z_1 + z_2)$. Now, it remains to prove that h is a homomorphism. For any $y_1, y_2 \in Y$ and $z_1, z_2 \in Z$, we have

$$
\begin{aligned}
h((y_1, z_1) + (y_2, z_2)) &= h(y_1 + y_2, z_1 + z_2) = (f(y_1 + y_2), g(z_1 + z_2)) \\
&= (f(y_1) + f(y_2), g(z_1) + g(z_2)) \\
&= (f(y_1), g(z_1)) + (f(y_2), g(z_2)) \\
&= h(y_1, z_1) + h(y_2, z_2)
\end{aligned}
$$

Finally, just remark that $h(0, 0) = (f(0), g(0)) = (0, 0)$.   □

For any prime p and any $n \in \mathbb{N}$, denote T_{p^n} the class of fDDS having a unique global attractor and such that the p^n states have the structure of an abelian group and the update rule is a homomorphism of this group.

Now, for any prime p and $n \in \mathbb{N}$, consider the set of fDDS $S_{p,n}$ defined as follows:

$$
S_{p,n} = \bigcup_{u_1 + u_2 + \ldots + u_k = n} X_p^{u_1} \odot X_p^{u_2} \odot \cdots \odot X_p^{u_k}
$$

Lemma 2. *For all prime p and $n \in \mathbb{N}$, $T_{p^n} \supseteq S_{p,n}$.*

Proof. Fix $u_1, u_2, \ldots, u_k$ such that $\sum_{i=1}^{k} u_i = n$. By the definition of Kronecker product, the number of states of $U = X_p^{u_1} \odot X_p^{u_2} \odot \cdots \odot X_p^{u_k}$ is $\prod_{i=1}^{k} p^{u_i} = p^{\sum_{i=1}^{k} u_i} = p^n$. By Lemma 1, we known that U is additive. Moreover, it is clear that U has a unique fixed point. Hence, $U \in T_{p^n}$ and $S_{p,n} \subseteq T_{p^n}$.   □

Lemma 3. *Let A, B and C be three fDDS belonging to $S_{p,i}, S_{p,j}$ and $S_{p,k}$, respectively, for $i, j, k \in \mathbb{N}$. If $A \not\cong C$, then $A \odot C \not\cong B \odot C$, where $\not\cong$ is graph non-isomorphism.*

Proof. Denote $\mathring{A}, \mathring{B}$ and $\mathring{C}$ the TG of A, B and C with orientation removed. Remark that $\mathring{C}$ has a loop and by the hypothesis $\mathring{A} \not\cong \mathring{B}$, then by [10, Proposition 9.6, pag. 109], we have that $\mathring{A} \odot \mathring{C} \not\cong \mathring{B} \odot \mathring{C}$. Now adding orientation to all edges towards the loop in $\mathring{A} \odot \mathring{C}$ and $\mathring{B} \odot \mathring{C}$ provides the result (Fig. 1).   □

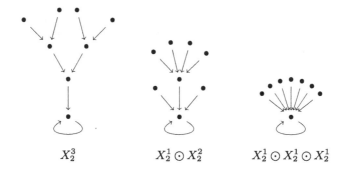

Fig. 1. The transition graphs of the fDDS in $S_{2,3}$.

Just by examining how the class $S_{p,n}$ is defined and by using Lemma 3, one finds the following.

Proposition 5. *For any prime p and any $n \in \mathbb{N}$, $|S_{p,n}| = P(n)$ where $P(n)$ is the number of the partitions of n.*

Lemma 4. *Let p be a prime number and $n, m \in \mathbb{N}$. Assume to have two non-void fDDS $A \in T_{p^n}$ and $B \in T_{p^m}$, then the fDDS $A \odot B$ strictly simulates both A and B.*

Proof. The TG of A can be identified in $A \odot B$ by considering the product of the nodes of the TG of A with the loop of B. The reasoning for B is similar. □

Theorem 1. *For any prime p and $n \in \mathbb{N}$, any fDDS in $S_{p,n}$ can be simulated by*

$$U_{p,n} = \bigodot_{k=1}^{n} (X_p^k)^{\lfloor \frac{n}{k} \rfloor}$$

where the notation $(X_p^i)^j$ is the j-times application of the Kronecker product of X_p^i with itself.

Proof. For $\ell > 0$, consider a set of integers $u_1, u_2, \ldots, u_\ell \in \mathbb{N}$ such that $n = \sum_{i=1}^{\ell} u_i$, then $\bigodot_{i=1}^{\ell} X_p^{u_i} \in S_{p,n}$. Using the commutativity of the Kronecker product, rewrite the previous fDDS as $\bigodot_{j=1}^{s} (X_p^j)^{v_j}$ by collecting the X_p^i with the same exponent i. It is clear that $s \le \ell$. For $1 \le j \le s$, consider $(X_p^j)^{v_j}$. Remark that v_j is the number of $u_i = j$ that occur in the sequence $u_1, u_2, \ldots, u_k$. Hence $v_j \le \lfloor \frac{n}{j} \rfloor$. By Lemma 4, $(X_p^j)^{v_j}$ is simulated by $U_{p,n}$. The rest of the proof follows by finite induction and Lemma 4.   □

Remark that by Lemma 1, $U_{p,n}$ is additive. It is also pretty clear that it has a unique global fixed point.

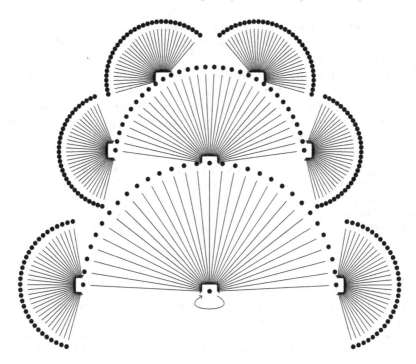

Fig. 2. The graph $U_{2,3}$ which is universal for the familiy $S_{2,3}$.

6   Conclusions and Perspectives

In this paper we defined local and global properties for fDDS by means of the TGs. Moreover, the corresponding computational complexity of the decision problems considered take in input TGs. Remark that this is not always the case in practical situations. Indeed, in many contexts, one has a succinct description of the fDDS and not the full TG. For example, call **parsimonious** a fDDS whose update rule can be expressed by a FO formula on some signature. Examples of parsimonious fDDS are reaction systems, (finite) cellular automata, boolean automata networks, Turing machines (with finite tape), *etc*. It would be an interesting research direction to study the succinct version of the complexity problems addressed in this paper. Indeed, we expect a complexity blow-up.

The notion of strict universality and of universal fDDS for a given family is tightly connected to the idea of universal graphs but the addition here is that only graphs of functions are considered and that some underlaying semantics are associated (e.g. the TGs of additive fDDS) which make these classes somewhat peculiar. It would be interesting to investigate the main characteristics and the growth parameters of universal graphs for these peculiar classes.

For example, Theorem 1 says that $U_{p,n}$ is universal for the family $S_{p,n}$. However, the number of states in $U_{p,n}$ is rather huge (see Fig. 2 to have an idea for a small value of p and n). Can we find a smaller universal fDDS for $S_{p,n}$ and having the same dynamical characteristics, namely it has a global fixed point attractor and it is additive?

Another interesting research direction which also concern universality consists in relaxing the fact that the simulation performed is one-to-one. One could imagine to allow the simulator to run through more than one step to perform the simulation of a transition of the simulated system. How complex would be to decide the universality in this case?

Acknowledgments. The author warmly thanks the *italian gang*: Luca Manzoni (Univ. of Trieste, Italy), Antonio E. Porreca (Aix-Marseille Univ., Marseille, France) and Alberto Dennunzio (Univ. of Milano-Bicocca, Milan, Italy) for many fruitful discussions and ideas which were at the basis of the present work.

I also warmly thank François Doré for having provided me with the picture of $U_{2,3}$.

References

1. Adamatzky, A., Goles, E., Martínez, G.J., Tsompanas, M.I., Tegelaar, M., Wosten, H.A.B.: Fungal automata. Complex Syst. **29**(4), 455–483 (2020)
2. Alonso-Sanz, R.: Cellular automata and other discrete dynamical systems with memory. In: Smari, W.W., Zeljkovic, V. (eds.) Proceedings of HPCS, p. 215. IEEE (2012)
3. Barrett, C.L., Hunt, H.B., Marathe, M.V., Ravi, S., Rosenkrantz, D.J., Stearns, R.E.: Complexity of reachability problems for finite discrete dynamical systems. J. Comput. Syst. Sci. **72**(8), 1317–1345 (2006)
4. Bridoux, F., Durbec, A., Perrot, K., Richard, A.: Complexity of fixed point counting problems in Boolean networks. J. Comput. Syst. Sci. **126**, 138–164 (2022)
5. Chaudhuri, P., Chowdhury, D., Nandi, S., Chattopadhyay, S.: Additive Cellular Automata Theory and Applications, vol. 1. IEEE Press (1997)
6. Dennunzio, A., Formenti, E., Manzoni, L., Porreca, A.E.: Complexity of the dynamics of reaction systems. Inf. Comput. **267**, 96–109 (2019)
7. Formenti, E., Manzoni, L., Porreca, A.E.: On the complexity of occurrence and convergence problems in reaction systems. Nat. Comput. **14**(1), 185–191 (2014). https://doi.org/10.1007/s11047-014-9456-3
8. Formenti, E., Papazian, C., Richard, A., Scribot, PA.: From additive flowers to additive automata networks. In: Adamatzky, A. (eds.) Automata and Complexity. Emergence, Complexity and Computation, vol. 42. Springer, Cham (2022). https://doi.org/10.1007/978-3-030-92551-2_18
9. Garey, M.R., Johnson, D.S.: Computers and intractability, vol. 174. freeman San Francisco (1979)
10. Hammack, R.H., Imrich, W., Klavžar, S.: Handbook of Product Graphs, vol. 2. CRC Press, Boca Raton (2011)
11. Immerman, N.: Descriptive Complexity. Texts in Computer Science. Springer, New York (2012). https://doi.org/10.1007/978-1-4612-0539-5
12. Marañón, G.Á., Encinas, L.H., del Rey, Á.M.: A multisecret sharing scheme for color images based on cellular automata. Inf. Sci. **178**(22), 4382–4395 (2008)

13. Miller, G.L.: Graph isomorphism, general remarks. In: Proceedings of the Ninth Annual ACM Symposium on Theory of Computing, pp. 143–150. STOC 1977, Association for Computing Machinery, New York, NY, USA (1977). https://doi.org/10.1145/800105.803404
14. Nandi, S., Kar, B.K., Chaudhuri, P.P.: Theory and applications of cellular automata in cryptography. IEEE Trans. Comput. **43**(12), 1346–1357 (1994)
15. Papadimitriou, C.: Computational Complexity. Addison-Wesley, Theoretical computer science (1994)

A Survey on Computationally Complete Accepting and Generating Networks of Evolutionary Processors

Bianca Truthe(✉)

Institut Für Informatik, Universität Giessen, Arndtstr. 2, 35392 Giessen, Germany
bianca.truthe@informatik.uni-giessen.de

Abstract. In this survey, we discuss accepting and generating networks of evolutionary processors in their various characteristics as presented in the literature over the years. We show several research directions with respect to reducing the resources needed for still being computationally complete and gather results obtained in these areas so far.

Keywords: Network · Evolutionary Processor · Computational Power

1 Introduction

Based on the idea of processing languages in a distributed and parallel manner by a system of simple agents,several models of language generating or accepting devices have been developed (for instance, grammar systems, evolutionary systems, networks of language processors, networks of splicing systems, networks of Watson–Crick D0L systems). Here, we focus on networks of evolutionary processors.

Starting from networks of language processors which have been introduced in [6] by E. CSUHAJ-VARJÚ and A. SALOMAA, networks of evolutionary processors have been developed in [4] by J. CASTELLANOS, C. MARTÍN-VIDE, V. MITRANA, and J. M. SEMPERE inspired by biological processes.

Such a network can be considered as a graph where the nodes represent processors which apply production rules to the words they contain and the edges are considered as communication channels for exchanging words between processors.

The computation consists of alternating derivation (evolutionary) and communication steps. In an evolutionary step, any node derives from its language all possible words according to its production rules as its new language (any word is assumed to exist in an arbitrary number such that there are enough words for the application of rules; only one rule is applied in one step at one place at most; if no rule is applicable, then the word itself will survive this derivation step, otherwise the original word will not exist anymore after the derivation). The allowed production rules are that one letter is substituted by a letter, a letter is inserted, or a letter is deleted; the nodes are then called substitution

J. Durand-Lose and G. Vaszil (Eds.): MCU 2022, LNCS 13419, pp. 12–26, 2022.
https://doi.org/10.1007/978-3-031-13502-6_2

nodes, insertion nodes, or deletion nodes, respectively. In a communication step, any node sends copies of those words to other nodes which satisfy an output condition given as a regular language (called the output filter) and any node adopts (copies of) words sent by the other nodes if the words satisfy an input condition also given by a regular language (called the input filter). Words not passing an output filter remain in the node for the next derivation step; words which have left node but do not pass an input filter to enter some node get lost (disappear from the network).

In the meantime, also other variants have been introduced and investigated, e. g., networks where the filters belong to edges not nodes (e. g., [19]) or networks where the filtering is realized by polarization (e. g., [17]).

Networks of evolutionary processors can be defined as language generating or language accepting devices. In case of a generating device, the processors start working with finite sets of axioms and all words which are in a designated processor at some time form the generated language. In case of an accepting device, input words are accepted if there is a computation which leads to a word in a designated processor.

Early results on generating networks of evolutionary processors can be found, e. g., in [4,5,23]. In [11] and [1], the generative capacity of networks of evolutionary processors was investigated where at most two types of rules occur. In [7], the generative capacity of networks of evolutionary processors was investigated for cases that all filters belong to a certain subfamily of the set of all regular languages. In [27], networks of evolutionary processors were investigated where the filters are restricted by bounded resources, namely the number of non-terminal symbols or the number of production rules which are necessary for generating the languages or the number of states of a minimal deterministic finite automaton over an arbitrary alphabet which are necessary for accepting the filters. In [15], the use of codes and ideals as filters was studied. In [14], the hierarchies of the language classes obtained before were merged.

Accepting networks of evolutionary processors were introduced in [22]. Further results, especially on accepting networks where the filters belong to certain subclasses of the family of the regular languages, were published in [8] and [20]. In [28], accepting networks of evolutionary processors were investigated where the filters are restricted by bounded resources (number of non-terminal symbols, number of production rules necessary for generating the languages or number of states of a minimal deterministic finite automaton over an arbitrary alphabet necessary for accepting the filters). In [16], the use of codes and ideals as filters was studied and compared to the impact of other filters.

In the present paper, we give an overview about classes of generating or accepting networks of evolutionary processors which generate or accept all recursively enumerable languages.

2   Definitions

We assume that the reader is familiar with the basic concepts of formal language theory (see, e. g., [25]). and recall here only some notations used in the paper.

Let V be an alphabet. By V^* we denote the set of all words (strings) over the alphabet V (including the empty word λ). The cardinality of a set A is denoted by $|A|$.

A phrase structure grammar is a quadruple $G = (N, T, P, S)$ where N is a finite set of non-terminal symbols, T is a finite set of terminal symbols, P is a finite set of production rules which are written as $\alpha \to \beta$ with $\alpha \in (N \cup T)^* \setminus T^*$ and $\beta \in (N \cup T)^*$, and $S \in N$ is the axiom. A grammar is right-linear if, for any rule $\alpha \to \beta$, the left-hand side α consists of a non-terminal symbol only and the right-hand side β contains at most one non-terminal symbol and this is at the right end of the word: $\alpha \in N$ and $\beta \in T^* \cup T^*N$. A special case of right-linearity is regularity where each rule contains exactly one terminal symbol (with the only possible exception $S \to \lambda$). Let $G = (N, T, P, S)$ be a grammar. A word $u \in (N \cup T)^*$ is derived in one step to a word $v \in (N \cup T)^*$ by the grammar G, written as $u \Longrightarrow v$, if there are a rule $\alpha \to \beta \in P$ and two subwords x and y of u such that $u = x\alpha y$ and $y = x\beta y$. By $\Longrightarrow^*$, we denote the reflexive and transitive closure of the derivation relation $\Longrightarrow$. The language $L(G)$ generated by the grammar G is the set of all words which consist of terminal symbols and which are derivable from the axiom S:

$$L(G) = \{\, w \mid w \in T^* \text{ and } S \Longrightarrow^* w \,\}.$$

Regular and right-linear grammars generate the same family of languages (the regular languages). Therefore, also right-linear grammars are often called regular. In the context of descriptional complexity, when the number of non-terminal symbols or the number of production rules which are necessary for generating a language are considered then there is a difference whether a language is generated by means of regular or right-linear rules. We use in this paper right-linear grammars.

By REG and RE, we denote the families of languages generated by regular and arbitrary phrase structure grammars, respectively.

A finite automaton is a quintuple $\mathcal{A} = (V, Z, z_0, F, \delta)$ where V is an alphabet called the input alphabet, Z is a non-empty finite set of elements which are called states, $z_0 \in Z$ is the so-called start state, $F \subseteq Z$ is the set of accepting states, and $\delta : Z \times V \to \mathcal{P}(Z)$ is a mapping which is also called the transition function where $\mathcal{P}(Z)$ denotes the power set of Z (the set of all subsets of Z). A finite automaton is called deterministic if every set $\delta(z, a)$ for $z \in Z$ and $a \in V$ is a singleton set.

The transition function δ can be extended to a function $\delta^* : Z \times V^* \to \mathcal{P}(Z)$ where $\delta^*(z, \lambda) = \{z\}$ and

$$\delta^*(z, va) = \bigcup_{z' \in \delta^*(z,v)} \delta(z', a).$$

We will use the same symbol δ in both the original and extended version of the transition function.

Let $\mathcal{A} = (V, Z, z_0, F, \delta)$ be a finite automaton. A word w is accepted by the finite automaton $\mathcal{A}$ if and only if the automaton has reached an accepting state after reading the input word w:

$$L(A) = \{\, w \mid \delta(z_0, w) \cap F \neq \emptyset \,\}.$$

The family of the languages accepted by finite automata is also the family of the regular languages.

In the sequel, let V be an alphabet. For a language L over V, we set

$$Comm(L) = \{\, a_{i_1} \ldots a_{i_n} \mid a_1 \ldots a_n \in L,\ n \geq 1,\ \{i_1, i_2, \ldots, i_n\} = \{1, 2, \ldots, n\} \,\},$$
$$Circ(L) = \{\, vu \mid uv \in L,\ u, v \in V^* \,\},$$
$$Suf(L) = \{\, v \mid uv \in L,\ u, v \in V^* \,\}.$$

We consider the following restrictions for regular languages (which yield so-called subregular families of languages). Let L be a language and $V = alph(L)$ the minimal alphabet of L. We say that the language L, with respect to the alphabet V, is

- *monoidal* if $L = V^*$,
- *combinational* if it has the form $L = V^*A$ for some subset $A \subseteq V$,
- *definite* if it can be represented in the form $L = A \cup V^*B$ where A and B are finite subsets of V^*,
- *nilpotent* if L is finite or $V^* \setminus L$ is finite,
- *commutative* if $L = Comm(L)$,
- *circular* if $L = Circ(L)$,
- *suffix-closed* if the relation $xy \in L$ for some words $x, y \in V^*$ implies that also the suffix y belongs to L or equivalently, $L = Suf(L)$,
- *non-counting* (or star-free) if there is an integer $k \geq 1$ such that, for any three words $x, y, z \in V^*$, the relation $xy^k z \in L$ holds if and only if also the relation $xy^{k+1}z \in L$ holds,
- *power-separating* if for any word $x \in V^*$ there is a natural number $m \geq 1$ such that either the equality $J_x^m \cap L = \emptyset$ or the inclusion $J_x^m \subseteq L$ holds where $J_x^m = \{\, x^n \mid n \geq m \,\}$,
- *ordered* if the language L is accepted by a finite automaton $\mathcal{A} = (Z, V, \delta, z_0, F)$ where $(Z, \preceq)$ is a totally ordered set and, for any $a \in V$, the relation $z \preceq z'$ implies the relation $\delta(z, a) \preceq \delta(z', a)$,
- *union-free* if L can be described by a regular expression which is only built by product and star.

Among the commutative, circular, suffix-closed, non-counting, and power-separating languages, we consider only those which are also regular.

By *FIN, MON, COMB, DEF, NIL, COMM, CIRC, SUF, NC, PS, ORD*, and *UF*, we denote the families of all finite, monoidal, combinational, definite, nilpotent, regular commutative, regular circular, regular suffix-closed, regular non-counting, regular power-separating, ordered, and union-free languages, respectively.

In several papers, also regular languages have been considered which are based on some kind of random context: A language over an alphabet V is defined by two subsets $P \subseteq V$ and $F \subseteq V$ and a mode (strong or weak) as the set of all words $w \in (V \setminus F)^*$ which contain every symbol of the permitting set P (in the strong mode) or at least one symbol (in the weak mode, if P is not empty) but, in any case, no symbol of the forbidding set F.

Additionally, families of languages are considered which are defined by bounding the resources which are necessary for accepting or generating these languages.

Let RLG be the set of all right-linear grammars and DFA the set of all deterministic finite automata. Further, let

$$G = (N, T, P, S) \in RLG \quad \text{and} \quad \mathcal{A} = (V, Z, z_0, F, \delta) \in DFA.$$

Then we define the following measures of descriptional complexity:

$$Var(G) = |N|, \quad Prod(G) = |P|, \quad State(\mathcal{A}) = |Z|.$$

For these complexity measures, we define the following families of languages (we abbreviate the measure *Var* by V, the measure *Prod* by P, and the measure *State* by Z):

$$RL_n^V = \{ L \mid \exists G \in RLG : L = L(G) \text{ and } Var(G) \le n \},$$
$$RL_n^P = \{ L \mid \exists G \in RLG : L = L(G) \text{ and } Prod(G) \le n \},$$
$$REG_n^Z = \{ L \mid \exists \mathcal{A} \in DFA : L = L(\mathcal{A}) \text{ and } State(\mathcal{A}) \le n \}.$$

We now introduce the notion of an ideal in V^* from the theory of rings and semigroups.

A non-empty language $L \subseteq V^*$ is called a right (left) ideal if and only if, for any word $v \in V^*$ and any word $u \in L$, we have $uv \in L$ ($vu \in L$, respectively). It is easy to see that the language L is a right (left) ideal if and only if there is a language L' such that $L = L'V^*$ ($L = V^*L'$, respectively).

We now present some notions from coding theory, especially some special codes. For details, we refer to [18] and [26].

For a word $x \in V^*$, let

$$E(x) = \{ y \mid y \in V^+, \, vyv' = x \text{ for some } v, v' \in V^* \},$$

(i.e., $E(x)$ is the set of all non-empty subwords of x).

A language $L \subseteq V^*$ is called

– a code if and only if, for any numbers $n \ge 1$, $m \ge 1$, and words

$$x_1, x_2, \ldots, x_n, y_1, y_2, \ldots y_m \in L$$

such that

$$x_1 x_2 \ldots x_n = y_1 y_2 \ldots y_m,$$

we have the equalities $n = m$ and $x_i = y_i$ for $1 \le i \le n$ (i.e., a word of L^* has a unique decomposition into code words.

– a solid code if and only if, for any numbers $n \geq 1$, $m \geq 1$, words

$$x_1, x_2, \ldots, x_n, y_1, y_2, \ldots y_m \in L,$$

and words

$$v_1, v_2, \ldots, v_{n+1}, w_1, w_2, \ldots, w_{m+1}$$

with $E(v_i) \cap L = \emptyset$ for $1 \leq i \leq n+1$, and $E(w_j) \cap L = \emptyset$ for $1 \leq j \leq m+1$ such that

$$v_1 x_1 v_2 x_2 \ldots v_n x_n v_{n+1} = w_1 y_1 w_2 y_2 \ldots w_m y_m w_{m+1},$$

we have $n = m$, $x_i = y_i$ for $1 \leq i \leq n$, and $v_j = w_j$ for $1 \leq j \leq n+1$;
– uniform if and only if $L \subseteq V^n$ for some $n \geq 1$ (all words have the same length);
– prefix if and only if, for any words $u \in L$ and $v \in V^*$ such that $uv \in L$, we have $v = \lambda$ (i.e., any proper prefix of a word in L is not in L);
– suffix if and only if, for any words $u \in L$ and $v \in V^*$ such that $vu \in L$, we have $v = \lambda$ (i.e., any proper suffix of a word in L is not in L);
– bifix if and only if it is prefix as well as suffix;
– infix if and only if, for any $u \in L$, and $v, v' \in V^*$ such that $vuv' \in L$, we have $v = v' = \lambda$ (i.e., any proper subword of a word in L is not in L).

Note that uniform, prefix, suffix, bifix, and infix languages are codes.

A code $L \subseteq V^*$ is called

– outfix if and only if, for any words $u \in V^*$ and $v, v' \in V^*$ such that $vv' \in L$ and $vuv' \in L$, we have $u = \lambda$;
– reflective if and only if, for any words $u, v \in V^*$ such that $uv \in L$, we have $vu \in L$.

By rId, lId, C, SC, PfC, SfC, BfC, IfC, OfC, RC, and UC, we denote the families of regular right ideals, regular left ideals, regular codes, regular solid codes, regular prefix codes, regular suffix codes, regular bifix codes, regular infix codes, regular outfix codes, regular reflective codes and uniform codes, respectively.

We now present networks of evolutionary processors. We call a production $\alpha \rightarrow \beta$ a substitution if $|\alpha| = |\beta| = 1$ and deletion if $|\alpha| = 1$ and $\beta = \lambda$. The productions are applied like context-free rewriting rules. We say that a word v derives a word w, written as $v \implies w$, if there are words x, y and a production $\alpha \rightarrow \beta$ such that $v = x\alpha y$ and $w = x\beta y$.

We introduce insertion as a counterpart of deletion. We write $\lambda \rightarrow a$, where a is a letter. The application of an insertion $\lambda \rightarrow a$ derives from a word w any word $w_1 a w_2$ with $w = w_1 w_2$ for some (possibly empty) words w_1 and w_2.

If the applied rule p should be mentioned, we write $v \implies_p w$. For a set P of rules, we write $v \implies_P w$ if and only if $v \implies_p w$ for some rule $p \in P$. The reflexive and transitive closure of the relation is denoted by $\implies_P^*$: we write $x \implies_P^* y$ if there are rules $p_1, \ldots, p_n$ ($n \geq 0$) in P and words $w_0, \ldots, w_n$

such that $x = w_0$, $w_i \Longrightarrow_{p_{i+1}} w_{i+1}$ for $i = 0, \ldots, n-1$, and $w_n = y$. If at least one rule is applied, we write $x \Longrightarrow_P^+ y$. For an alphabet V, we denote by SUB_V, DEL_V, and INS_V the sets of all substitution, deletion, or insertion rules, respectively, over the alphabet V.

We first define networks of evolutionary processors for generating languages. In the literature, they are abbreviated as NEPs but in order to better distiguish them from accepting networks, for say here GNEPs.

Definition 1.

1. *A generating network of evolutionary processors (of size n) is an $(n+3)$-tuple*
   $\mathcal{N} = (V, N_1, N_2, \ldots, N_n, E, n_o)$ *where*
   - *V is a finite alphabet (the working alphabet of the network),*
   - *for $1 \leq i \leq n$, there is a processor $N_i = (M_i, A_i, I_i, O_i)$ where*
     - *M_i is a set of evolution rules of a certain type, i. e., $M_i \subseteq SUB_V$ or $M_i \subseteq DEL_V$ or $M_i \subseteq INS_V$,*
     - *A_i is a finite subset of V^* (the language of axioms, from where the processing starts in this processor),*
     - *I_i and O_i are regular sets over V (called the input and output filter, respectively),*
   - *E is a subset of $\{1, 2, \ldots, n\} \times \{1, 2, \ldots, n\}$, and*
   - *n_o is a natural number from the set $\{1, 2, \ldots, n\}$; the processor N_{n_o} is called the output node of the network.*
2. *A configuration C of $\mathcal{N}$ is an n-tuple $C = (C(1), C(2), \ldots, C(n))$ where $C(i)$ is a subset of V^* for $1 \leq i \leq n$.*
3. *Let $C = (C(1), C(2), \ldots, C(n))$ and $C' = (C'(1), C'(2), \ldots, C'(n))$ be two configurations of $\mathcal{N}$. We say that C derives C' in one*
   - *evolution step (written as $C \Longrightarrow C'$) if, for $1 \leq i \leq n$, the set $C'(i)$ consists of all words $w \in C(i)$ to which no rule of M_i is applicable and of all words w for which there are a word $v \in C(i)$ and a rule $p \in M_i$ such that $v \Longrightarrow_p w$ holds,*
   - *communication step (written as $C \vdash C'$) if, for $1 \leq i \leq n$,*

$$C'(i) = (C(i) \setminus O_i) \cup \bigcup_{(k,i) \in E} C(k) \cap O(k) \cap I(i).$$

The computation of $\mathcal{N}$ is a sequence of configurations

$$C_t = (C_t(1), C_t(2), \ldots, C_t(n)), \text{ for } t \geq 0,$$

such that
   - *$C_0 = (A_1, A_2, \ldots, A_n)$,*
   - *for any $t \geq 0$, C_{2t} derives C_{2t+1} in one evolution step:*

$$C_{2t} \Longrightarrow C_{2t+1},$$

– *for any $t \geq 0$, C_{2t+1} derives C_{2t+2} in one communication step:*

$$C_{2t+1} \vdash C_{2t+2}.$$

4. *The language $L(\mathcal{N})$ generated by $\mathcal{N}$ is defined as*

$$L(\mathcal{N}) = \bigcup_{t \geq 0} C_t(n_o)$$

where $C_t = (C_t(1), C_t(2), \ldots, C_t(n))$ with $t \geq 0$ is the computation of $\mathcal{N}$.

Before we define accepting networks, we briefly describe how such a network works. The underlying structure of a GNEP is a graph consisting of some, say n, nodes $N_1, N_2, \ldots, N_n$ (called processors) and edges given by E such that there is a directed edge from N_k to N_i if and only if $(k, i) \in E$. Any processor N_i consists of a set M_i of evolution rules (also called mutation rules), a set A_i of start words, an input filter I_i and an output filter O_i. We say that N_i is a substitution node or a deletion node or an insertion node if $M_i \subseteq \{a \to b \mid a, b \in V\}$ or $M_i \subseteq \{a \to \lambda \mid a \in V\}$ or $M_i \subseteq \{\lambda \to b \mid b \in V\}$, respectively. The input filter I_i and the output filter O_i control the words which are allowed to enter and to leave the node, respectively. With any node N_i and any time moment $t \geq 0$, we associate a set $C_t(i)$ of words (the words contained in the node N_i at time t). Initially, N_i contains the words of A_i. In an evolutionary step, we derive from $C_t(i)$ all words by applying rules from the set M_i (each word occurs in a sufficiently large number, each rule is applied at an arbitrary possible position in a word, but only one rule at one place is applied in one step, if no rule can be applied to a word, then it remains unchanged, if a rule can be applied, then the original word will be consumed). In a communication step, any processor N_i sends out all words $C_t(i) \cap O_i$ (which pass the output filter) to all processors to which a directed edge exists (only the words from $C_t(i) \setminus O_i$ remain in the set associated with N_i) and, moreover, it receives from any processor N_k such that there is an edge from N_k to N_i all words sent by N_k and passing the input filter I_i of N_i, i.e., the processor N_i gets in addition all words of $(C_t(k) \cap O_k) \cap I_i$. The computation starts with an evolutionary step and then communication steps and evolutionary steps are alternately performed. The language generated consists of all words which are in the output node N_{n_o} at some moment t with $t \geq 0$.

We now define networks of evolutionary processors for accepting languages (ANEPs for short).

Definition 2. 1. *An accepting network of evolutionary processors (of size n) is a $(n + 5)$-tuple $\mathcal{N} = (V, U, N_1, N_2, \ldots, N_n, E, n_i, n_o)$ where*
   – *V is a finite alphabet, called the input alphabet of the network,*
   – *U is a finite alphabet with $V \subseteq U$, called the working alphabet of the network,*
   – *$N_i = (M_i, I_i, O_i)$ for $1 \leq i \leq n$ are the processors where*

- M_i is a set of rules of a certain type: $M_i \subseteq SUB_U$ or $M_i \subseteq DEL_U$ or $M_i \subseteq INS_U$,
- I_i and O_i are regular sets over U (called the input and output filter, respectively),

  – E is a subset of $\{1, 2, \ldots, n\} \times \{1, 2, \ldots, n\}$, and
  – n_i and n_o are two natural numbers from the set $\{1, 2, \ldots, n\}$; the processor N_{n_i} is called the input node and N_{n_o} the output node of the network.

2. Configuration, evolutionary steps, and communication steps are defined as for generating networks.

   The computation of an evolutionary network $\mathcal{N}$ on an input word $w \in V^*$ is a sequence of configurations $C_t^w = (C_t^w(1), C_t^w(2), \ldots, C_t^w(n))$ with $t \geq 0$, such that

   – $C_0^w(n_i) = \{w\}$ and $C_0^w(j) = \emptyset$ for $j \in \{1, \ldots, n\} \setminus \{n_i\}$,
   – for any $t \geq 0$, C_{2t}^w derives C_{2t+1}^w in one evolutionary step,
   – for any $t \geq 0$, C_{2t+1}^w derives C_{2t+2}^w in one communication step.

   The computation of an evolutionary network $\mathcal{N}$ on an input word $w \in V^*$ is said to be accepting if there exists a step $t \geq 0$ in which the component $C_t^w(n_o)$ of the configuration representing the content of the output node is not empty.

3. The language $L(\mathcal{N})$ accepted by $\mathcal{N}$ is defined as

$$L(\mathcal{N}) = \{ \, w \mid w \in V^* \text{ and the computation of } \mathcal{N} \text{ on } w \text{ is accepting} \, \}.$$

An accepting network of evolutionary processors works in the same manner as a generating one. The differences are that, in an ANEP, only one processor has a word in the beginning (called the input word) and that a word in the output processor in an ANEP indicates the acceptance of the input word whereas in a GNEP it belongs to the generated language.

For a language class X, we denote the class of languages accepted by networks of evolutionary processors where all filters belong to the class X by $\mathcal{A}(X)$ and the class of languages generated by networks of evolutionary processors where all filters belong to the class X by $\mathcal{E}(X)$. We consider the filters independently from the environment. A filter language belongs to some family X if it belongs to it with respect to its smallest alphabet, not necessarily to the the alphabet of all letters which might occur in the node or even in the entire network. A word passes a filter if it is an element of the language representing the filter otherwise it does not pass the filter.

In the literature, also other definitions have been used. In the first paper [4] and subsequent ones, the underlying graph was a complete one and the insertion and deletion rules were allowed only to be applied at the end of a word (substitution was allowed everywhere). Later, the so-called hybrid networks of evolutionary processors were introduced (generating HNEPs in [24] and accepting HNEPs in [22]) where each processor is equipped also with a position where its rules must be applied (either all to the left end of a word or all to the right end of a word, or at an arbitrary place). Another difference regards what happens with words to which not all rules or even no rule can be applied in an evolutionary step. Consider, for instance, the word a. If it is in a processor with the deletion rule $a \to \lambda$ and only this rule, then the word is derived to λ. If further a deletion rule $b \to \lambda$ is present, then this rule does not change the word. Hence, the words obtained are a (by the b-rule) and λ (by the a-rule). In [2], a variant has been introduced, called obligatory HNEPs, where only the evolved words belong to the derived language (in this example, only λ because a together with the b-rule yields the empty set). Hence, in OHNEPs, the original words disappear in an evolutionary step (their evolution is obligatory). In [11], a weaker variant has been introduced where in an evolutionary step a word survives if no rule can be applied to it but if a rule can be applied, then the original word will not be present any longer (after all rules have been applied at every possible position). In all these cases, computational completeness was obtained (for every recursively enumerable language, there is a network of evolutionary processors generating or accepting it, no matter what details have been used).

In the sequel, we refer here to papers where the same definition as above has been used. Some results appeared already earlier in other publications but based on another definition.

The following theorem is known (see [7] and [20]).

Theorem 1 ([7], [20]). *We have $\mathcal{E}(REG) = \mathcal{A}(REG) = RE$.*

As usual for powerful models, one asks what can be reduced to what extend without leaving this power.

3   Restrictions Without Decreasing Computational Power

The size of a system is always interesting since smaller systems need fewer resources (space, time for the construction). Regarding resources, the size is not only the number of components but also the sum of the sizes of the components. So, there are many aspects to consider.

3.1   Number of Processors

While in the introductory paper to GNEPs [4] the size of the constructed network was still unbounded (depending on the size of the problem), it has been shown in [5] that for any recursively enumerable language, there is a GNEP with five processors generating the language. Already between these two papers, the definition changed (in the first one, deletion and insertion rules were allowed to be applied only at the ends of a word whereas in the second paper, they could be applied everywhere in a word). In [3], the number was reduced to four (if one takes only terminal words of the generated language (the intersection of the language with a monoid), then even three processors are sufficient). In the same paper, it was shown that, with again another definition (any type of rule is allowed in any processor), any recursively enumerable language can be generated by a network with two processors (even one with intersection with a monoid). Back to processors specialized in one type of rules only, the network with four/three nodes used each type of rules. Hence, a natural question was whether the number of rule types could be reduced. This question was investigated in [1] where it was shown that any recursively enumerable language can be generated by a network which has one node for insertion rules, one node for deletion rules, and one node without rules (which is for collecting the terminal words) only. If one allows intersection with a monoid, the node without rules can be omitted. This yielded also an optimal result for the total number of processors needed to be still computational complete.

Regarding accepting NEPs, any recursively enumerable language can be accepted by a network with three nodes: one substitution or deletion node, one insertion node and one without rules [10].

3.2   Number of Production Rule Types

As mentioned above, in [1], it was shown that any recursively enumerable language can be generated by a network which has one node for insertion rules one node for deletion rules, and one node without rules. In the same paper, it was shown that networks with an arbitrary number of deletion and substitution nodes only generate finite languages (and, for each finite language, one deletion node or one substitution node is sufficient) and networks with an arbitrary number of insertion and substitution nodes only generate context-sensitive languages (and, up to an intersection with a monoid, every context-sensitive language can be generated by a network with one substitution node and one insertion node). So, one type alone would not suffice for computational completeness.

Also ANEPs do not need all three types of rules for being computationally complete; two types are sufficient: one node with substitution or deletion rules, one node with insertion rules, and one node without rules [10]. In [9], it has been shown that networks with only substitution and deletion rules accept context-sensitive languages only (and that every context-sensitive language is accepted by such a network). So, insertion rules are essential for being computational complete.

3.3   Restrictions to the Filters

In several papers, generating or accepting networks haven been investigated where the filters are not arbitrary regular languages but special ones like finite, union-free, suffix-closed languages or languages which are codes or languages which can be generated with a certain number of variables or rules in their generating right-linear grammarsor accepted by deterministic finite automata with a certain number of states. Also networks where the filters are given by permitting and forbidding sets (random-context filters) belong to this area.

For generating NEPs, we refer to the papers [7] and [14] for overviews about hierarchies where the language classes obtained are put into set theoretic relations.

In [7], it was shown that the use of filters from the class of ordered, non-counting, power-separating, circular, suffix-closed regular, union-free, definite, and combinational languages is as powerful as the use of arbitrary regular languages and yields networks that can generate all the recursively enumerable languages. On the other hand, the use of filters that are only finite languages allows only the generation of regular languages, but not every regular language can be generated. If filters are used which are monoids, nilpotent languages, or commutative regular languages, we obtain one and the same family of languages which contains non-context-free languages but not all regular languages.

In [12] and [13], generating networks have been investigated where the minimal determinstic finite automata accepting the filter languages are restricted with respect to the number of their states. It was shown that if the number of states is bounded by two, then every recursively enumerable language can be generated by such a network. If the number of states is bounded by one, then not all regular languages but non-context-free languages can be generated.

In [27], other restrictions on the resources needed for the filters, namely the number of variables or production rules which are needed by a right-linear grammar generating a filter were investigated and set into relation with the restrictions of the papers [12] and [13].

In [15], the generative capacity of GNEPs has been studied where the filters are codes (arbitrary and special ones) or ideals. The hierarchy of the generated language classes obtained there has been merged which that one from [27] in the paper [14].

If the filters are all taken from one of the classes PS, NC, ORD, DEF, $CIRC$, UF, SUF, $COMB$, lId, rId, $(RL_i^V)_{i\geq 1}$, $(REG_i^Z)_{i\geq 2}$, then any recursively enumerable language can be generated. With filters from the other cosidered classes, the GNEPs are less powerful.

Theorem 2 ([7,14,15]). *We have*

$$RE = \mathcal{E}(PS) = \mathcal{E}(NC) = \mathcal{E}(ORD) = \mathcal{E}(DEF) = \mathcal{E}(CIRC)$$
$$= \mathcal{E}(UF) = \mathcal{E}(SUF) = \mathcal{E}(COMB)$$
$$= \mathcal{E}(lId) = \mathcal{E}(rId) = \mathcal{E}((RL_i^V)_{i\geq 1}) = \mathcal{E}((REG_i^Z)_{i\geq 2}).$$

For accepting NEPs, we refer to the papers [21] and [16] for overviews about hierarchies where the language classes obtained are put into set theoretic relations.

In [21], it was shown that the use of filters from the class of non-counting, ordered, power-separating, suffix-closed regular, union-free, definite and combinational languages is as powerful as the use of arbitrary regular languages and yields networks that can accept all the recursively enumerable languages. On the other hand, by using filters that are only finite languages, monoids, nilpotent languages, commutative regular languages, or circular regular languages, one cannot generate all recursively enumerable languages. Hence, for such filters, the only difference between generating and accepting NEPs is the class $CIRC$. Networks with circular filters only can still generate every recursively enumerable language whereas they cannot accept every such language.

In [28], the aforementioned restrictions on the resources needed for the filters, namely the number of variables or production rules which are needed by a right-linear grammar generating a filter and the number of states which are needed by a minimal determinstic finite automaton accepting a filter were investigated and set into relation with the restrictions of the paper [21]. Here, the results for GNEPs and ANEPs coincide: In both cases, the classes $(RL_i^V)_{i \geq 1}$ and $(REG_i^Z)_{i \geq 2}$ yield computationally complete networks whereas filter restrictions to the classes REG_1^Z or RL_i^P for any number $i \geq 1$ are less powerful.

In [16], the generative capacity of ANEPs has been studied where the filters are codes (arbitrary and special ones) or ideals. The hierarchy of the generated language classes obtained there has been merged which that one from [28]. For ideals, the results for GNEPs and ANEPs coincide: In both cases, the classes lId and rId yield computationally complete networks. For codes, the situation is different: Whereas filter restrictions to the classes C, PfC, SfC, BfC, IfC, or SC do not decrease the computational power of accepting networks (such filters are equally powerful as arbitrary regular languages), generating networks with filters from such classes are less powerful.

Summarizing, for accepting networks with filters from subregular language classes, we have the following results.

Theorem 3 ([16,21]). *We have*

$$
\begin{aligned}
RE = \mathcal{A}(PS) &= \mathcal{A}(NC) = \mathcal{A}(ORD) = \mathcal{A}(DEF) \\
&= \mathcal{A}(UF) = \mathcal{A}(SUF) = \mathcal{A}(COMB) \\
&= \mathcal{A}(lId) = \mathcal{A}(rId) = \mathcal{A}((RL_i^V)_{i \geq 1}) = \mathcal{A}((REG_i^Z)_{i \geq 2}) \\
&= \mathcal{A}(C) = \mathcal{A}(PfC) = \mathcal{A}(SfC) = \mathcal{A}(BfC) = \mathcal{A}(IfC) = \mathcal{A}(SC).
\end{aligned}
$$

4   Further Research

Various kinds of generating and accepting networks of evolutionary processors have been developed. Every kind has its own motivation (for instance, biological background). However, from the theoretical point of view, it would be interesting to close the gaps such that networks and their properties are better comparable.

Further, there are still open questions about the computational power of certain networks (e. g., networks with insertion processors only or where the filters belong to a class such that not every recursively enumerable language can be generated or accepted by such a network). Also other restrictions could be considered (other subregular language classes for the filters) or restrictions regarding other resources or combinations thereof.

References

1. Alhazov, A., Dassow, J., Martín-Vide, C., Rogozhin, Y., Truthe, B.: On networks of evolutionary processors with nodes of two types. Fundam. Informaticae **91**, 1–15 (2009)

2. Alhazov, A., Enguix, G.B., Rogozhin, Y.: Obligatory hybrid networks of evolutionary processors. In: Filipe, J., Fred, A.L.N., Sharp, B. (eds.) ICAART 2009 - Proceedings of the International Conference on Agents and Artificial Intelligence, Porto, Portugal, 19–21 January 2009, pp. 613–618. INSTICC Press (2009)
3. Alhazov, A., Martín-Vide, C., Rogozhin, Y.: On the number of nodes in universal networks of evolutionary processors. Acta Informatica **43**(5), 331–339 (2006). https://doi.org/10.1007/s00236-006-0024-x
4. Castellanos, J., Martín-Vide, C., Mitrana, V., Sempere, J.M.: Solving NP-complete problems with networks of evolutionary processors. In: Mira, J., Prieto, A. (eds.) IWANN 2001. LNCS, vol. 2084, pp. 621–628. Springer, Heidelberg (2001). https://doi.org/10.1007/3-540-45720-8_74
5. Castellanos, J., Martín-Vide, C., Mitrana, V., Sempere, J.M.: Networks of evolutionary processors. Acta Informatica **39**(6–7), 517–529 (2003). https://doi.org/10.1007/s00236-003-0114-y
6. Csuhaj-Varjú, E., Salomaa, A.: Networks of parallel language processors. In: Păun, G., Salomaa, A. (eds.) New Trends in Formal Languages. LNCS, vol. 1218, pp. 299–318. Springer, Heidelberg (1997). https://doi.org/10.1007/3-540-62844-4_22
7. Dassow, J., Manea, F., Truthe, B.: Networks of evolutionary processors: the power of subregular filters. Acta Informatica **50**(1), 41–75 (2013). https://doi.org/10.1007/s00236-012-0172-0
8. Dassow, J., Mitrana, V.: Accepting networks of non-inserting evolutionary processors. In: Petre, I., Rozenberg, G. (eds.) Proceedings of NCGT 2008 - Workshop on Natural Computing and Graph Transformations, Leicester, United Kingdom, 8 September 2008, pp. 29–41. University of Leicester (2008)
9. Dassow, J., Mitrana, V.: Accepting networks of non-inserting evolutionary processors. In: Priami, C., Back, R.-J., Petre, I. (eds.) Transactions on Computational Systems Biology XI. LNCS, vol. 5750, pp. 187–199. Springer, Heidelberg (2009). https://doi.org/10.1007/978-3-642-04186-0_9
10. Dassow, J., Mitrana, V., Truthe, B.: The role of evolutionary operations in accepting hybrid networks of evolutionary processors. Inf. Comput. **209**(3), 368–382 (2011)
11. Dassow, J., Truthe, B.: On the power of networks of evolutionary processors. In: Durand-Lose, J., Margenstern, M. (eds.) MCU 2007. LNCS, vol. 4664, pp. 158–169. Springer, Heidelberg (2007). https://doi.org/10.1007/978-3-540-74593-8_14
12. Dassow, J., Truthe, B.: On networks of evolutionary processors with state limited filters. In: Bordihn, H., Freund, R., Hinze, T., Holzer, M., Kutrib, M., Otto, F. (eds.) Second Workshop on Non-Classical Models of Automata and Applications (NCMA), Jena, Germany, 23–24 August 2010, Proceedings. books@ocg.at, vol. 263, pp. 57–70. Österreichische Computer Gesellschaft, Austria (2010)
13. Dassow, J., Truthe, B.: On networks of evolutionary processors with filters accepted by two-state-automata. Fundam. Informaticae **112**(2–3), 157–170 (2011)
14. Dassow, J., Truthe, B.: Generating networks of evolutionary processors with resources restricted and structure limited filters. J. Automata Lang. Comb. **25**(2–3), 83–113 (2020)
15. Dassow, J., Truthe, B.: Networks with evolutionary processors and ideals and codes as filters. Int. J. Found. Comput. Sci. **31**(1), 73–89 (2020)
16. Dassow, J., Truthe, B.: Accepting networks of evolutionary processors with resources restricted and structure limited filters. RAIRO Theor. Inform. Appl. **55**, 8 (2021)

17. Freund, R., Rogojin, V., Verlan, S.: Variants of networks of evolutionary processors with polarizations and a small number of processors. Int. J. Found. Comput. Sci. **30**(6–7), 1005–1027 (2019)
18. Jürgensen, H., Konstantinidis, S.: Codes[1]. In: Rozenberg, G., Salomaa, A. (eds.) Handbook of Formal Languages, pp. 511–607. Springer, Heidelberg (1997). https://doi.org/10.1007/978-3-642-59136-5_8
19. Loos, R., Manea, F., Mitrana, V.: Small universal accepting networks of evolutionary processors with filtered connections. J. Automata Lang. Comb. **15**(1–2), 155–174 (2010)
20. Manea, F., Truthe, B.: Accepting networks of evolutionary processors with subregular filters. Theory of Computing Systems **55**(1), 84–109 (2014)
21. Manea, F., Truthe, B.: Accepting networks of evolutionary processors with subregular filters. Theor. Comput. Syst. **55**(1), 84–109 (2013). https://doi.org/10.1007/s00224-013-9502-z
22. Margenstern, M., Mitrana, V., Pérez-Jiménez, M.J.: Accepting hybrid networks of evolutionary processors. In: Ferretti, C., Mauri, G., Zandron, C. (eds.) DNA 2004. LNCS, vol. 3384, pp. 235–246. Springer, Heidelberg (2005). https://doi.org/10.1007/11493785_21
23. Martín-Vide, C., Mitrana, V.: Networks of evolutionary processors: results and perspectives. In: Molecular Computational Models: Unconventional Approaches, pp. 78–114 (2005)
24. Martín-Vide, C., Mitrana, V., Pérez-Jiménez, M.J., Sancho-Caparrini, F.: Hybrid networks of evolutionary processors. In: Cantú-Paz, E. (ed.) GECCO 2003. LNCS, vol. 2723, pp. 401–412. Springer, Heidelberg (2003). https://doi.org/10.1007/3-540-45105-6_49
25. Rozenberg, G., Salomaa, A. (eds.): Handbook of Formal Languages. Springer, Heidelberg (1997). https://doi.org/10.1007/978-3-642-59136-5
26. Shyr, H.J.: Free Monoids and Languages. Hon Min Book Company, Taichung, Taiwan (1991)
27. Truthe, B.: Networks of evolutionary processors with resources restricted filters. In: Freund, R., Hospodár, M., Jirásková, G., Pighizzini, G. (eds.) Tenth Workshop on Non-Classical Models of Automata and Applications (NCMA), Košice, Slovakia, 21–22 August 2018, Proceedings. books@ocg.at, vol. 332, pp. 165–180. Österreichische Computer Gesellschaft (2018)
28. Truthe, B.: Accepting networks of evolutionary processors with resources restricted filters. In: Freund, R., Holzer, M., Sempere, J.M. (eds.) Eleventh Workshop on Non-Classical Models of Automata and Applications (NCMA), Valencia, Spain, 2–3 July 2019, Proceedings. books@ocg.at, vol. 336, pp. 187–202. Österreichische Computer Gesellschaft (2019)

Prescribed Teams of Rules Working on Several Objects

Artiom Alhazov[1], Rudolf Freund[2(✉)], Sergiu Ivanov[3], and Sergey Verlan[4]

[1] Vladimir Andrunachievici Institute of Mathematics and Computer Science,
Academiei 5, 2028 Chişinău, Moldova
`artiom@math.md`
[2] Faculty of Informatics, TU Wien,
Favoritenstraße 9–11, 1040 Vienna, Austria
`rudi@emcc.at`
[3] IBISC, Univ. Évry, Paris-Saclay University,
23, boulevard de France, 91034 Évry, France
`sergiu.ivanov@ibisc.univ-evry.fr`
[4] Univ. Paris Est Creteil, LACL, 94010 Creteil, France
`verlan@u-pec.fr`

Abstract. In this paper we consider prescribed sets of rules working on several objects either in parallel – in this case the rules have to take different objects – or else sequentially in any order – in this case several rules may take the same object to work on.

We show that prescribed teams of size two, i.e., containing exactly two rules, are sufficient to obtain computational completeness for strings with the simple rules being of the form $aI_R(b)$ – meaning that a symbol b can be inserted on the right-hand side of a string ending with a – and $D_R(b)$ meaning that a symbol b is erased on the right-hand side of a string. This result is established for systems starting with three initial strings. Using prescribed teams of size three, we may start with only two strings, ending up with the output string and the second string having been reduced to the empty string. We also establish similar results when using the generation of the anti-object b^- on the right-hand side of a string instead of deleting the object b, i.e. $bI_R(b^-)$ inserts the anti-object b^- and the annihilation rule bb^- assumed to happen immediately whenever b and b^- *meet* deletes the b.

Keywords: Computational completeness · Insertion-deletion systems · Prescribed teams · Anti-objects

1 Introduction

Cooperation in its different forms is a feature which has attracted a lot of research in formal languages and theory of computation. Indeed, the family of context-free languages is quite well studied, and it is folklore that some easy to describe languages are not context free, e.g. $\{a^n b^n c^n \mid n \in \mathbb{N}\}$, the copy language

J. Durand-Lose and G. Vaszil (Eds.): MCU 2022, LNCS 13419, pp. 27–41, 2022.
https://doi.org/10.1007/978-3-031-13502-6_6

$\{ww \mid w \in V^*\}$, for some alphabet V, etc. On the other hand, it is just as well-known that full cooperation – classically expressed by allowing multiple symbols in the left-hand side of the rewriting rules – yields computational completeness in many situations. We refer to [7] for a comprehensive overview of the multiple facets of cooperation.

This situation aroused interest in the expressive power of intermediate forms, in which some cooperation is allowed, but full cooperation is avoided. One of the possible implementations is by forcing some rules to only be applied together, a classic example being matrix grammars, in which the rules are grouped into sequences, and must be applied one after another, in order. Here, we focus on a less strict variant, in which the rules of a group must be applied together, but the order of their application is not imposed. This control mechanism is known as *prescribed teams* and was introduced in [1].

In this paper, we define prescribed teams in a general framework for rewriting as a control mechanism over abstract rules. In order to study the computational power of this device, we specialize the rules to string insertion and deletion operations. More concretely, we focus on insertions and deletions which are only allowed to occur at the right end of a string and which may depend on a finite context. We show that by allowing computation to happen on two strings at the same time, such insertion and deletion rules grouped in prescribed teams containing three rules can simulate any Turing machine (Theorem 1). We remark that even though insertion-deletion operations with matrix control have been quite extensively investigated (e.g., [3–6]), the power of insertion and deletion operations restricted to the right of the string and equipped with matrix control has never been studied to the best of our knowledge.

2   Definitions

For an alphabet V, by V^* we denote the free monoid generated by V under the operation of concatenation, i.e., containing all possible strings over V. The *empty string* is denoted by λ. Given a string $w = w_1 \ldots w_n$ over V, with $w_i \in V$, $1 \leq i \leq n$, its mirror image is $w^R = w_n \ldots w_1$. Moreover, instead of $w = w_1 \ldots w_n$ we may also write $w = w(1) \ldots w(n)$.

The cardinality of a set M is denoted by $|M|$. For further notions and results in formal language theory we refer to textbooks like [2] and [7].

2.1   Systems with Prescribed Teams of Rules

The main model we consider in this paper is a system of arbitrary objects which starts on a finite set of such objects and has prescribed teams of rules to work on these objects until no such team can be applied any more.

Definition 1. *A system with prescribed teams of rules is a construct*

$$G = (O, O_T, P, R, A) \quad \text{where}$$

- O *is a set of objects;*
- $O_T \subseteq O$ *is a set of* terminal objects*;*
- P *is a finite set of* rules, *i.e.,* $P = \{p_i \mid 1 \le i \le m\}$, *for some* $m \ge 0$, *and* $p_i \subseteq O \times O$*;*
- $R = \{T_1, \ldots, T_n\}$ *is a finite set of sets of rules from* P *called* prescribed teams, *i.e.,* $T_i \subseteq P$, $1 \le i \le n$*;*
- A *is a finite set of initial objects in* O.

A rule $p \in P$ is called *applicable* to an object $x \in O$ if and only if there exists at least one object $y \in O$ such that $(x, y) \in p$; in this case we also write $x \Longrightarrow_p y$.

$|T_i|$ is called the *size* of the prescribed team T_i. If all prescribed teams have at most size s, then G is called a *system (with prescribed teams) of size s*. If all prescribed teams have the same size s, then G is called a *homogenous system (with prescribed teams) of size s*. The number of initial objects in A is called the *degree* of the system.

Computations in a System with Prescribed Teams of Rules. We may consider different variants of applications of the prescribed teams of rules as already indicated above when working on several objects, starting with the initial objects in A; in any case, at the beginning of a computation step we first have to choose a suitable team T_k:

parallel each rule in T_k is applied to a different object in the current set of objects; T_k can only be applied if every rule in T_k can be applied; we observe that in the parallel case the number of rules in any prescribed team must not exceed the number of initial objects;

sequential the rules in T_k are applied sequentially in any order – in this case several rules may take the same object to work on in several sequential derivation steps, yet again each rule is to be applied exactly once.

T_k can only be applied if every rule in T_k can be applied in the given derivation mode.

We mention that we do not consider the case where several rules from T_k may be applied to the same object at the same moment in parallel.

In case the mode of application is not clear from the context, we may specify it in the definition of the system, i.e., we then write

$$G = (O, O_T, P, T_1, \ldots, T_n, A, d)$$

where $d \in \{parallel, sequential\}$.

A *derivation step* in G using T_k in the mode d then can be written as

$$\{O_1, \ldots, O_m\} \Longrightarrow_{T_k, d} \{O'_1, \ldots, O'_m\}$$

where $\{O_1, \ldots, O_m\}$ is the current set of objects and $\{O'_1, \ldots, O'_m\}$ is the set of objects obtained after the application of T_k in mode d.

The derivation relation $\Longrightarrow_{G,d}$ of the system G in mode d then is the union of all derivation relations $\Longrightarrow_{T_k,d}$, $1 \leq k \leq n$. Given two objects $u, v \in O$, we write $u \Longrightarrow_d v$ ($u \Longrightarrow_{T_k,d} v$) to indicate that v can be obtained from u in one derivation/computation step from u (using the prescribed team T_k) in the derivation mode d. The reflexive and transitive closure of $\Longrightarrow_{G,d}$ is denoted by $\Longrightarrow_{G,d}*$. If the derivation mode d is obvious from the context, d is omitted in all these notations.

For arbitrary systems working in the sequential mode, we can prove the following complexity result:

Lemma 1. *Given a homogenous system*

$$G = (O, O_T, P, T_1, \ldots, T_n, A, sequential)$$

of size 1, its computations are the union of the computations of the m systems

$$G_k = (O, O_T, P, T_1, \ldots, T_n, A_k, sequential),$$

$1 \leq k \leq m$, *where* $A = \{A_k \mid 1 \leq k \leq m\}$.

Proof. In the sequential mode, a prescribed team can only work on one of the m subjects. Hence, the computations on the initial objects are independent of each other. Therefore also the terminal objects must be obtained from one of these initial objects A_k by the corresponding system G_k. □

2.2   Matrix Grammars Working on Several Objects

A model quite closely related to systems with prescribed teams of rules is the model of matrix grammars usually only considered to work on one object:

Definition 2. *A* matrix grammar working on several objects *is a construct*

$$G = (O, O_T, P, M, A) \quad where$$

- *O is a set of objects;*
- *$O_T \subseteq O$ is a set of terminal objects;*
- *P is a finite set of rules, i.e., $P = \{p_i \mid 1 \leq i \leq n\}$, for some $n \geq 0$, and $p_i \subseteq O \times O$;*
- *M is a finite set of sequences of the form $(p_1, \ldots, p_n)$, $n \geq 1$, of rules in P; an element of M is called a* matrix;
- *A is a finite set of initial objects in O.*

A derivation step in the matrix grammar consists of choosing a matrix and applying the sequence of rules in the matrix in this order, yet allowing several rules to be applied to the same object.

Lemma 2. *Any system with prescribed teams of rules $G = (O, O_T, P, R, A)$ working in the sequential mode can be simulated by a matrix grammar $G = (O, O_T, P, M, A)$.*

Proof. From a prescribed team T in R we immediately get the corresponding set of matrixes for M by taking every possible sequence of the rules in T, i.e.,

$$M = \{[p_1, \ldots, p_n] \mid \{p_1, \ldots, p_n\} \in R, |\{p_1, \ldots, p_n\}| = n\}.$$

Hence, matrix grammars are at least as powerful as systems with prescribed teams of rules working in the sequential mode.   □

2.3 Turing Machines

The computational model we will simulate for showing computational completeness for the systems with prescribed teams of rules defined above are Turing machines with one tape with left boundary marker Z_0:

Definition 3. *A Turing machine is a construct*

$$M = (Q, V, T_1, T_2, \delta, q_0, q_1, Z_0, B)$$

where

- Q *is a finite set of* states,
- V *is the* tape alphabet,
- $T_1 \subset V \setminus (\{Z_0, B\})$ *is the* input alphabet,
- $T_2 \subset V \setminus (\{Z_0, B\})$ *is the* output alphabet,
- $\delta \subset (Q \times V) \to (Q \times V \times \{L, R\})$ *is the* transition function,
- q_0 *is the* initial state,
- q_1 *is the* final state,
- $Z_0 \in V$ *is the* left boundary marker,
- $B \in V$ *is the* blank symbol.

A configuration of the Turing machine M can be written as $Z_0 uqvB^\omega$, where $u \in (V \setminus (\{Z_0\}))^*$, $v \in (V \setminus (\{Z_0\}))^+ \cup \{\lambda\}$, and B^ω indicates the remaining empty part of the tape, offering an unbounded number of tape cells initially carrying the blank symbol B; moreover, the current state $q \in Q$ is written to the right of the tape cell on which the read-write head of the Turing machine currently stands.

A transition between configurations is carried out according to the transition function δ in the following way for $(q, X; p, Y, D) \in \delta$:

- the state changes from q to p,
- the symbol X currently read is replaced by the symbol Y,
  and for
    $D = R$ the read-write head goes one step to the right; i.e.,
        $Z_0 uXqUvB^\omega \Longrightarrow Z_0 uYUpvB^\omega$;
    $D = L$ the read-write head goes one step to the left, i.e.,
        $Z_0 uXqvB^\omega \Longrightarrow Z_0 upYvB^\omega$;
        observe that the read-write head can never go to the left of Z_0.

For the derivation relation $\Longrightarrow$ as defined above, its reflexive and transitive closure is defined by $\Longrightarrow^*$.

Turing machines are well-known automata which can compute any partial recursive relation $f : T_1{}^* \rightarrow T_2{}^*$:

A successful computation of the Turing machine M starts with the input string w_{input} on its tape with the configuration

$$Z_0 w_{input} q_0 B^\omega$$

and ends up with the output string w_{output} on its tape with the configuration

$$Z_0 w_{output} q_1 B^\omega,$$

i.e.,

$$Z_0 w_{input} q_0 B^\omega \Longrightarrow^* Z_0 w_{output} q_1 B^\omega.$$

A successful computation *halts* in the final state q_1; without loss of generality, we may assume that from the final state q_1 no transition is possible.

The *generation* of a language $L \subseteq T_2{}^*$ can be seen as computing a partial recursive relation $g_L : \{\lambda\} \rightarrow T_2{}^*$, *acceptance* of a language $L \subseteq T_1{}^*$ as computing a partial recursive function $h_L : T_2{}^* \rightarrow \{\lambda\}$.

In order to show that another (string) computing device is computationally complete, an option is to simulate Turing machines, which is exactly what we will do in the next section.

3   Prescribed Teams of Rules on Strings

In this section we consider the objects to be strings. Moreover, we will restrict ourselves to special variants of insertion and deletion rules to be applied to strings.

3.1   Definitions for Prescribed Teams of Insertion and Deletion Rules on Strings

We are going to use the following notations:

Definition 4.
   Right insertions and deletions with contexts:

$uI_R(v)$ *to a string ending with u, v is appended;*
$uD_R(v)$ *from a string ending with uv, the end v is deleted.*

   left insertions and deletions with contexts:

$uI_L(v)$ *to a string beginning with u, v is added as prefix;*
$uD_L(v)$ *from a string beginning with vu, the prefix v is deleted.*

   right and left substitutions

$S_R(u, v)$ *in a string ending with* u, u *is replaced by* v;
$S_L(u, v)$ *in a string beginning with* u, u *is replaced by* v.

Both insertions and deletions can easily be replaced by substitutions:

Lemma 3. *Right and left insertions and deletions can be replaced by right and left substitutions, respectively.*

Proof. Right and left insertions and deletions are replaced by right and left substitutions, respectively, in the following way:

- $uI_R(v)$ by $S_R(u, uv)$;
- $uI_L(v)$ by $S_L(u, vu)$;
- $uD_R(v)$ by $S_R(uv, u)$;
- $uD_L(v)$ by $S_L(vu, u)$.

We remark that contexts need not be considered with substitutions as they can be deleted and re-inserted immediately. $\qquad\square$

Example 1. Consider the system

$$G = (T'^* \{c'c\} T^*, T'^* \{c'c\} T^*, P, T_1, \ldots, T_n, \{c'c\})$$

working in the sequential derivation mode, where T is an arbitrary alphabet, $T' = \{a' \mid a \in T\}$, $c \notin T$, cc' is the only initial string, the set P consists of two disjoint sets of rules R and R',

$$R = \{aI_R(b) \mid a \in T \cup \{c\}, b \in T\},$$
$$R' = \{a'I_L(b') \mid a \in T \cup \{c\}, b \in T\},$$

i.e., for each rule $p = aI_R(b)$ in R we have the corresponding rule $p' = a'I_L(b')$. The set of prescribed teams then is formed by all possible couples p, p', i.e.,

$$\bigcup_{1 \le i \le n} T_i = \bigcup_{p \in R} \{p, p'\}.$$

As both sets of rules work with disjoint alphabets, we get the derivations

$$\{c'c\} \Longrightarrow_{\{cI_R(b_1), c'I_L(b'_1)\}} \{b'_1 c' c b_1\} \ldots$$
$$\Longrightarrow_{\{b_{m-1}I_R(b_m), b'_{m-1}I_L(b'_{m-1})\}} \{b'_m \ldots b'_1 c' c b_1 \ldots b_m\}$$

Hence, for the language generated by G we obtain (the context-free, but non-regular) language

$$\{(w')^R c' c w \mid w \in T^*\}.$$

We observe that we have started with only one string and only used left and right insertion of one symbol in the context of another symbol.

We now are going to show that right insertion rules inserting just one symbol at the end of a string in the left context of just another single symbol together with right deletion rules eliminating the last symbol of a string, even without using any context, are already sufficient to obtain computational completeness. A similar result holds for the corresponding variants of left insertion and deletion rules.

3.2   Results for Prescribed Teams of Insertion and Deletion Rules on Strings

We first establish a result for systems of degree 2 and size 3.

Theorem 1. *The computations of a Turing machine M can be simulated by a homogenous string system with prescribed teams of size 3 and degree 2 using only rules of the form $aI_R(b)$ and $D_R(b)$.*

Proof. Let

$$M = (Q, V, T_1, T_2, \delta, q_0, q_1, Z_0, B)$$

be a Turing machine. In order to represent the configurations of M as finite strings, we use a right end marker Z_1 to mark the end of a finite representation $Z_0uqvB^mZ_1$ of the configuration Z_0uqvB^ω, where m may be any natural number ≥ 0; m depends on how far on the tape the read-write head has already proceeded during a computation.

We now construct a system G with prescribed teams using only rules of the form $aI_R(b)$ and $D_R(b)$ which can simulate the computations of the given Turing machine M. The basic idea is folklore – a configuration $Z_0uqvB^mZ_1$ is represented by two strings Z_0uq and $(vB^mZ_1)^R = Z_1B^mv^R$, which like stacks are only affected at the end of the strings. A special technical detail is that when we reach a situation where the second string is Z_1, no transition to the right is possible immediately, we first have to insert an additional blank B to then continue with the second string Z_1B. Moreover, in order to allow the rules to distinguish between the two strings, the second string is written in the primed alphabet $V' = \{X' \mid X \in V\}$.

The system with prescribed teams using only rules of the form $aI_R(b)$ and $D_R(b)$ is constructed with only two strings being processed, which represent these two parts of the configuration; the size of the teams can be restricted to be exactly three. Moreover, the system is constructed in such a way that the teams have to be applied in a sequential way, but the sequence of the application of the rules does not matter, yet the sequence in which the rules are given in the sets indicates in which sequence the rules are to be applied to obtain the desired result.

The main idea is that in every derivation step using a prescribed team of size 3 we only simulate one right insertion or deletion on one of the two strings in the second step, whereas the first step eliminates the symbol representing the current state and the third step inserts the symbol representing the next state. The state symbols always are placed at the end of the first string. Moreover, the three rules always must be applied exactly in this order, and each of the rules is applied exactly once.

$$G = ((V \cup Q) \cup (V \cup Q)' \cup Q'')^*, \{Z_0\}T_2^*, P, R, A, sequential),$$
$$A = \{Z_0w_{input}q_0, Z_1'\}.$$

The set of rules P can be collected from the prescribed teams of rules described in the following for the transitions given by δ, and the intermediate states defined below are collected in Q'':

$(\mathbf{q}, \mathbf{X}; \mathbf{p}, \mathbf{Y}, \mathbf{L})$ With the first prescribed team the symbol X at the end of the first string is eliminated remembering the rule to be applied and the symbol W to the left of X in the intermediate state $[W; q, X; p, Y, L; U]$, where U is the first symbol at the end of the second string. Then the new symbol Y in its primed version is inserted to the second string using the second prescribed team.

Observe that the two teams must be applied exactly in this order, as the intermediate state $[W; q, X; p, Y, L; U]$ carrying all necessary information cannot be used otherwise:

1. $\{D_R(q), D_R(X), WI_R([W; q, X; p, Y, L; U])\}$, $W, U \in V$;
   the symbol W to the left of X and the symbol U at the end of the second string have to be guessed in a non-deterministic way.
   The rule $D_R(X)$ cannot be applied before the rule $D_R(q)$, as the deletions can only happen in the order the symbols appear at the end of the first string.
   $WI_R([W; q, X; p, Y, L; U])$ cannot be applied before the other two rules, as these then would not be applicable any more.
2. $\{D_R([W; q, X; p, Y, L; U]), U'I_R(Y'), WI_R(p)\}$.
   The rule $D_R([W; q, X; p, Y, L; U])$ must be applied before the rule $WI_R(p)$, because W is not a state symbol.
   The rule $U'I_R(Y')$ on the second string can be applied at any moment.

   With these two teams, we obtain the following derivation:
   $\{uWXq, Z_1'B'^m v'^R U'\} \Longrightarrow$
   $\{uW[W; q, X; p, Y, L; U], Z_1'B'^m v'^R U'\} \Longrightarrow$
   $\{uWp, Z_1'B'^m v'^R U'Y'\}$

$(\mathbf{q}, \mathbf{X}; \mathbf{p}, \mathbf{Y}, \mathbf{R})$ With the first prescribed team the symbol X at the end of the first string is eliminated, then the new symbol Y is inserted to the first string instead of X; with the third prescribed team the last symbol U (in its primed version) of the second string is deleted and remembered in the intermediate state $[q, X; p, Y, L; U']$; finally, using the fourth prescribed team, this symbol U' is inserted at the end of the first string.

Observe that the four teams must be applied exactly in this order, as the intermediate states

$$[W; q, X; p, Y, L; U], \quad [W; q, X; p, Y, L; U'], \quad \text{and} [W; q, X; p, Y, L; U'']$$

carrying all necessary information cannot be used otherwise.

1. $\{D_R(q), D_R(X), WI_R([W; q, X; p, Y, L; U])\}$, $W, U \in V$;
   the symbol W to the left of X and the symbol U at the end of the second string have to be guessed in a non-deterministic way.
   The rule $D_R(X)$ cannot be applied before the rule $D_R(q)$, as the deletions can only happen in the order the symbols appear at the end of the first string.
   $WI_R([W; q, X; p, Y, L; U]$ cannot be applied before the other two rules, as these rules then would not be applicable any more.

2. $\{D_R([W;q,X;p,Y,L;U]),WI_R(Y),YI_R([q,X;p,Y,L;U'])\}$;
   The rule $D_R([W;q,X;p,Y,L;U])$ must be applied first, i.e., before the other two rules, as these rules require a left context not being a state. Using the same argument it follows that the rule $WI_R(Y)$ must be applied before the rule $YI_R([q,X;p,Y,L;U'])$.

3. $\{D_R([W;q,X;p,Y,L;U'])),D_R(U'),YI_R([q,X;p,Y,L;U''])\}$;
   The rule $D_R([W;q,X;p,Y,L;U'])$ must be applied before the rule $YI_R([q,X;p,Y,L;U''])$, because Y is not a state symbol. The rule $D_R(U')$ on the second string can be applied at any moment.

4. $\{D_R([W;q,X;p,Y,L;U'']),YI_R(U),UI_R(p)\}$.
   The rule $D_R([W;q,X;p,Y,L;U''])$ must be applied first, i.e., before the other two rules, also working on the first string, as these rules require a left context not being a state. Using the same argument it follows that the rule $UI_R(p)$ must be applied after the rule $YI_R(U)$.

With these four teams, we obtain the following derivation:

$\{uWXq,Z_1'B'^m v'^R U'\} \Longrightarrow$
$\{uW[W;q,X;p,Y,L;U],Z_1'B'^m v'^R U'\} \Longrightarrow$
$\{uWY[W;q,X;p,Y,L;U'],Z_1'B'^m v'^R U'\} \Longrightarrow$
$\{uWY[W;q,X;p,Y,L;U''],Z_1'B'^m v'^R\} \Longrightarrow$
$\{uWYUp,Z_1'B'^m v'^R\}$

insertion of B If one more blank is needed in front of the right end marker Z_1', an intermediate step for any state q being part of a rule $(q,B;p,Y,R)$ to be applied must be carried out:
$\{D_R(q),Z_1'I_R(B'),WI_R(q)\}$, $W \in V$;
the symbol W at the end of the first string has to be guessed in a non-deterministic way.

Derivation:
$\{uWq,Z_1'\} \Longrightarrow \{uWq,Z_1'B'\}$

final cleaning First the remaining blanks are removed:
$\{D_R(q_1),D_R(B'),aI_R(q_1)\}$, $a \in T_2 \cup \{Z_0\}$.
The rule $D_R(q_1)$ must be applied before the rule $aI_R(q_1)$, because a is not a state symbol. The rule $D_R(B')$ on the second string can be applied at any moment.

Moreover, observe that with the final state q_1 of the Turing machine no transitions are defined any more, i.e., with q_1 the Turing machine has halted.

Applying this team of rules m times, we obtain the following derivation:
$\{Z_0 w_{output} q_1,Z_1'B'^m\} \Longrightarrow^m \{Z_0 w_{output} q_1,Z_1'\}$

When all the blank symbols on the second string have been erased, finally, the second string is completely eliminated, at the same time also the final state at the end of the terminal string is erased; in order to have exactly teams of size 3 we insert one blank again in an intermediate step using the intermediate state q_1':
$\{D_R(q_1),Z_1'I_R(B'),aI_R(q_1')\}$, $a \in T \cup \{Z_0\}$;
The rule $D_R(q_1)$ must be applied before the rule $aI_R(q_1')$, because a is not a state symbol. The rule $Z_1'I_R(B')$ on the second string can be applied at any moment.

Finally, we use the following prescribed team of rules:
$$\{D_R(q_1'), D_R(B'), D_R(Z_1')\};$$
When using this final team, the only restriction on the sequence how they are to be applied is that $D_R(B')$ must be applied before $D_R(Z_1')$.
Derivation:
$$\{Z_0 w_{output} q_1, Z_1'\} \implies \{Z_0 w_{output} q_1', Z_1' B'\} \implies^m \{Z_0 w_{output}, \lambda\}$$

In sum, we observe that every computation of the Turing machine M

$$Z_0 w_{input} q_0 B^\omega \implies Z_0 w_{output} q_1 B^\omega$$

can be simulated in G by a computation

$$\{Z_0 w_{input} q_0, Z_1'\} \implies \{Z_0 w_{output}, \lambda\}.$$

A result $Z_0 w_{output}$ obtained in G represents the string w_{output}. Observe that Z_0 cannot be avoided as only non-empty strings can be handled on the first string of the system. □

We now show the somehow symmetric case using three initial strings, but only teams of size two:

Theorem 2. *The computations of a Turing machine M can be simulated by a homogenous string system with prescribed teams of size 2 and degree 3 using only rules of the form $a I_R(b)$ and $D_R(b)$, either working in the sequential or the parallel derivation mode.*

Proof. For $d \in \{sequential, parallel\}$, we construct the system

$$G' = ((V \cup Q) \cup (V \cup Q)' \cup Q'')^*, \{Z_0\} T_2^*, P, R, A', d),$$
$$A' = \{Z_0 w_{input} q_0, Z_1', p_0\}.$$

and follow the constructions given in the proofs of Theorem 1.

The initial set of strings now contains a third string which step by step will collect the (labels of) the rules applied in the computation steps. Except for the last cleaning step, the prescribed teams in the proof of Theorem 1 all are of the form $\{D_R(p), rule, W I_R(q)\}$, where W is an arbitrary symbol, but not a state symbol, and *rule* is an insertion or deletion rule on the first or second string. With the help of the third string, the two rules $\{D_R(p), W I_R(q)\}$ now can be replaced by one single insertion rule $p I_R(q)$.

In contrast to the final cleaning established in the proof of Theorem 1, the final team now is the following:

$$\{q_1 I_R(q_1'), D_R(Z_1')\}.$$

At the end, the result of a successful computation is given by the first string and the second string has been reduced to the empty string as in the preceding proof, but the third string remains as a kind of garbage.

We finally remark that this construction, in contrast to the one given in the proof of Theorem 1, now not only works in the *sequential* derivation mode, but as well in the *parallel* derivation mode, as the rules in each prescribed team work on different strings.   □

Remark 1. As outlined in the preceding proof, the prescribed teams of rules of size 2 only work on one the two strings representing the left and right part of the Turing tape by either deleting or inserting one symbol. The left context of the insertion rules is only needed to indicate to which string the new symbol has to be added.

In that sense, instead of simulating the computations of a Turing machine we could also have simulated the computations of a 2-stack automaton which also used the operations of deleting (*pop*) one symbol oder inserting (*push*) one symbol on one of its two stacks, together with changing state.

Whereas the preceding proof might have become even easier when just simulating *pop* and *push* actions on the two stacks, the intuition what these two stacks in fact represent would have got lost, especially why we need to insert a blank symbol when reaching the bottom of the second stack.

Remark 2. The third string remaining in the construction of the system G' constructed in the proof of Theorem 2 can be interpreted as the Szilard word of the computation in the system, hence, it is not only garbage, but carries useful information.

We now use the idea of anti-objects to replace the deletions of a symbol b by the insertion of the corresponding anti-symbol b^-, where in addition we assume that b and b^- immediately annihilate each other immediately before the next rules are applied. Therefore, any deletion rule $D_R(b)$ can be replaced by the corresponding insertion rule $bI_R(b^-)$. Hence, based on the preceding results, we immediately obtain the following ones:

Corollary 1. *The computations of a Turing machine M can be simulated by a homogenous string system with prescribed teams of size 3 and degree 2 using only rules of the form $aI(b)$ and $bI(b^-)$.*

Corollary 2. *The computations of a Turing machine M can be simulated by a homogenous string system with prescribed teams of size 2 and degree 3 using only rules of the form $aI(b)$ and $bI(b^-)$.*

3.3   Complexity Considerations for Prescribed Teams of Rules on Strings

In the preceding subsection we have already seen that there seems to be a trade-off between the size and the degree of string system with prescribed teams using only rules of the form $aI_R(b)$ and $D_R(b)$, where one parameter has to be three and the other one can be restricted to two. We now especially consider the generating case.

- According to Lemma 1, having only systems of size 1, we only can get finite unions of languages generated by systems of size 1 and degree 1.
- Moreover, as matrix grammars according to Lemma 2 are at least as powerful as string systems with prescribed teams, an upper bound for string systems with prescribed teams of degree 1 are usual matrix grammars working on one string with the same rules.
- According to Lemma 3, insertions and deletions on the right can be replaced by substitutions on the right.

The proof of the following lemma is left to the interested reader.

Lemma 4. *The effect of a matrix using right substitution rules on one string can be simulated by just one right substitution rule, i.e., for any matrix grammar using right substitution rules on one string we can construct a standard sequential grammar using right substitution rules.*

In order to show that systems of either size 1 or degree 1 cannot generate more than regular languages, it therefore suffices to prove the following result:

Lemma 5. *Sequential grammars using only right substitution rules can only generate regular languages.*

Proof. Let us start with a sequential grammar using right substitution rules

$$G = (N, T, P, S) \text{ where}$$

- N is a set of *nonterminal symbols*;
- T is a set of *terminal symbols*;
- P is a finite set of *right substitution rules* over V, where $V = N \cup T$;
- $S \in V^+$ is the *axiom*.

Now let $n := max\{|uv| \mid S_R(u, v) \in P)\}$. Moreover, let A_0 be the set of all terminal strings of lengths k, $0 \leq k \leq 2n$ that can be derived in G, and A be the set of all strings of lengths k with $n \leq k \leq 2n$ which can be derived in G. The language generated by G then is the union of the (terminal) strings in A_0 and the languages generated by the sequential grammars $G(A') = (N, T, P(A'), A')$ for $A' \in A$. In $P(A')$ we will only allow the substitutions in P which do not decrease the lengths of sentential forms any more:

Those strings in the language generated by G of lengths at most $2n$ are already contained in A_0, therefore we only need to aim at terminal strings of lengths bigger than $2n$.

Starting from a string w with u at the end, $|u| = n$, there can only be a finite number of derivations from w, not decreasing the length, but increasing the length by at most n symbols, which can be captured by right substitution rules $S_R(u, v)$ with $|u| \leq |v| \leq |u| + n$. For all possible u, we now collect all the possible right substitution rules fulfilling these conditions, which in sum yields $P(A')$.

We remark that this part of the proof is not constructive – we are only interested in the result itself.

For every such system $G(A') = (N, T, P(A'), A')$ we now can easily construct an extended regular grammar $G'(A') = (N', T, P'(A'), A')$ with extended regular rules of the forms $A \rightarrow wC$ and $A \rightarrow w$, $w \in T^*$, $A, C \in N'$.

The nonterminals in $N' \setminus \{S\}$ are of the form $[X]$ where $X \in (N \cup T)^n$. We start with the rule

$$S \rightarrow A'(1) \ldots A'(|A'| - n)[A'(|A'| - n + 1) \ldots A'(|A'|)]$$

in $P'(A')$. Observe that $A'(1) \ldots A'(|A'| - n)$ must be a terminal string, as otherwise nonterminals there will remain forever, hence, $L(G'(A')) = \emptyset$. If A' only consists of terminal symbols, we also take $S \rightarrow A'(1) \ldots A'(|A'|)$ into $P'(A')$.

Now let $S_R(u, v)$ be a rule in $P(A')$ with $|u| = n$ and $|u| \leq |v| \leq |u| + n$:

- If $|u| = |v|$, then we take the rule $[u] \rightarrow [v]$ into $P'(A')$.
- If $|u| = |v|$ and v is a terminal string, then we also take the rule $[u] \rightarrow v$ into $P'(A')$.
- If $|u| < |v|$, we take the rule $[u] \rightarrow v(1) \ldots v(|v| - n)[v(|v| - n + 1) \ldots v(|v|)]$ into $P'(A')$, but only if $v(1) \ldots v(|v| - n)$ is a terminal string.
- If $|u| < |v|$ and v is a terminal string, then we also take the rule $[u] \rightarrow v$ into $P'(A')$.

The extended regular grammar $G'(A') = (N', T, P'(A'), S)$ now exactly simulates all possible terminal derivations in $G(A') = (N, T, P(A'), A')$, which observation completes the proof. □

As the family of regular languages are closed under union, putting together all the lemmas mentioned above, we obtain the following result:

Theorem 3. *String systems of either size 1 or degree 1 using only right insertion and deletion rules of the forms $aI_R(b)$ and $D_R(b)$ cannot generate more than regular languages.*

In sum, the main complexity question left open is the characterization of the languages which can be generated by string systems of size 2 and degree 2, homogenous or not. A thorough investigation of such systems will be given in an extended version of this paper.

4   Conclusion

In this paper we have considered the concept of applying prescribed teams of rules to a bounded number of initially given objects, with the rules to be applied either in parallel to different objects or sequentially to these objects. Each rule in a team has to be applied exactly once with a successful application of a team.

When using prescribed teams for string objects either two initial strings and teams with three rules or else three initial strings and teams with two rules are sufficient to obtain computational completeness. As string operations we use very simple insertion and deletion rules, i.e., inserting one object in the left context of another symbol or the deletion of a symbol on the right-hand side of a string. It remains an open question for future research how computational completeness can be obtained with even less ingredients, i.e., with only two initial strings and teams with two rules.

Moreover, we have shown that systems with either only one initial string or else with teams of only one rule can generate only regular languages.

We have also considered the insertion of anti-symbols which annihilate the corresponding symbols instead of deleting a symbol.

Similar results can be obtained when using these operations of insertion and deletion on the left-hand sides of the strings.

Acknowledgements. The authors gratefully thank the three referees for their useful comments.

Artiom Alhazov acknowledges project 20.80009.5007.22 "Intelligent information systems for solving ill-structured problems, processing knowledge and big data" by the National Agency for Research and Development.

References

1. Csuhaj-Varjú, E., Dassow, J., Kelemen, J.: Grammar Systems: A Grammatical Approach to Distribution and Cooperation. Topics in Computer Mathematics, Gordon and Breach (1994)
2. Dassow, J., Păun, Gh.: Regulated Rewriting in Formal Language Theory. Springer, Cham (1989)
3. Fernau, H., Kuppusamy, L., Raman, I.: Investigations on the power of matrix insertion-deletion systems with small sizes. Nat. Comput. **17**(2), 249–269 (2017). https://doi.org/10.1007/s11047-017-9656-8
4. Fernau, H., Kuppusamy, L., Raman, I.: On the computational completeness of matrix simple semi-conditional grammars. Inf. Comput. **284**, 104688 (2022). https://doi.org/10.1016/j.ic.2021.104688
5. Fernau, H., Kuppusamy, L., Verlan, S.: Universal matrix insertion grammars with small size. In: Patitz, M.J., Stannett, M. (eds.) UCNC 2017. LNCS, vol. 10240, pp. 182–193. Springer, Cham (2017). https://doi.org/10.1007/978-3-319-58187-3_14
6. Petre, I., Verlan, S.: Matrix insertion-deletion systems. Theor. Comput. Sci. **456**, 80–88 (2012). https://doi.org/10.1016/j.tcs.2012.07.002
7. Rozenberg, G., Salomaa, A. (eds.): Handbook of Formal Languages. Springer, Heidelberg (1997). https://doi.org/10.1007/978-3-642-59136-5

From Networks of Reaction Systems to Communicating Reaction Systems and Back

Bogdan Aman[1,2]([✉])

[1] Alexandru Ioan Cuza University of Iaşi, Iaşi, Romania
bogdan.aman@info.uaic.ro, bogdan.aman@iit.academiaromana-is.ro
[2] Romanian Academy, Institute of Computer Science, Iaşi, Romania

Abstract. A network of reaction systems is a graph such that each of its nodes contains a reaction system, and the context of each such reaction system is achieved by considering the products obtained at the previous step from all the enabled reactions of its neighbours. On the other hand, communicating reaction systems with direct communication are networks of reaction systems without context but each of the reaction systems is able to communicate products or reactions to its neighbours. In this paper we prove that these variants of networks of reaction systems can be related by establishing translations of networks of reaction systems into communicating reaction systems with direct communication and back.

1 Introduction

Reaction systems [14] are a formal framework for modelling the interactions of biochemical entities. Two major assumptions are made in order to define the reaction systems:

(i) threshold assumption: an available resource can be used by any number of reactions without causing conflicts between them (mathematically, this amounts to consider that each resource has an infinite multiplicity);
(ii) no permanency assumption: only resources created by the enabled rules in one state are available in the next one.

The reaction systems were extended to take into account also aspects as time [10], context [6,7], structure [8,16] and reversibility [2,3,5]. While in standard reaction systems, the set of reactions remains unchanged for the entire evolution, a different approach is considered in [13] where the set of reactions can change over time. Also while in standard reaction systems, there are no constraints between rules, in [4] is defined a priority relation between rules using a directed graph encoded in the rules of the reaction system and in [3] is defined a relation between rules that forbids two rules to be used in parallel in the same step.

A network of reaction systems [8] is a (un)directed graph such that each of its nodes contains a reaction system. While the behaviour of reaction systems is influenced by an arbitrary context, in networks of reaction systems the context of each reaction system is achieved by considering the products obtained at the previous step from all the enabled reactions of its neighbours. In networks of reaction systems, all edges of the graph act as communication channels and the behaviours of all reaction systems (residing in the nodes of the graph) are synchronized (a global clock is used).

Recently, communicating reaction systems with direct communication (cdcR systems) [11, 12] were introduced as variants of networks of reaction systems. A cdcR system consists of several components defined over the same background set, each of them containing several extended reactions of the same type. Besides performing reactions, the components communicate with some of their neighbours by sending products or even reactions.

In this paper we prove that these variants of networks of reaction systems can be related by establishing mappings from networks of reaction systems to communicating reaction systems with direct communication and back.

The paper is structured as follows. In Sect. 2 we recall general mathematical notions used throughout the paper and provide specific notions for reaction systems. In Sect. 3 we present networks of reaction systems, while in Sect. 4 we present two variants of communicating reaction systems with direct communication. In Sect. 5 we investigate how to simulate the behaviour of networks of reaction systems using communicating reaction systems with direct communication, and the other way around. In Sect. 6 we conclude, suggesting also some future research lines.

2   Reaction Systems

Reaction systems (abbreviated as RS) are a formal framework for modelling the interactions of biochemical entities; the main idea is that these interactions are based on facilitation and inhibition [9]. Thus, a reaction is a triplet of sets of: reactants, inhibitors and products. A reaction is enabled in a state that contains all its reactants but none of its inhibitors. Applying a reaction, means that its reactants are consumed and its products are created. Next, we present the notions of notations of reaction systems as given in [9].

An empty set is denoted by $\emptyset$, while an empty sequence is denoted by ε. Given a finite set X, its cardinality, set of subsets and set of (nonempty) finite sequences over X are denoted by $|X|$, 2^X and (X^+) X^* respectively. Given two sets X and Y, their difference, union, intersection, Cartesian product and (not necessarily strict) inclusion are denoted by $X \backslash Y$, $X \cup Y$, $X \cap Y$, $X \times Y$ and $X \subseteq Y$, respectively. Given a sequence $\tau = (x_1, \ldots, x_k)$, its length is denoted by $|\tau|$, while its tail of length n is defined using the function $tail : X^+ \times \mathbb{N} \to X^*$, where $tail(\tau, n) = (x_{n+1}, \ldots, x_k)$ if $n < k$ and $tail(\tau, n) = \varepsilon$ if $n \geq k$.

A reaction over a background set S of symbols (or molecules) is given as a triple $a = (R, I, P)$, where R, I, P are the sets of reactants, inhibitors and products, respectively, such that $\emptyset \neq R, I, P \subseteq S$ and $R \cap I = \emptyset$. If one wants to stress that the sets R, I and P belong to reaction a, then the used notations are R_a, I_a and P_a, respectively. Also, the set of all reactions in S is denoted $rac(S)$. According to [9], since every reaction with $I = \emptyset$ can be simulated by a reaction with $I \neq \emptyset$ containing a dummy variable that is never consumed or produced by other reactions, in what follows we consider that I can be also the empty set $\emptyset$.

A reaction $a \in rac(S)$ is enabled in a configuration $T \subseteq S$ (denoted by $a\ en\ T$) if $R_a \subseteq T$ and $I_a \cap T = \emptyset$, while the result of applying the reaction is $res_a(T) = P_a$. The effect of reaction a on configuration T can be written as $T \xrightarrow{a} res_a(T)$. If $a\ en\ T$ does not hold, then $res_a(T) = \emptyset$; the fact that reaction a is not enabled in configuration T and cannot be applied is written as $T \xslashed{a}{\not\rightarrow}$.

The previous notations can be extended to a finite set A of reactions. A set of reactions from A that is enabled in a configuration T is $en(A,T) = \{a \in A \mid a\ en\ T\}$, while the result of applying the reaction from A is $res_A(T) = \bigcup_{a \in A} res_a(T)$. The effect of the set A of reactions on configuration T can be written as $T \xrightarrow{A} res_A(T)$. Since $res_a(T) = \emptyset$ for any reaction $a \in A$ not enabled in configuration T, it holds that $res_A(T) = res_{en(A,T)}(T)$. According to [15], if $R_A \cap I_A = \emptyset$ then the set A of reactions is said to be consistent.

A *reaction system* is denoted by $\mathcal{A}$ and is given as an ordered pair (S, A), where the set of reactions A is built over the background set S, namely $A \subseteq rac(S)$. In order to capture the dynamic behaviour of the reaction systems the notion of an interactive process is defined as follows.

Definition 1 ([9]). *Let $\mathcal{A} = (S, A)$ be a reaction system. An interactive process π in $\mathcal{A}$ is a pair (γ, δ) of finite sequences such that $\gamma = C_0, C_1, \ldots, C_n$, $\delta = D_1, \ldots, D_n$ with $n \geq 1$, where $C_0, \ldots, C_n, D_1, \ldots, D_n \subseteq S$, $D_1 = res_A(C_0)$, and $D_i = res_A(D_{i-1} \cup C_{i-1})$ for each $2 \leq i \leq n$.*

For an interactive process π the sequences γ and δ are called the context and result sequence, respectively. The initial state of the interactive process π is represented by the context C_0, while the influence of the environment in the step $i \geq 1$ of the computation is represented by the context C_i. If $C_i \neq \emptyset$ for some $i \geq 1$, then the reaction system $\mathcal{A}$ is open [17] as its behaviour is influenced by the environment. If $C_i = \emptyset$ for all $i \geq 1$, then the reaction system $\mathcal{A}$ is closed as its behaviour is not influenced by the environments after C_0 is initially provided.

The state sequence of interactive process π is $sts(\pi) = W_0, \ldots, W_n$, where the initial state is $W_0 = C_0$, and $W_i = D_i \cup C_i$ for all $1 \leq i \leq n$. Then the distribution sequence of interactive process π is $\theta(\pi) = H_0, \ldots, H_n$, where $H_i = (C_i, D_i)$ for all $0 \leq i \leq n$. Also, the activity sequence of the interactive process π is $act(\pi) = E_0, \ldots, E_{n-1}$, where $E_i = en(A, W_i) \subseteq A$ for all $0 \leq i \leq n-1$. Thus, the effect of the activity sequence on the state sequence can be written as:

$$W_0 \xrightarrow{E_0} W_1 \xrightarrow{E_1} \ldots \xrightarrow{E_{n-1}} W_n.$$

Note that the threshold assumption allows each molecule to appear in several reactions as reactant or inhibitor, while the no permanency assumption allows to use at each step of the computation only molecules produced at the previous step and those received from the environment.

In what follows for a reaction system $\mathcal{A}$ the set of all its interactive (n-step) processes is denoted by ($\mathbf{Proc}^n(\mathcal{A})$) $\mathbf{Proc}(\mathcal{A})$, while the set of the state sequences of all interactive processes in $\mathbf{Proc}(\mathcal{A})$ is denoted by $\mathbf{STS}(\mathcal{A})$.

3   Networks of Reaction Systems

A network of reaction systems [8] is a (un)directed graph such that each of its nodes contains a reaction system. While the behaviour of reaction systems is influenced by an arbitrary context, in networks of reaction systems the context of each reaction system is achieved by considering the products obtained at the previous step from all the enabled reactions of its neighbours. As we are interested in the behaviour of all reaction systems we omit the notion of central reaction system from [8]. In what follows a finite graph G is an ordered pair (V, E), where V and E are finite sets of nodes and edges, respectively. An undirected graph is said to be connected if there exists a path between every two nodes, while a directed graph is weakly connected if its undirected version is connected; also $in(v)$ denotes the set of incoming neighbours of a node v.

Definition 2 ([8]). *A network of reaction systems (abbreviated RS network) is a tuple $\mathcal{N} = (G, \mathcal{F}, \mu)$, where:*

- *$G = (V, E)$ is a finite graph;*
- *$\mathcal{F}$ is a nonempty finite set of reaction systems;*
- *$\mu : V \to \mathcal{F}$ is a location function, assigning reaction systems to nodes.*

Moreover, if G is undirected, then it is connected and if G is directed, then G is weakly connected.

Given a network of reaction systems $\mathcal{N}$, G is its graph, while $(V, \mathcal{F}, \mu)$ its reaction structure. We assume that V is totally ordered; thus $V = (v_1, \ldots, v_m)$, for some $m \geq 1$. For a node $v_i \in V$, reaction system residing at it is obtained through the function μ such that $\mu(v_i) = \mathcal{A}^i = (S^i, A^i)$, where the background and reaction sets of the reaction system $\mathcal{A}^i$ are denoted by S^i and A^i, respectively. Also, the background set of a network of reaction systems $\mathcal{N}$ is $S(\mathcal{N}) = \bigcup_{j=1}^m S^j$. Note that a network of reaction systems $\mathcal{N}$ such that $m = 1$, is in fact a closed reaction system $\mathcal{A}^1$.

Definition 3 ([8]). *Let $\mathcal{N} = (G, \mathcal{F}, \mu)$ be a RS network with $|V| = m$ for some $m \geq 1$. For $n \in \mathbb{N}^+$, an interactive (n-step) network process is a tuple $\Pi = (\pi^1, \ldots, \pi^m)$, where, for $j \in \{1, \ldots, m\}$, $\pi^j = (\gamma^j, \delta^j) \in \mathbf{Proc}^n(\mathcal{A}^j)$, and $\gamma^j = (C_0^j, \ldots, C_n^j)$, $\delta^j = (D_0^j, \ldots, D_n^j)$, are such that:*

(1) $C_k^j = S^j \cap \left(\bigcup \{D_{k-1}^i | v_i \in in(v_j)\} \right)$, for $k \in \{1, \ldots, n\}$, and
(2) $D_k^j = res_{A^j}(D_{k-1}^j \cup C_{k-1}^j)$ for $k \in \{1, \ldots, n\}$.
(3) Moreover, if $in(v_j) = \emptyset$, then $C_0^j = \emptyset$.

Thus, an interactive network process is constructed using the interactive processes of the m reaction systems placed in the nodes V of the graph G. For any reaction system $\mathcal{A}^j$ with initial distribution (C_0^j, D_0^j), the set D_i^j contains all products of the enabled reactions from A^j, while the set C_i^j contains only the objects from the set S^j produced, at the previous step, by all the reaction systems $\mathcal{A}^i$ such that $v_i \in in(v_j)$.

Given an interactive network process Π, the vector of contexts at step i is $\mathbf{C}_i^{\Pi} = (C_i^1, \ldots, C_i^m)$, the vector of results is $\mathbf{D}_i^{\Pi} = (D_i^1, \ldots, D_i^m)$, the vector of states is $\mathbf{W}_i^{\Pi} = (W_i^1, \ldots, W_i^m)$, and the vector of distributions is $\mathbf{H}_i^{\Pi} = (H_i^1, \ldots, H_i^m)$. In what follows for a RS network $\mathcal{N}$, the set of its interactive (n-step) network processes is denoted by $(\mathbf{PROC}^n(\mathcal{N}))$ $\mathbf{PROC}(\mathcal{N})$.

4 Communicating Reaction Systems

The communicating reaction systems (cdcR systems) with two variants of direct communication were introduced and studied in [11,12]. A cdcR system is composed from a finite amount of components over the same background set, where a finite set of extended reactions is a component. Each component can perform standard reaction, but also can send to a specified component the obtained products from a reaction or to a set of specified components each used reaction. Note that the receiving component of the products or reactions can also be the sending component. Once all components apply the enabled reactions and communicate the products or reactions, the entire process can be repeated.

Definition 4 ([11]). *A cdcR system communicating by products (a cdcR(p) system), of degree n, $n \geq 1$, is an $(n+1)$-tuple $\Delta = (S, A_1, \ldots, A_n)$, where:*

- *S is a finite nonempty set, the background set of Δ;*
- *A_i, $1 \leq i \leq n$, is the ith component of Δ, where:*
  - *A_i is a finite nonempty set of extended reactions of type pc (pc-reactions).*
  - *Each pc-reaction ρ of A_i is of the form $\rho : (R_\rho, I_\rho, \Pi_\rho)$, where R_ρ and I_ρ are nonempty subsets of S, $R_\rho \cap I_\rho = \emptyset$, and $\Pi_\rho \subseteq P_\rho \times \{1, \ldots, n\}$ is a nonempty set with P_ρ being a nonempty subset of S. R_ρ, I_ρ, Π_ρ are called the set of reactants, the set of inhibitors, and the set of products with targets. A pair (b, j), $1 \leq j \leq n$ in Π_ρ means that product $b \in S$ is communicated to component A_j.*

A pc-reaction, standing for product communication reaction, is a standard reaction equipped with a target and that communicates the created products to another component. Just like for standard reactions, a pc-reaction $\rho : (R_\rho, I_\rho, \Pi_\rho)$ is enabled for the set $U \subseteq S$ (denoted by $en_\rho(U)$) if $R_\rho \subseteq U$ and $I_\rho \cap U = \emptyset$, while the result of applying the pc-reaction is $res_\rho(U) = \{b | (b, i) \in \Pi_\rho\}$. If $en_\rho(U)$ does not hold, then $res_\rho(U) = \emptyset$ otherwise.

For a cdcR(p) system $\Delta = (S, A_1, \ldots, A_n)$ and a set $U \subseteq S$, the result of applying the enabled pc-reaction in A_i is $res_{A_i}(U) = \{b | (b, i) \in \Pi_\rho, \rho \in A_i, en_\rho(U)\}$, while if no pc-reaction in A_i is enabled the result is $res_{A_i}(U) = \emptyset$. The behaviour of a cdcR(p) system Δ is characterized by transitions between states of the form $(D_1, \ldots, D_n)$ where to each component A_i, $1 \leq i \leq n$, corresponds the state $\emptyset \subseteq D_i \subseteq S$. This means that in each component A_i, $1 \leq i \leq n$, all its enabled pc-reactions are applied to the current state D_i and the created products are sent to the corresponding component as indicated by the target of each pc-reaction. Note that due to the threshold assumption even if the same objects is received from several components, only one copy will be available in the next state.

For a cdcR(p) system Δ starting from an initial state and applying the reactions as described above, the sequence of transitions forms a state sequence. Note that, for a given cdcR(p) system Δ its state sequence is deterministic as it depends only on the initial state.

Definition 5 ([11]). *Let $\Delta = (S, A_1, \ldots, A_n)$, $n \geq 1$, be a cdcR(p) system. The sequence $\overline{D}_0, \ldots, \overline{D}_j, \ldots$ is called the state sequence of Δ starting with initial state $\overline{D}_0$ if the following conditions are met:*

For every $\overline{D}_j$, $j \geq 0$ where $\overline{D}_j = (D_{1,j}, \ldots, D_{n,j})$, $1 \leq i \leq n$ it holds that $\overline{D}_{j+1} = (D_{1,j+1}, \ldots, D_{n,j+1})$ with $D_{i,j+1} = \bigcup_{1 \leq k \leq n} Com_{k \to i}(res_{A_k}(D_{k,j}))$ where $Com_{k \to i}(res_{A_k}(D_{k,j})) = \{b | (b,i) \in \Pi_\rho, \rho : (R_\rho, I_\rho, \Pi_\rho) \in en_{A_k}(D_{k,j})\}$.

Sequence $D_{i,0}, D_{i,1}, \ldots$ is said to be the state sequence of component A_i of Δ, $1 \leq i \leq n$.

Note that for a component A_i of cdcR(p) system Δ it holds that $res_{A_i}(D_{i,j}) = \emptyset$ does not lead to a stop in the state sequence as the component may receive resources at subsequent steps from other components. A transition in Δ has the form $(\overline{D}_i; \overline{D}_{i+1})$, $i \geq 0$ and can also be written as $\overline{D}_i \to \overline{D}_{i+1}$.

Definition 6 ([11]). *A cdcR system communicating by reactions (a cdcR(r) system) of degree n, $n \geq 1$, is a triplet $\Delta = (n, S, \mathcal{R})$ where:*

- *n is the number of components,*
- *S is a finite nonempty set, called the background set of Δ,*
- *$\mathcal{R}$ is a finite nonempty set of extended reactions of type rc (rc-reactions), where:*
  - *each rc-reaction is of the form $\rho : (R_\rho, I_\rho, P_\rho); target(\rho)$,*
  - *R_ρ, I_ρ, P_ρ are nonempty subsets of S, the set of reactants, the set of inhibitors, and the set of products of the rc-reaction, respectively,*
  - *$target(\rho) \subseteq \{1, \ldots, n\}$ is a nonempty set, the set of indices (labels) of the target components to which the rc-reaction is communicated.*

A rc-reaction, standing for reaction communication reaction, is a standard reaction equipped with at least one target that moves to other components after it was used. Note that the components are identified by numbers i, $1 \leq i \leq n$. The core of an rc-reaction $\rho : (R_\rho, I_\rho, P_\rho); target(\rho)$ is $core(\rho) = (R_\rho, I_\rho, P_\rho)$, while the core of a nonempty set of rc-reactions $\mathcal{R}' \subseteq \mathcal{R}$ is $core(\mathcal{R}') = \{core(\rho) | \rho \in \mathcal{R}'\}$. If $core(\rho)$ is enabled for a set $U \subseteq S$, then also the rc-reaction ρ is said to be enabled for the set U. The result of applying the enables re-reaction ρ on the set U is the same as applying the reaction $core(\rho)$ on the set U. Given a rc-reaction ρ and a set of rc-reaction $\mathcal{R}'$ the notations $en_\rho(U)$, $res_\rho(U)$, and $en_{\mathcal{R}'}(U)$, $res_{\mathcal{R}'}(U)$ are similar with those from standard reaction systems.

As a cdcR(r) system Δ works with configuration containing the sets of reaction and reactants that can change during the evolution, by starting from an initial configuration and applying the reactions as described above, the sequence of transitions forms a configuration sequence.

Definition 7 ([11]). *Let $\Delta = (n, S, \mathcal{R})$, $n \geq 1$, be a cdcR(r) system with n components. Let $\overline{C}_0$ be the initial configuration of Δ where $\overline{C}_0 = ((A_{1,0}, D_{1,0}), \ldots, (A_{n,0}, D_{n,0}))$ with $A_{i,0} \subseteq \mathcal{R}$ (the initial rc-reaction set of component i) and $D_{i,0} \subseteq S$ (the initial reactant set of component i), $1 \leq i \leq n$. The pair $(A_{i,0}, D_{i,0})$ is called the initial configuration of component i.*

The configuration sequence $\overline{C}_0, \overline{C}_1, \ldots$ of Δ, where $\overline{C}_j = ((A_{1,j}, D_{1,j}), \ldots, (A_{n,j}, D_{n,j}))$, $j \geq 0$, is defined as follows:

For each component i, $1 \leq i \leq n$, for each j, $j \geq 0$ and all subsequent configurations $(A_{i,j}, D_{i,j}), (A_{i,j+1}, D_{i,j+1})$ of component i the following hold:

- $A_{i,j+1} = \{\rho \in \mathcal{R} | i \in target(\rho), \rho \in A_{k,j}, en_{core(\rho)}(D_{k,j}), 1 \leq k \leq n\}$ *and*
- $D_{i,j+1} = res_{core(A_{i,j})}(D_{i,j})$.

This means, that unlike cdcR(p) systems where the products obtained from the enabled reactions were send to other components while the reaction set remains unchanged, in cdcR(r) systems the products obtained from the enabled reactions remain while the reaction set is modified. This implies that a reaction set from one component loses the applied reactions that are communicated to other components, and gains reactions communicated by other components to it. In cdcR(r) systems is considered a no permanency assumption: only the reactions that were communicated at one state are available in the next one.

5   Connections Between RS Networks and CdcR Systems

Next we show that the behaviour of every network of reaction systems can be expressed through the behaviour of a cdcR(p) system. As it can be seen from the next result this implies using a double number of components in the cdcR(p) system with respect to the simulated network of reaction systems. The additional components in the network of reaction systems are used for filtering purposes.

Theorem 1. *Let $\mathcal{N} = (G, \mathcal{F}, \mu)$ be a network of reaction systems with $|V| = m$ for some $m \geq 1$ and initial distribution $\mathbf{H}_0^{\Pi}$. Then there exists a cdcR(p) system $\Delta = (S, A_1', \ldots, A_m', A_1, \ldots, A_m)$, $m \geq 1$ with initial state $\overline{D}_0$ such that $\mathbf{W}_i^{\Pi} = tail(\overline{D}_i, m)$, for all $i \geq 0$.*

Proof. Let $\mathcal{N} = (G, \mathcal{F}, \mu)$ be a network of reaction systems such that $V = \{v_1, \ldots, v_m\}$. First we construct the background set S of the cdcR(p) system Δ as $S = \bigcup_{1 \leq j \leq m} S^j$, where S^j is the background set of the reaction system $\mu(v_j) = \mathcal{A}^j = (S^j, A^j)$, with $1 \leq j \leq m$.

For every node v_j in $\mathcal{N}$, with $1 \leq j \leq m$, we construct two components A_j' and A_j, such that for any reaction $a = (R, I, P) \in A^j$ we add the following pc-reactions to the component A_j of Δ:

- $\rho_a^j = (R, I, (P, j))$ - representing the fact that the created resources remain in the node v_j;

- $\rho_a^{j'} = (R, I, (P, j'))$ - representing the fact that the resources created are sent towards the node v_j' to be available in the next step to be sent to the nodes v_k such that $v_j \in in(v_k)$.

Also, to each component A_j' of Δ we add the following pc-reactions:

- $\rho_a^k = (s, \emptyset, (s, k))$, for all $s \in S_k$ if $v_j \in in(v_k)$ - representing the fact that the resources created at the previous step in node v_j are sent towards the node v_k. Note that by defining rules only from the objects from S_k only objects from S_k will be sent to v_k, while the other will vanish as they are not consumed.

Finally, we assume that $\overline{D}_0 = (\mathbf{D}_0^{II}, \mathbf{W}_0^{II})$, namely we consider that the first m components of Δ hold the initial m results of the network of reaction systems $\mathcal{N}$, while the last m components of Δ hold the initial m states of the network of reaction systems $\mathcal{N}$.

We prove that the state sequence of $\mathcal{A}^j$, with $1 \leq j \leq m$, starting from W_0^j corresponds to the state sequence of component A_j of Δ starting from initial state $D_{j,0}$. The proof is by induction on the last applied step:

- Case $i = 0$. There was no step applied yet, and the system is in the initial state. From $\overline{D}_0 = (\mathbf{D}_0^{II}, \mathbf{W}_0^{II})$ it follows that $W_0^j = D_{j,0}$ as required.
- Case $i = 1$. This implies that this is the first applied step using the existing resources. Since $W_1^j = C_1^j \cup D_1^j$, due to Definition 3, it holds that $W_1^j = (S^j \cap (\bigcup \{D_0^k | v_k \in in(v_j)\})) \cup res_{A^j}(W_0^j)$. Also, due to Definition 5 it holds that $D_{j,1} = \bigcup Com_{k \rightarrow j}(res_{A_k}(D_{k,0}))$ where $Com_{k \rightarrow j}(res_{A_k}(D_{k,0})) = \{b | (b, j) \in \Pi_\rho, \rho : (R_\rho, I_\rho, \Pi_\rho) \in en_{A_k}(D_{k,0})\}$. As the only rules to send resources from a component A_j to itself are of the form $\rho_a^j = (R, I, (P, j))$, then $Com_{j \rightarrow j}(res_{A_j}(D_{j,0})) = res_{A_j}(D_{j,0}) = res_{A_j}(D_{j,0}) = res_{A^j}(W_0^j)$. Also, as the only rules sending resources to component A_j are placed in the components A_k' and are of the form $\rho_a^j = (s, \emptyset, (s, j))$, for all $s \in S_k$ if $v_k \in in(v_j)$, it implies that $Com_{k' \rightarrow j}(res_{A_k'}(D_{k',0})) = res_{A_k'}(D_{k',0}) = D_{k',0}$. As the resources placed initially in node v_k' are D_0^k, it implies that $D_{k',0} = D_0^k \cap S_j$, and thus $W_1^j = D_{j,1}$ as required.
- Case $i > 1$. Assume the statement holds for $i - 1$, namely $W_{i-1}^j = D_{j,i-1}$. We show that $W_i^j = D_{j,i}$ holds as well. Since $W_i^j = C_i^j \cup D_i^j$, due to Definition 3, it holds that $W_i^j = (S^j \cap (\bigcup \{D_{i-1}^k | v_k \in in(v_j)\})) \cup res_{A^j}(W_{i-1}^j)$. Also, due to Definition 5 it holds that $D_{j,i} = \bigcup Com_{k \rightarrow j}(res_{A_k}(D_{k,i-1}))$ where $Com_{k \rightarrow j}(res_{A_k}(D_{k,i-1})) = \{b | (b, j) \in \Pi_\rho, \rho : (R_\rho, I_\rho, \Pi_\rho) \in en_{A_k}(D_{k,i-1})\}$. As the only rules to send resources from a component A_j to itself are of the form $\rho_a^j = (R, I, (P, j))$, then $Com_{j \rightarrow j}(res_{A_j}(D_{j,i-1})) = res_{A_j}(D_{j,i-1}) = res_{A^j}(W_{i-1}^j)$. Also, as the only rules sending resources to component A_j are placed in the components A_k' and are of the form $\rho_a^j = (s, \emptyset, (s, j))$, for all $s \in S_j$ if $v_k \in in(v_j)$, it implies that $Com_{k' \rightarrow j}(res_{A_k'}(D_{k',i-1})) = res_{A_k'}(D_{k',i-1}) = D_{k',i-1}$. But the resources from node v_j' forwarded to node v_j were received from node v_k in the previous step by using the rules of the form $\rho_a^{j'} = (R, I, (P, j'))$, and thus $D_{k',i-1} = S^j \cap res_{A_k}(D_{k,i-2}) = S^j \cap res_{A^k}(W_{i-2}^k) = S^j \cap D_{i-1}^k$. It follows that $W_i^j = D_{j,i}$ as required.

Also it holds that the behaviour of every cdcR(p) system can be expressed through the behaviour of a network of reaction systems. As it can be seen from the next result this in the network of reaction systems requires a number of components equal to the number of components and edges of the simulated cdcR(p) system. The additional components in the network of reaction systems are used for filtering purposes.

Theorem 2. *Let $\Delta = (S, A_1, \ldots, A_m)$, $m \geq 1$ be a cdcR(p) system with initial state $\overline{D}_0$. Then there exists a network of reaction systems $\mathcal{N} = (G, \mathcal{F}, \mu)$ with G directed and the initial distribution $\mathbf{H}_0^{\Pi}$ such that $\overline{D}_i = tail(\mathbf{W}_{4i}^{\Pi}, m)$, for all $i \geq 0$.*

Proof. Let $\Delta = (S, A_1, \ldots, A_m)$, $m \geq 1$ be a cdcR(p) system. For every component A_j of Δ, with $1 \leq j \leq m$, we construct a node v_j such that $\mu(v_j) = \mathcal{A}^j = (S^j, A^j)$, where $S^j = S \cup \left(\bigcup_{1 \leq k \leq m} \tau_k \right)$ and for any pc-reaction $\rho = (R, I, (P, k)) \in A_j$ we add the following reactions to A^j of $\mathcal{N}$.

– $a_\rho^j = (R, I, P\tau_k)$ - the additional object τ_k will be used to remove the resources from system $\mathcal{A}^j$ at a subsequent step;
– $a_\tau^j = (a, \left(\bigcup_{1 \leq k \leq m} \tau_k \right), a)$ - these rules are used to remove all resources from a system $\mathcal{A}^j$ if any of the resources $\tau_1, \ldots, \tau_m$ was created in a previous step by a reaction a_ρ^j.

Also, for each edge (k, j) in Δ we construct two nodes v_{kj} and v_{jk} and add to E the directed edges (k, kj), (kj, j), (j, jk) and (jk, k). Each node v_{kj} is such that $\mu(v_{kj}) = \mathcal{A}^{kj} = (S^{kj}, A^{kj})$, where $S^{kj} = S \cup \left(\bigcup_{1 \leq l \leq m} \tau_l \right)$ and to A^{kj} we add the following reactions:

– $a_{\tau_j}^{kj} = (a\tau_j, \emptyset, a)$ - if the existing resources are meant to be sent to node v_j then the resource τ_j exists and thus all resources are kept alive.

We assume that $V = (\ldots, v_1, \ldots, v_m)$ where on the first places are the nodes v_{kj} created as above. Thus, using this given order of nodes, we assume that $\mathbf{W}_0^{\Pi} = (\emptyset, \ldots, \emptyset, \overline{D}_0)$, such that $C_0^j = D_{j,0}$ and $D_0^j = \emptyset$.

We prove that the state sequence of component A_j of Δ starting from initial state $D_{j,0}$ corresponds to the state sequence of $\mathcal{A}^j$, with $1 \leq j \leq m$, starting from W_0^j. The proof is by induction on the last applied step:

– Case $i = 0$. There was no step applied yet, and the system is in the initial state. From $\mathbf{W}_0^{\Pi} = (\emptyset, \ldots, \emptyset, \overline{D}_0)$ it follows that $D_{j,0} = W_0^j$ as required.
– Case $i = 1$. This implies that this is the first applied step using the existing resources. Due to Definition 5 it holds that $D_{j,1} = \bigcup Com_{k \to j}(res_{A_k}(D_{k,0}))$ where $Com_{k \to j}(res_{A_k}(D_{k,0})) = \{b | (b, j) \in \Pi_\rho, \rho : (R_\rho, I_\rho, \Pi_\rho) \in en_{A_k}(D_{k,0})\}$. Due to Definition 3 it holds that:
  • $C_1^j = \bigcup D_0^{kj} = \emptyset$ and $D_1^j = res_{A^j}(W_0^j)$;
  • $C_1^{kj} = D_0^k = \emptyset$ and $D_1^{kj} = res_{A^{kj}}(W_0^{kj}) = \emptyset$;
  • $C_2^j = \bigcup D_1^{kj} = \emptyset$ and $D_2^j = res_{A^j}(W_1^j) = \emptyset$;

- $C_2^{kj} = D_1^k = res_{A^k}(W_0^k)$ and $D_2^{kj} = res_{A^{kj}}(W_1^{kj}) = \emptyset$;
- $C_3^j = \bigcup D_2^{kj} = \emptyset$ and $D_3^j = res_{A^j}(W_2^j) = \emptyset$;
- $C_3^{kj} = D_2^k = \emptyset$ and $D_3^{kj} = res_{A^{kj}}(W_2^{kj}) = res_{A^{kj}}(res_{A^k}(W_0^k))$;
- $C_4^j = \bigcup D_3^{kj} = \bigcup res_{A^{kj}}(res_{A^k}(W_0^k))$ and $D_4^j = res_{A^j}(W_3^j) = \emptyset$;
- $C_4^{kj} = D_3^k = \emptyset$ and $D_4^{kj} = res_{A^{kj}}(W_3^{kj}) = \emptyset$;

Since the rules of $\mathcal{N}$ were constructed such that the obtained resources are the same, namely $res_{A_k}(D_{k,0}) = res_{A^{kj}}(res_{A^k}(W_0^k))$, it follows that $D_{j,1} = W_4^j$ as required. Also note that $C_4^j \neq \emptyset$, while $D_4^j = C_4^{kj} = D_4^{kj} = \emptyset$.

- Case $i > 1$. Assume the statement holds for $i-1$, namely $D_{j,i-1} = W_{4i-4}^j$ and also $C_{4i-4}^j \neq \emptyset$, while $D_{4i-4}^j = C_{4i-4}^{ij} = D_{4i-4}^{ij} = \emptyset$. We show that $D_{j,i} = W_{4i}^j$ as well. Due to Definition 5 it holds that $D_{j,i} = \bigcup Com_{k \to j}(res_{A_k}(D_{k,i-1}))$ where the communicated resources are $Com_{k \to j}(res_{A_k}(D_{k,i-1})) = \{b | (b,j) \in \Pi_\rho, \rho : (R_\rho, I_\rho, \Pi_\rho) \in en_{A_k}(D_{k,i-1})\}$. Due to Definition 3 it holds that:

- $C_{4i-3}^j = \bigcup D_{4i-4}^{kj} = \emptyset$ and $D_{4i-3}^j = res_{A^j}(W_{4i-4}^j)$;
- $C_{4i-3}^{kj} = D_{4i-4}^k = \emptyset$ and $D_{4i-3}^{kj} = res_{A^{kj}}(W_{4i-4}^{kj}) = \emptyset$;
- $C_{4i-2}^j = \bigcup D_{4i-3}^{kj} = \emptyset$ and $D_{4i-2}^j = res_{A^j}(W_{4i-3}^j) = \emptyset$;
- $C_{4i-2}^{kj} = D_1^k = res_{A^k}(W_{4i-3}^i)$ and $D_{4i-2}^{kj} = res_{A^{kj}}(W_{4i-3}^{kj}) = \emptyset$;
- $C_{4i-1}^j = \bigcup D_{4i-2}^{kj} = \emptyset$ and $D_{4i-1}^j = res_{A^j}(W_{4i-2}^j) = \emptyset$;
- $C_{4i-1}^{kj} = D_{4i-2}^k = \emptyset$ and $D_{4i-1}^{kj} = res_{A^{kj}}(W_{4i-2}^{kj}) = res_{A^{kj}}(res_{A^k}(W_{4i-4}^k))$;
- $C_{4i}^j = \bigcup D_{4i-1}^{kj} = \bigcup res_{A^{kj}}(res_{A^k}(W_{4i-4}^k))$ and $D_{4i}^j = res_{A^j}(W_{4i-1}^j) = \emptyset$;
- $C_{4i}^{kj} = D_{4i-1}^k = \emptyset$ and $D_{4i}^{kj} = res_{A^{kj}}(W_{4i-1}^{kj}) = \emptyset$;

Since the rules of $\mathcal{N}$ were constructed such that the obtained resources are the same, namely $res_{A_k}(D_{k,i-1}) = res_{A^{kj}}(res_{A^k}(W_{4i-4}^k))$, it follows that $D_{j,i} = W_{4i}^j$ as required.

Next we show that the behaviour of every network of reaction system can be expressed through the behaviour of a cdcR(r) system. As it can be seen from the next result this implies using a double number of components in the cdcR(r) system with respect to the simulated network of reaction systems. The additional components in the network of reaction systems are used for filtering purposes.

In order to express the translation we will use objects of the form (x, y, z) (their meaning will be explained in the following proof) and functions $\downarrow_t$ such that $\downarrow_z (x, y, t) = x$ if $z = t$ and $\downarrow_z (x, y, t) = \emptyset$ if $z \neq t$.

Theorem 3. *Let $\mathcal{N} = (G, \mathcal{F}, \mu)$ be a network of reaction systems with $|V| = m$ for some $m \geq 1$ and initial distribution $\mathbf{H}_0^\Pi$. Then there exists a cdcR(r) system $\Delta = (n, S, \mathcal{R})$, where $n \geq 1$, with initial state $\overline{C}_0$ such that $\mathbf{W}_i^\Pi(j) = \downarrow_j (tail(\overline{C}_i, m)(j))$, for all $i \geq 0$ and all $1 \leq j \leq m$, where j represents the position in the tuple $tail(\overline{C}_i, m)$.*

Proof. Let $\mathcal{N} = (G, \mathcal{F}, \mu)$ be a network of reaction systems such that $V = \{v_1, \ldots, v_m\}$. First we construct the background set S of the cdcR(r) system Δ as $S = \bigcup_{1 \leq j \leq m} \{(x, d, j), (x, c, j) \mid x \in S^j\}$, where S^j is the background set of the reaction system $\mu(v_j) = \mathcal{A}^j = (S^j, A^j)$, with $1 \leq j \leq m$. An object

(x, d, j) will represent an object x of the reaction system $\mathcal{A}^j$ that belongs to the result set D_k^j, where $k \geq 0$. In a similar manner, an object (x, c, j) will represent an object x of the reaction system $\mathcal{A}^j$ that belongs to the context set C_k^j, where $k \geq 0$.

For every node v_j in $\mathcal{N}$ with initial distribution (C_0^j, D_0^j), where $1 \leq j \leq m$, we construct two components; a component $\mathcal{A}_j = (A_j, D_j)$ with initial configuration $(A_{j,0}, D_{j,0})$ such that:

- $D_{j,0} = \left(\bigcup_{1 \leq k \leq m} \{(x, c, k) \mid x \in C_0^k\} \right) \cup \left(\bigcup_{1 \leq k \leq m} \{(x, d, k) \mid x \in D_0^k\} \right)$;
- for any reaction $a = (R, I, P) \in A^k$, where $1 \leq k \leq m$, we add to $A_{j,0}$ the rc-reaction

$$\rho_a : \left(\left(\bigcup_{x \in R, y=c \vee y=d}(x, y, k) \right), \left(\bigcup_{x \in I, y=c \vee y=d}(x, y, k) \right), \left(\bigcup_{x \in P}(x, d, k) \right) \right); \{j'\};$$

- for every v_k such that $v_j \in in(v_k)$ and for every $x \in S^k$ we add to $A_{j,0}$ the rc-reaction $\rho_{j \to k} : ((x, d, j), \emptyset, (x, c, k)); \{j'\}$.

Since the unused rules from $A_{j,0}$ will not be available for the next computational steps, we need components that will provide to the component $\mathcal{A}_j$ the rules from $A_{j,0}$ at every step of the computation. Thus, we construct a component $\mathcal{A}_j' = (A_j', D_j')$ with initial configuration $(A_{j,0}', D_{j,0}')$ such that:

- $D_{j,0}' = S$;
- $A_{j,0}' = \{\rho : (R, I, P); \{j, j'\} \mid \rho : (R, I, P); \{j'\} \in A_{j,0}\} \cup \{\rho_z : (z, \emptyset, z); \{j'\} \mid z \in S\}$.

Thus, in Δ, the number of components is $n = 2m$, while the set of rules is $\mathcal{R} = \left(\bigcup_{1 \leq j \leq m} A_{j,0} \right) \cup \left(\bigcup_{1 \leq j \leq m} A_{j,0}' \right)$.

Finally, we assume that

$$\overline{C}_0 = ((A_{1,0}', D_{1,0}'), \ldots, (A_{m,0}', D_{m,0}'), (A_{1,0}, D_{1,0}), \ldots, (A_{m,0}, D_{m,0})).$$

We prove that the state sequence of $\mathcal{A}^j$, with $1 \leq j \leq m$, starting from W_0^j corresponds to the reactant sequence $\downarrow_j D_j$ of component $\mathcal{A}_j$ of Δ starting from initial reactant set $D_{j,0}$. The proof is by induction on the last applied step:

- Case $i = 0$. There was no step applied yet, and the system is in the initial state. Applying $\downarrow_j$ to initial reactant set $D_{j,0}$ it holds that: $\downarrow_j D_{j,0} = \downarrow_j \left(\left(\bigcup_{1 \leq k \leq m} \{(x, c, k) \mid x \in C_0^k\} \right) \cup \left(\bigcup_{1 \leq k \leq m} \{(x, d, k) \mid x \in D_0^k\} \right) \right) = \{x \mid x \in C_0^j\} \cup \{x \mid x \in D_0^j\} = C_0^j \cup D_0^j = W_0^j$ as required.
- Case $i = 1$. This implies that this is the first applied step using the existing resources and rules from each component. Since $W_1^j = C_1^j \cup D_1^j$, due to Definition 3, it holds that $W_1^j = \left(S^j \cap \left(\bigcup \{D_0^k | v_k \in in(v_j)\} \right) \right) \cup res_{\mathcal{A}^j}(W_0^j)$. Also, due to Definition 7 it holds that $D_{j,1} = res_{core(A_{j,0})}(D_{j,0})$ and $A_{j,1} = \{\rho \in \mathcal{R} | j \in target(\rho), \rho \in A_{k,0}, en_{core(\rho)}(D_{k,0}), 1 \leq k \leq m\} \cup \{\rho \in \mathcal{R} | j \in target(\rho), \rho \in A_{k,0}', en_{core(\rho)}(D_{k,0}'), 1 \leq k \leq m\}$. As the rules ρ_a of $A_{j,0}$ transform the sets

$\{(x, c, j) \mid x \in C_0^j\}$ and $\{(x, d, j) \mid x \in D_0^j\}$ into the set $\{(x, d, j) \mid x \in D_1^j\}$, while the rules $\rho_{k \to j}$ transform the set $\{(x, d, k) \mid x \in D_0^k, x \in S^j, v_k \in in(v_j)\}$ into the set $\{(x, c, j) \mid x \in C_1^j, x \in S^j, v_k \in in(v_j)\}$, it results that $\downarrow_j D_{j,1} = \downarrow_j \left(\left(\bigcup_{1 \le k \le m} \{(x, d, k) \mid x \in D_1^k\} \right) \cup \left(\bigcup_{1 \le k \le m} \{(x, c, k) \mid x \in C_1^k, x \in S^k, v_k \in in(v_j)\} \right) \right) = D_1^j \cup \left(\bigcup_{1 \le k \le m} \{C_1^j \cap S^j \mid v_k \in in(v_j)\} \right) = D_1^j \cup \left(\bigcup_{1 \le k \le m} \{D_0^k \cap S^j \mid v_k \in in(v_j)\} \right) = W_1^j$, as required.

Also note that $A_{j,1} = \{\rho \in \mathcal{R} \mid j \in target(\rho), \rho \in A'_{k,0}, en_{core(\rho)}(D'_{k,0}), 1 \le k \le m\} = \{\rho : (R, I, P); \{j, j'\} \mid \rho : (R, I, P); \{j'\} \in A_{j,0}\} = A_{j,i}$, namely for any step $i \ge 1$ the set of rules $A_{j,i}$ contains the same rules as $A_{j,0}$ except that the target j is replaced now by the targets j and j', just to keep the rules alive in the component $\mathcal{A}'_j$.

- Case $i > 1$. Assume the statement holds for $i - 1$, namely $\downarrow_j D_{j,i-1} = W_{i-1}^j$. We show that $\downarrow_j D_{j,i} = W_i^j$ holds as well. Since $W_i^j = C_i^j \cup D_i^j$, due to Definition 3, it holds that $W_i^j = (S^j \cap (\bigcup \{D_{i-1}^k \mid v_k \in in(v_j)\})) \cup res_{A^j}(W_{i-1}^j)$. Also, due to Definition 7 it holds that $D_{j,i} = res_{core(A_{j,i-1})}(D_{j,i-1})$. As the rules ρ_a of $A_{j,i-1}$ transform the sets $\{(x, c, j) \mid x \in C_{i-1}^j\}$ and $\{(x, d, j) \mid x \in D_{i-1}^j\}$ into the set $\{(x, d, j) \mid x \in D_i^j\}$, while the rules $\rho_{k \to j}$ transform the set $\{(x, d, k) \mid x \in D_{i-1}^k, x \in S^j, v_k \in in(v_j)\}$ into the set $\{(x, c, j) \mid x \in C_i^j, x \in S^j, v_k \in in(v_j)\}$, it results that $\downarrow_j D_{j,i} = \downarrow_j \left(\left(\bigcup_{1 \le k \le m} \{(x, d, k) \mid x \in D_i^k\} \right) \cup \left(\bigcup_{1 \le k \le m} \{(x, c, k) \mid x \in C_i^k, x \in S^k, v_k \in in(v_j)\} \right) \right) = D_i^j \cup \left(\bigcup_{1 \le k \le m} \{C_i^j \cap S^j \mid v_k \in in(v_j)\} \right) = D_i^j \cup \left(\bigcup_{1 \le k \le m} \{D_{i-1}^k \cap S^j \mid v_k \in in(v_j)\} \right) = W_i^j$, as required.

Also it holds that the behaviour of every cdcR(r) system can be expressed through the behaviour of a network of reaction systems. As it can be seen from the next result this implies using in the network of reaction systems a number of components equal to the number of components and edges of the simulated cdcR(r) system. The additional components in the network of reaction systems are used for filtration purposes.

Theorem 4. *Let $\Delta = (m, S, \mathcal{R})$, where $m \ge 1$, be a cdcR(r) system with initial state $\overline{C}_0$. Then there exists a network of reaction systems $\mathcal{N} = (G, \mathcal{F}, \mu)$ with G directed and initial distribution $\mathbf{H}_0^\Pi$ such that $\overline{D}_i = tail(\mathbf{W}_{5i}^\Pi, m) \cap S$, for all $i \ge 0$.*

Proof. Let $\Delta = (m, S, \mathcal{R})$, where $m \ge 1$, be a cdcR(r) system with initial configuration $\overline{C}_0 = ((A_{1,0}, D_{1,0}), \ldots, (A_{m,0}, D_{m,0}))$. For every component A_j of Δ, with $1 \le j \le m$, we construct a node v_j such that $\mu(v_j) = \mathcal{A}^j = (S^j, A^j)$, where $S^j = \{x, x', x'', x'''\} \mid x \in S\} \cup \{\tau_\rho, \tau'_\rho, \overline{\tau}_\rho \mid \rho \in \mathcal{R}\}$ and for any rc-reaction $\rho : (R, I, P); target\{\rho\} \in \mathcal{R}$ we add the following reactions to A^j of $\mathcal{N}$:

- $a_\rho = (R, I\tau_\rho, P'\tau_\rho\tau'_\rho)$ - the object τ_ρ will be use to block the application of rule ρ in the current node in the next step;
- $a_\rho^\tau = (\tau_\rho, \overline{\tau}_\rho, \tau_\rho)$ - the object τ_ρ is kept alive till an object $\overline{\tau}_\rho$ arrives in the node;
- $a'_x = (x', \emptyset, x'')$ - such a rule is added for each $x \in S$;
- $a''_x = (x'', \emptyset, x''')$ - such a rule is added for each $x \in S$;
- $a'''_x = (x''', \emptyset, x)$ - such a rule is added for each $x \in S$.

Also, for each edge (k, j) in Δ we construct two nodes v_{kj} and v_{jk} and add to E the directed edges (k, kj), (kj, j), (j, jk) and (jk, k). Each node v_{kj} is such that $\mu(v_{kj}) = \mathcal{A}^{kj} = (S^{kj}, A^{kj})$, where $S^{kj} = \{\tau'_\rho, \overline{\tau}_\rho \mid \rho \in \mathcal{R}\}$ and to A^{kj} we add the following reactions for every $\rho \in \mathcal{R}$:

- $a_\rho^{kj} = (\tau'_\rho, \emptyset, \overline{\tau}_\rho)$ - the object $\overline{\tau}_\rho$ is used to activate a rule blocked by an existing τ_ρ object in node v_j.

We assume that $V = (\ldots, v_1, \ldots, v_m)$ where on the first places are the nodes v_{kj} created as above. Thus, using this given order of nodes, we assume that $\mathbf{W}_0^{\Pi} = (\emptyset, \ldots, \emptyset, W_0^1, \ldots, W_0^m)$, such that $W_0^j = C_0^j \cup D_0^j$ where $C_0^j = D_{j,0}$ and $D_0^j = \bigcup_{\rho \in \mathcal{R} \setminus A_{j,0}} \tau_\rho$. Thus, the objects τ_ρ added initially in D_0^j inhibit the application of the rules, except for the ones from $A_{j,0}$.

We prove that the state sequence of component A_j of Δ starting from initial state $D_{j,0}$ corresponds to the state sequence of $\mathcal{A}^j$, with $1 \leq j \leq m$, restricted to the elements of S and starting from W_0^j. The proof is by induction on the last applied step:

- Case $i = 0$. There was no step applied yet, and the system is in the initial state. From $\mathbf{W}_0^{\Pi} = (\emptyset, \ldots, \emptyset, W_0^1, \ldots, W_0^m)$ it follows that $W_0^j \cap S = (C_0^j \cup D_0^j) \cap S = (D_{j,0} \cup (\bigcup_{\rho \in \mathcal{R} \setminus A_{j,0}} \tau_\rho)) \cap S = D_{j,0}$ as required.
- Case $i = 1$. This implies that this is the first applied step using the existing resources. Due to Definition 7 it holds that $D_{j,1} = res_{core(A_{j,0})}(D_{j,0})$ and $A_{j,1} = \{\rho \in \mathcal{R} \mid j \in target(\rho), \rho \in A_{k,0}, en_{core(\rho)}(D_{k,0}), 1 \leq k \leq m\}$. Due to Definition 3 it holds that:
  - $C_1^j = (\bigcup D_0^{kj}) \cap S^j = \emptyset$ and $D_1^j = res_{A^j}(W_0^j)$;
  - $C_1^{kj} = D_0^k \cap S^{kj} = \emptyset$ and $D_1^{kj} = res_{A^{kj}}(W_0^{kj}) = \emptyset$;
  - $C_2^j = (\bigcup D_1^{kj}) \cap S^j = \emptyset$ and $D_2^j = res_{A^j}(W_1^j) = res_{A^j}(D_1^j)$;
  - $C_2^{kj} = D_1^k \cap S^{kj} = res_{A^k}(W_0^k) \cap S^{kj} = \bigcup_{a \in en(A^k, W_0^k)} \tau'_a$ and $D_2^{kj} = res_{A^{kj}}(W_1^{kj}) = \emptyset$;
  - $C_3^j = (\bigcup D_2^{kj}) \cap S^j = \emptyset$ and $D_3^j = res_{A^j}(W_2^j) = res_{A^j}(D_2^j)$;
  - $C_3^{kj} = D_2^k \cap S^{kj} = \emptyset$ and $D_3^{kj} = res_{A^{kj}}(W_2^{kj}) = res_{A^{kj}}(res_{A^k}(W_0^k)) = res_{A^{kj}}(\bigcup_{a \in en(A^k, W_0^k)} \tau'_a) = \bigcup_{a \in en(A^k, W_0^k)} \overline{\tau}_a$;
  - $C_4^j = (\bigcup D_3^{kj}) \cap S^j = \bigcup(\bigcup_{a \in en(A^k, W_0^k)} \overline{\tau}_a)$ and $D_4^j = res_{A^j}(W_3^j) = res_{A^j}(D_3^j)$;
  - $C_4^{kj} = D_3^k \cap S^{kj} = \emptyset$ and $D_4^{kj} = res_{A^{kj}}(W_3^{kj}) = \emptyset$;
  - $C_5^j = (\bigcup D_4^{kj}) \cap S^j = \emptyset$ and $D_5^j = res_{A^j}(W_4^j)$;
  - $C_5^{kj} = D_4^k \cap S^{kj} = \emptyset$ and $D_5^{kj} = res_{A^{kj}}(W_4^{kj}) = \emptyset$.

  Since the rules of $\mathcal{N}$ were constructed such that $res_{A_k}(D_{k,0}) = D_5^{kj} \cap S$, it follows that $D_{j,1} = W_5^j \cap S$ as required. Also note that $C_5^j = C_5^{kj} = D_5^{kj} = \emptyset$.
- Case $i > 1$. Assume the statement holds for $i - 1$, namely $D_{j,i-1} = W_{5i-5}^j \cap S$ and also $C_{5i-5}^j = C_{5i-5}^{ij} = D_{5i-5}^{ij} = \emptyset$. We show that $D_{j,i} = W_{5i}^j \cap S$ holds as well. Due to Definition 7 it holds that $D_{j,i} = res_{core(A_{j,i-1})}(D_{j,i-1})$ and

$A_{j,i} = \{\rho \in \mathcal{R} | j \in target(\rho), \rho \in A_{k,i-1}, en_{core(\rho)}(D_{k,i-1}), 1 \le k \le m\}$. Due to Definition 3 it holds that:

- $C_{5i-4}^{j} = (\bigcup D_{5i-5}^{kj}) \cap S^{j} = \emptyset$ and $D_{5i-4}^{j} = res_{A^{j}}(W_{5i-5}^{j})$;
- $C_{5i-4}^{kj} = D_{5i-5}^{k} \cap S^{kj} = \emptyset$ and $D_{5i-4}^{kj} = res_{A^{kj}}(W_{5i-5}^{kj}) = \emptyset$;
- $C_{5i-3}^{j} = (\bigcup D_{5i-4}^{kj}) \cap S^{j} = \emptyset$ and $D_{5i-3}^{j} = res_{A^{j}}(W_{5i-4}^{j}) = res_{A^{j}}(D_{5i-4}^{j})$;
- $C_{5i-3}^{kj} = D_{5i-4}^{k} \cap S^{kj} = res_{A^{k}}(W_{5i-5}^{k}) \cap S^{kj} = \bigcup_{a \in en(A^{k}, W_{5i-5}^{k})} \tau_{a}'$ and

  $D_{5i-3}^{kj} = res_{A^{kj}}(W_{5i-4}^{kj}) = \emptyset$;
- $C_{5i-2}^{j} = (\bigcup D_{5i-3}^{kj}) \cap S^{j} = \emptyset$ and $D_{5i-2}^{j} = res_{A^{j}}(W_{5i-3}^{j}) = res_{A^{j}}(D_{5i-3}^{j})$;
- $C_{5i-2}^{kj} = D_{5i-3}^{k} \cap S^{kj} = \emptyset$ and $D_{5i-2}^{kj} = res_{A^{kj}}(W_{5i-3}^{kj}) = res_{A^{kj}}(\bigcup_{a \in en(A^{k}, W_{5i-5}^{k})} \tau_{a}') = \bigcup_{a \in en(A^{k}, W_{5i-5}^{k})} \overline{\tau}_{a}$;
- $C_{5i-1}^{j} = (\bigcup D_{5i-2}^{kj}) \cap S^{j} = \bigcup(\bigcup_{a \in en(A^{k}, W_{5i-5}^{k})} \overline{\tau}_{a})$ and

  $D_{5i-1}^{j} = res_{A^{j}}(W_{5i-2}^{j}) = res_{A^{j}}(D_{5i-2}^{j})$;
- $C_{5i-1}^{kj} = D_{5i-2}^{k} \cap S^{kj} = \emptyset$ and $D_{5i-1}^{kj} = res_{A^{kj}}(W_{5i-2}^{kj}) = \emptyset$;
- $C_{5i}^{j} = (\bigcup D_{5i-1}^{kj}) \cap S^{j} = \emptyset$ and $D_{5i}^{j} = res_{A^{j}}(W_{5i-1}^{j})$;
- $C_{5i}^{kj} = D_{5i-1}^{k} \cap S^{kj} = \emptyset$ and $D_{5i}^{kj} = res_{A^{kj}}(W_{5i-1}^{kj}) = \emptyset$.

Since the rules of $\mathcal{N}$ were constructed such that $res_{A_{k}}(D_{k,5i-5}) = D_{5i}^{kj} \cap S$, it follows that $D_{j,i} = W_{5i}^{j} \cap S$ as required.

6   Conclusion

In this paper we considered, on one hand, networks of reaction systems that are graphs such that in each node resides a reaction system, and the context of each reaction system is obtained from all its neighbours. On the other hand, we considered communicating reaction systems with direct communication that are networks of reaction systems without context but able to send products or reactions between neighbours. We proved that these types of networks of reaction systems can be related by establishing mappings from network of reaction systems to communicating reaction systems with direct communication and back.

Membrane computing [18] and reaction systems [14] represent two well-known research fields in natural computing; both were created by modelling various aspects from the behaviour of living cells. While the networks of reaction systems consider sets of resources placed in the components, membrane systems consider multisets rather than sets. By considering the thresholds and no permanency assumptions from reaction systems in the context of membrane systems, a connection between these two fields was studied in [19]. Also membrane systems were used to simulate reaction systems in [1]. Starting from these existing connections, we intend to establish other connections between the various classes of networks of reaction systems and various classes of P systems.

References

1. Alhazov, A., Aman, B., Freund, R., Ivanov, S.: Simulating R systems by P systems. In: Leporati, A., Rozenberg, G., Salomaa, A., Zandron, C. (eds.) CMC 2016. LNCS, vol. 10105, pp. 51–66. Springer, Cham (2017). https://doi.org/10.1007/978-3-319-54072-6_4
2. Aman, B., Ciobanu, G.: Controlled reversibility in reaction systems. In: Gheorghe, M., Rozenberg, G., Salomaa, A., Zandron, C. (eds.) CMC 2017. LNCS, vol. 10725, pp. 40–53. Springer, Cham (2018). https://doi.org/10.1007/978-3-319-73359-3_3
3. Aman, B., Ciobanu, G.: Mutual exclusion and reversibility in reaction systems. J. Memb. Comput. **2**(3), 171–178 (2020). https://doi.org/10.1007/s41965-020-00043-1
4. Azimi, S., Iancu, B., Petre, I.: Reaction system models for the heat shock response. Fund. Inform. **131**(3–4), 299–312 (2014). https://doi.org/10.3233/FI-2014-1016
5. Bagossy, A., Vaszil, G.: Simulating reversible computation with reaction systems. J. Memb. Comput. **2**(3), 179–193 (2020). https://doi.org/10.1007/s41965-020-00049-9
6. Barbuti, R., Gori, R., Levi, F., Milazzo, P.: Generalized contexts for reaction systems: definition and study of dynamic causalities. Acta Inform. **55**(3), 227–267 (2017). https://doi.org/10.1007/s00236-017-0296-3
7. Bottoni, P., Labella, A., Rozenberg, G.: Reaction systems with influence on environment. J. Memb. Comput. **1**(1), 3–19 (2019). https://doi.org/10.1007/s41965-018-00005-8
8. Bottoni, P., Labella, A., Rozenberg, G.: Networks of reaction systems. Int. J. Found. Comput. Sci. **31**(1), 53–71 (2020). https://doi.org/10.1142/S0129054120400043
9. Brijder, R., Ehrenfeucht, A., Main, M.G., Rozenberg, G.: A tour of reaction systems. Int. J. Found. Comput. Sci. **22**(7), 1499–1517 (2011). https://doi.org/10.1142/S0129054111008842
10. Brijder, R., Ehrenfeucht, A., Rozenberg, G.: Reaction systems with duration. In: Kelemen, J., Kelemenová, A. (eds.) Computation, Cooperation, and Life. LNCS, vol. 6610, pp. 191–202. Springer, Heidelberg (2011). https://doi.org/10.1007/978-3-642-20000-7_16
11. Csuhaj-Varjú, E., Sethy, P.K.: Communicating reaction systems with direct communication. In: Freund, R., Ishdorj, T.-O., Rozenberg, G., Salomaa, A., Zandron, C. (eds.) CMC 2020. LNCS, vol. 12687, pp. 17–30. Springer, Cham (2021). https://doi.org/10.1007/978-3-030-77102-7_2
12. Csuhaj-Varjú, E., Sethy, P.K.: Properties of communicating reaction systems. In: Brejová, B., et al. (eds.) 21st Conference Information Technologies - Applications and Theory (ITAT 2021). CEUR Workshop Proceedings, vol. 2962, pp. 217–221. CEUR-WS.org (2021)
13. Ehrenfeucht, A., Kleijn, J., Koutny, M., Rozenberg, G.: Evolving reaction systems. Theoret. Comput. Sci. **682**, 79–99 (2017). https://doi.org/10.1016/j.tcs.2016.12.031
14. Ehrenfeucht, A., Rozenberg, G.: Reaction systems. Fund. Inform. **75**(1–4), 263–280 (2007)
15. Ehrenfeucht, A., Rozenberg, G.: Introducing time in reaction systems. Theoret. Comput. Sci. **410**(4–5), 310–322 (2009). https://doi.org/10.1016/j.tcs.2008.09.043
16. Ehrenfeucht, A., Rozenberg, G.: Zoom structures and reaction systems yield exploration systems. Int. J. Found. Comput. Sci. **25**(3), 275–306 (2014). https://doi.org/10.1142/S0129054114500142

17. Kleijn, J., Koutny, M., Rozenberg, G.: Plug-in context providers for reaction systems. Theoret. Comput. Sci. **834**, 26–42 (2020). https://doi.org/10.1016/j.tcs.2020.01.033
18. Păun, Gh.: Computing with membranes. J. Comput. Syst. Sci. **61**(1), 108–143 (2000). https://doi.org/10.1006/jcss.1999.1693
19. Păun, Gh., Pérez-Jiménez, M.J.: Towards bridging two cell-inspired models: P systems and R systems. Theoret. Comput. Sci. **429**, 258–264 (2012). https://doi.org/10.1016/j.tcs.2011.12.046

A Characterization of Polynomial Time Computable Functions from the Integers to the Reals Using Discrete Ordinary Differential Equations

Manon Blanc[1,2] and Olivier Bournez[1(✉)]

[1] Institut Polytechnique de Paris, Ecole Polytechnique,
Laboratoire d'Informatique de l'X (LIX), 91128 Palaiseau Cedex, France
{manon.blanc,olivier.bournez}@lix.polytechnique.fr
[2] ENS Paris-Saclay, Gif-Sur-Yvette, France

Abstract. The class of functions from the integers to the integers computable in polynomial time has been recently characterized using discrete ordinary differential equations (ODE), also known as finite differences. Doing so, the fundamental role of linear (discrete) ODEs and classical ODE tools such as changes of variables to capture computability and complexity measures, or as a tool for programming was pointed out.

In this article, we extend the approach to a characterization of functions from the integers to the reals computable in polynomial time in the sense of computable analysis. In particular, we provide a characterization of such functions in terms of the smallest class of functions that contains some basic functions, and that is closed by composition, linear length ODEs, and a natural effective limit schema.

1 Introduction

Ordinary differential equations are a natural tool for modeling many phenomena in applied sciences, with a very abundant literature (see e.g. [1,3,13]) and are rather well understood under many aspects. In a series of recent articles, they have been shown to also correspond to some natural computational model, with a nice computability and complexity theory: See [7] for a survey.

In a recent article [5,6], their discrete counterpart, which are called discrete ODEs, also known as difference equations have been investigated. The basic principle is, for a function $\mathbf{f}(x)$ to consider its discrete derivative defined as $\Delta\mathbf{f}(x) = \mathbf{f}(x+1) - \mathbf{f}(x)$. We will intentionally also write $\mathbf{f}'(x)$ for $\Delta\mathbf{f}(x)$ to help to understand statements with respect to their classical continuous counterparts. This associated derivative notion, called *finite differences*, has been widely studied in numerical optimization for function approximation [14] and in *discrete calculus* [15–17,19] for combinatorial analysis. While the underlying computational content of finite differences theory is clear and has been pointed out many

---

This work has been partially supported by ANR Project $\partial IFFERENCE$.

J. Durand-Lose and G. Vaszil (Eds.): MCU 2022, LNCS 13419, pp. 58–74, 2022.
https://doi.org/10.1007/978-3-031-13502-6_4

times, no fundamental connections with algorithms and complexity had been formally established before [5,6], where it was proved that many complexity and computability classes from computation theory can actually be characterized algebraically using discrete ODEs. Even if such results were initially motivated by helping to understand the relationships between analog computations and classical discrete models of computation theory, the relation between the two is currently unclear.

In the context of algebraic classes of functions, a classical notation is the following: Call *operation* a scheme of definition that takes finitely many functions, and returns some new function defined from them. Then,

$$[f_1, f_2, \ldots, f_k; op_1, op_2, \ldots, op_\ell],$$

denotes the smallest set of functions containing functions $f_1, f_2, \ldots, f_k$ that is closed under operations op_1, op_2, $\ldots op_\ell$. Call *discrete function* a function of type $f : S_1 \times \cdots \times S_d \to S_1' \times \ldots S_{d'}'$, where each S_i, S_i' is either $\mathbb{N}$ or $\mathbb{Z}$. Write **FPTIME** for the class of functions computable in polynomial time. A main result of [5,6] is the following ($\mathbb{LDL}$ stands for linear derivation on length):

Theorem 1 ([6]). *For discrete functions, we have*

$$\mathbb{LDL} = \textbf{FPTIME}$$

where $\mathbb{LDL} = [\mathbf{0}, \mathbf{1}, \pi_i^k, \ell(x), +, -, \times, sg(x) \ ; composition, linear \ length \ ODE]$.

That is to say, $\mathbb{LDL}$ (and hence **FPTIME** for discrete functions) is the smallest subset of functions, that contains

- the constant functions $\mathbf{0}$ and $\mathbf{1}$,
- the projections $\pi_i^k : \mathbb{R}^k \to \mathbb{R}$ given by $\pi_i^k(x_1, \ldots, x_k) = x_i$, for various integers i and k,
- the length function $\ell(x)$, which maps an integer to the length of its binary representation,
- the addition function $x + y$,
- the subtraction function $x - y$,
- the multiplication function $x \times y$ (that we will also often denote $x \cdot y$),
- the sign function $sg(x) : \mathbb{Z} \to \mathbb{Z}$ that takes value 1 for $x > 0$ and 0 in the other case,

and closed under composition (when defined) and linear length-ODE scheme: The linear length-ODE scheme basically (a formal definition is provided in Definition 4) corresponds in defining functions from linear ODEs with respect to derivation with respect to the length of the argument, that is to say, of the form

$$\frac{\partial \mathbf{f}(x, \mathbf{y})}{\partial \ell} = \mathbf{A}[\mathbf{f}(x, \mathbf{y}), x, \mathbf{y}] \cdot \mathbf{f}(x, \mathbf{y}) + \mathbf{B}[\mathbf{f}(x, \mathbf{y}), x, \mathbf{y}],$$

In all what follows, when we write some variable using some boldface letter, like $\mathbf{y}$, this means that it can be a vector of variable. A usual typography, like for the x above, means it is a single variable. In the above description, we use the notation $\frac{\partial \mathbf{f}(x,\mathbf{y})}{\partial \ell}$, which corresponds in derivation of $\mathbf{f}$ along the length function: Given some function $\mathcal{L} : \mathbb{N}^{p+1} \to \mathbb{Z}$, and in particular for the case of where $\mathcal{L}(x,\mathbf{y}) = \ell(x)$,

$$\frac{\partial \mathbf{f}(x,\mathbf{y})}{\partial \mathcal{L}} = \frac{\partial \mathbf{f}(x,\mathbf{y})}{\partial \mathcal{L}(x,\mathbf{y})} = \mathbf{h}(\mathbf{f}(x,\mathbf{y}),x,\mathbf{y}), \tag{1}$$

is a formal synonym for

$$\mathbf{f}(x+1,\mathbf{y}) = \mathbf{f}(x,\mathbf{y}) + (\mathcal{L}(x+1,\mathbf{y}) - \mathcal{L}(x,\mathbf{y})) \cdot \mathbf{h}(\mathbf{f}(x,\mathbf{y}),x,\mathbf{y}).$$

Remark 1. This concepts, introduced in [5,6], is motivated by the fact that the latter expression is similar to classical formula for classical continuous ODEs:

$$\frac{\delta f(x,\mathbf{y})}{\delta x} = \frac{\delta \mathcal{L}(x,\mathbf{y})}{\delta x} \cdot \frac{\delta f(x,\mathbf{y})}{\delta \mathcal{L}(x,\mathbf{y})},$$

and hence this is similar in spirit to a change of variable. Consequently, a linear length-ODE is basically a linear ODE over variable t, once the change of variable $t = \ell(x)$ is done.

In particular, writing as usual B^A for functions from A to B, we have:

Theorem 2 ([6]). $\mathbb{LDL} \cap \mathbb{N}^{\mathbb{N}} = \mathbf{FPTIME} \cap \mathbb{N}^{\mathbb{N}}$.

This provides a characterization of **FPTIME** for discrete functions that does not require to specify an explicit bound in the recursion, in contrast to Cobham's work [12], nor to assign a specific role or type to variables, in contrast to safe recursion or ramification [2,20]. The characterization happens to be very simple using only natural notions from the world of ODE.

Our purpose in this article is to extend this to more general classes of functions. In particular, this makes sense to try to characterize polynomial time functions from the reals to the reals. We consider here computability and complexity over the reals in the most classical sense, that is to say, computable analysis (see e.g. [27]). Indeed, considering that $\mathbb{N} \subset \mathbb{R}$, most of the basic functions and operations in the above characterization (for example, $+$, $-$, ...) have a clear meaning over the reals. One clear difficulty is that discrete ODEs are about discrete schemata, while we would like to talk about functions over the continuum. We did not succeed to do so yet, but we propose here a substantial step towards this direction: We provide a characterization of polynomial time computable functions *from the integers to the reals* using discrete linear ODEs: considering linear ODEs is very natural in the context of ODEs.

To do so, we naturally go to talking about algebra of functions more general than discrete functions, that is to say over more general space than $\mathbb{N}$ and $\mathbb{Z}$. This introduces some subtleties, and difficulties, that we discuss in this article, with our various concepts, definitions and statements. Hence, we consider in this article functions of type $f : S_1 \times \cdots \times S_d \to S_0$, where each S_i is either $\mathbb{N}$, $\mathbb{Z}$ or $\mathbb{Q}$ or $\mathbb{R}$, or is possibly vectorial functions whose components (that is to say coordinates/projections) are of this type. We denote $\mathcal{F}$ for the class of such functions. Clearly, we can consider $\mathbb{N} \subset \mathbb{Z} \subset \mathbb{Q} \subset \mathbb{R}$, but as functions may have different type of outputs, composition is an issue. We simply admit that composition may not be defined in some cases. In other words, we consider that composition is a partial operator: for example, given $f : \mathbb{N} \to \mathbb{R}$ and $g : \mathbb{R} \to \mathbb{R}$, the composition of g and f is defined as expected, but f cannot be composed with a function such as $h : \mathbb{N} \to \mathbb{N}$.

We then consider the class

$$\mathbb{LDL}^{\bullet} = [\mathbf{0}, \mathbf{1}, \pi_i^k, \ell(x), +, -, \times, \overline{\mathrm{cond}}(x), \frac{x}{2}; composition, linear\ length\ ODE]$$

of functions of $\mathcal{F}$. Here

- $\ell : \mathbb{N} \to \mathbb{N}$ is the length function, mapping some integer to the length of its binary representation,
- $\frac{x}{2} : \mathbb{R} \to \mathbb{R}$ is the function that divides by 2, and all other basic functions are defined exactly as for $\mathbb{LDL}$, but considered here as functions from the reals to reals.
- $\overline{\mathrm{cond}}(x) : \mathbb{R} \to \mathbb{R}$ is some piecewise affine function that takes value 1 for $x > \frac{3}{4}$ and 0 for $x < \frac{1}{4}$, and continuous piecewise affine. In particular, its restrictions to the integer is the function $\mathrm{sg}(x)$ considered in $\mathbb{LDL}$.

We prove the following ($\|.\|$ stands for the sup-norm).

Theorem 3 (Main Theorem 1). *A function* $\mathbf{f} : \mathbb{N}^d \to \mathbb{R}^{d'}$ *is computable in polynomial time if and only if there exists* $\tilde{\mathbf{f}} : \mathbb{N}^{d+1} \to \mathbb{R}^{d'} \in \mathbb{LDL}^{\bullet}$ *such that for all* $\mathbf{m} \in \mathbb{N}^d$, $n \in \mathbb{N}$, $\|\tilde{\mathbf{f}}(\mathbf{m}, 2^n) - \mathbf{f}(\mathbf{m})\| \leq 2^{-n}$.

From the fact that we have the reverse direction in the previous theorem, it is natural to consider the operation that maps $\tilde{\mathbf{f}}$ to $\mathbf{f}$. Namely, we introduce the operation $ELim$ ($ELim$ stands for Effective Limit):

Definition 1 (Operation $ELim$). *Given* $\tilde{\mathbf{f}} : \mathbb{N}^{d+1} \to \mathbb{R}^{d'} \in \mathbb{LDL}^{\bullet}$ *such that for all* $\mathbf{m} \in \mathbb{N}^d$, $n \in \mathbb{N}$, $\|\tilde{\mathbf{f}}(\mathbf{m}, 2^n) - \mathbf{f}(\mathbf{m})\| \leq 2^{-n}$ *for some function* $\mathbf{f}$, *then* $ELim(\tilde{\mathbf{f}})$ *is the (clearly uniquely defined) corresponding function* $\mathbf{f} : \mathbb{N}^d \to \mathbb{R}^{d'}$.

We obtain our main result, that provides a characterization of polynomial time computable functions for functions from the integers to the reals.

Theorem 4 (Main theorem 2). *A function* $\mathbf{f} : \mathbb{N}^d \to \mathbb{R}^{d'}$. *is computable in polynomial time if and only if all it components can be written through the* $\overline{\mathbb{LDL}^{\bullet}}$ *scheme, where:*
$\overline{\mathbb{LDL}^{\bullet}} = [\mathbf{0}, \mathbf{1}, \pi_i^k, \ell(x), +, -, \times, \overline{cond}(x), \frac{x}{2}; composition, linear\ length\ ODE, ELim]$.

In particular:

Theorem 5. $\overline{\mathbb{LDL}^{\bullet}} \cap \mathbb{R}^{\mathbb{N}} = \mathbf{FPTIME} \cap \mathbb{R}^{\mathbb{N}}$

In Sect. 2, we recall the theory of discrete ODEs. In Sect. 3, we recall required concepts from computable analysis. In Sect. 4, we prove that functions from $\mathbb{LDL}^\bullet$ are polynomial time computable. Section 5 is proving a kind of reverse implication for functions over words. Then this is extended in Sect. 6 to functions from integers to the reals, and we obtain a proof of Theorem 3. Section 7 then proves Theorems 4 and 5. Section 8 is some generalizations of these results. Section 9 discusses future work and difficulties to go to functions of $\mathbb{R}^\mathbb{R}$.

Related Work. Various computability and complexity classes have been recently characterized using (classical) continuous ODEs: The most up-to-date survey is [7]. Dealing with discrete ODEs is really different, as most of the constructions heavily rely on some closure properties of continuous ODEs not true for discrete ODEs, in particular because there is no chain rule formula for discrete derivation. The idea of considering discrete ODEs as a model of computation is due to [5,6].

In a non-ODE centric point of view, we are characterizing some complexity classes using particular discrete schemata. Recursion schemes constitute a major approach of computability theory and to some extent of complexity theory. The foundational characterization of **FPTIME** due to Cobham [12], and then others based on safe recursion [2] or ramification [21,22], or for other classes [23], gave birth to the very vivid field of *implicit complexity* at the interplay of logic and theory of programming: See [10,11] for monographs.

Our ways of simulating Turing machines have some reminiscence of similar constructions used in other contexts such as Neural Networks [25,26]. But with respect to all previous contexts, as far as we know, only a few papers have been devoted to characterizations of complexity, and even computability, classes in the sense of computable analysis. There have been some attempts using continuous ODEs [4], or the so-called $\mathbb{R}$-recursive functions [7]. For discrete schemata, we only know [8] and [24], focusing on computability and not complexity.

2   Some Concepts from the Theory of Discrete ODEs

In this section, we recall some concepts and definitions from discrete ODEs, either well-known or established in [5,6]. We need to slightly extend the concept of sg-polynomial expression from [5,6] to allow expressions with $\overline{\text{cond}}()$ instead of sg().

Definition 2 (Extension of [5,6]). *A $\overline{\text{cond}}$-polynomial expression $P(x_1, ..., x_h)$ is an expression built-on $+, -, \times$ (often denoted $\cdot$) and $\overline{\text{cond}}()$ functions over a set of variables $V = \{x_1, ..., x_h\}$ and integer constants. The degree $\deg(x, P)$ of a term $x \in V$ in P is defined inductively as follows: $\deg(x, x) = 1$ and for $x' \in V \cup \mathbb{Z}$ such that $x' \neq x$, $\deg(x, x') = 0$; $\deg(x, P + Q) = \max\{\deg(x, P), \deg(x, Q)\}$; $\deg(x, P \times Q) = \deg(x, P) + \deg(x, Q)$; $\deg(x, sg(P)) = 0$. A $\overline{\text{cond}}$-polynomial expression P is essentially constant in x if $\deg(x, P) = 0$.*

Compared to the classical notion of degree in polynomial expression, all sub-terms that are within the scope of a sign (that is to say $\overline{\text{cond}}()$) function con-tributes 0 to the degree. A vectorial function (respectively a matrix or a vector) is said to be a $\overline{\text{cond}}$-polynomial expression if all its coordinates (respectively coefficients) are. It is said to be *essentially constant* if all its coefficients are.

Definition 3 ([5,6]). *A $\overline{\text{cond}}$-polynomial expression $\mathbf{g}(\mathbf{f}(x,\mathbf{y}),x,\mathbf{y})$ is essen-tially linear in $\mathbf{f}(x,\mathbf{y})$ if it is of the form $\mathbf{g}(\mathbf{f}(x,\mathbf{y}),x,\mathbf{y}) = \mathbf{A}[\mathbf{f}(x,\mathbf{y}),x,\mathbf{y}] \cdot \mathbf{f}(x,\mathbf{y}) + \mathbf{B}[\mathbf{f}(x,\mathbf{y}),x,\mathbf{y}]$ where $\mathbf{A}$ and $\mathbf{B}$ are $\overline{\text{cond}}$-polynomial expressions essen-tially constant in $\mathbf{f}(x,\mathbf{y})$.*

For example, the expression $P(x,y,z) = x \cdot \overline{\text{cond}}((x^2 - z) \cdot y) + y^3$ is essentially linear in x, essentially constant in z and not linear in y. The expression: $z + (1 - \overline{\text{cond}}(x)) \cdot (1 - \overline{\text{cond}}(-x)) \cdot (y - z)$ is essentially constant in x and linear in y and z.

Definition 4 (Linear length ODE [5,6]). *Function $\mathbf{f}$ is linear $\mathcal{L}$-ODE defin-able (from $\mathbf{u}$, $\mathbf{g}$ and $\mathbf{h}$) if it corresponds to the solution of*

$$\mathbf{f}(0,\mathbf{y}) = \mathbf{g}(\mathbf{y}) \quad and \quad \frac{\partial \mathbf{f}(x,\mathbf{y})}{\partial \ell} = \mathbf{u}(\mathbf{f}(x,\mathbf{y}), \mathbf{h}(x,\mathbf{y}), x, \mathbf{y}) \tag{2}$$

where $\mathbf{u}$ is essentially linear in $\mathbf{f}(x,\mathbf{y})$.

3 Some Concepts from Computable Analysis

When we say that a function $f : S_1 \times \cdots \times S_d \to \mathbb{R}^{d'}$ is (respectively: polynomial-time) computable this will always be in the sense of computable analysis. We recall here the basic concepts and definitions, mostly following the book [18], whose subject is complexity theory in computable analysis. Alternative presen-tations include [9,27]. Actually, as we want to talk about functions in $\mathcal{F}$, we need to mix complexity issues dealing with integer and real arguments.

A dyadic number d is a rational number with a finite binary expansion. That is to say $d = m/2^n$ for some integers $m \in \mathbb{Z}$, $n \in \mathbb{N}$, $n \geq 0$. Let $\mathbb{D}$ be the set of all dyadic rational numbers. We denote by $\mathbb{D}_n$ the set of all dyadic rationals d with a representation s of precision $\text{prec}(s) = n$; that is, $\mathbb{D}_n = \{m \cdot 2^{-n} \mid m \in \mathbb{Z}\}$.

Definition 5 ([18]). *For each real number x, a function $\phi : \mathbb{N} \to \mathbb{D}$ is said to binary converge to x if for all $n \in \mathbb{N}, \text{prec}(\phi(n)) = n$ and $|\phi(n) - x| \leq 2^{-n}$. Let CF_x (Cauchy function) denote the set of all functions binary converging to x.*

Intuitively Turing machine M computes a real function f in the following way: 1. The input x to f, represented by some $\phi \in CF_x$, is given to M as an oracle; 2. The output precision 2^{-n} is given in the form of integer n as the input to M; 3. The computation of M usually takes two steps, though sometimes these two steps may be repeated for an indefinite number of times: 4. M computes, from the output precision 2^{-n}, the required input precision 2^{-m}; 5. M queries the oracle to get $\phi(m)$, such that $\|\phi(m) - x\| \leq 2^{-m}$, and computes from $\phi(m)$ an output $d \in \mathbb{D}$ with $\|d - f(x)\| \leq 2^{-n}$.

More formally:

Definition 6 ([18]). *A real function* $f : \mathbb{R} \to \mathbb{R}$ *is computable if there is a function-oracle TM M such that for each* $x \in \mathbb{R}$ *and each* $\phi \in CF_x$, *the function* ψ *computed by M with oracle* ϕ *(i.e.,* $\psi(n) = M^\phi(n)$*) is in* $CF_{f(x)}$.

Assume that M is an oracle machine which computes f on domain G. For any oracle $\phi \in CF_x$, with $x \in G$, let $T_M(\phi, n)$ be the number of steps for M to halt on input n with oracle ϕ, and $T'_M(x, n) = \max\{T_M(\phi, n) \mid \phi \in CF_x\}$. The time complexity of f is defined as follows.

Definition 7 ([18]). *Let G be bounded closed interval* $[a, b]$. *Let* $f : G \to \mathbb{R}$ *be a computable function. Then, we say that the time complexity of f on G is bounded by a function* $t : G \times \mathbb{N} \to \mathbb{N}$ *if there exists an oracle TM M which computes f such that for all* $x \in G$ *and all* $n > 0$, $T'_M(x, n) \le t(x, n)$.

In other words, the idea is to measure the time complexity of a real function based on two parameters: input real number x and output precision 2^{-n}. Sometimes, it is more convenient to simplify the complexity measure to be based on only one parameter, the output precision. For this purpose, we say the uniform time complexity of f on G is bounded by a function $t' : \mathbb{N} \to \mathbb{N}$ if the time complexity of f on G is bounded by a function $t : G \times \mathbb{N} \to \mathbb{N}$ with the property that for all $x \in G$, $t(x, n) \le t'(n)$.

However, if we do so, it is important to realize that if we had taken $G = \mathbb{R}$ in the previous definition, for unbounded functions f, the uniform time complexity would not exist, because the number of moves required to write down the integral part of $f(x)$ grows as x approaches $+\infty$ or $-\infty$. Therefore, the approach of [18] is to do as follows (the bounds -2^X and 2^X are somewhat arbitrary, but are chosen here because the binary expansion of any $x \in (-2^n, 2^n)$ has n bits in the integral part).

Definition 8 (Adapted from [18]). *For functions* $f(x)$ *whose domain is* $\mathbb{R}$, *we say that the (non-uniform) time complexity of f is bounded by a function* $t' : \mathbb{N}^2 \to \mathbb{N}$ *if the time complexity of f on* $[-2^X, 2^X]$ *is bounded by a function* $t : \mathbb{N}^2 \to \mathbb{N}$ *such that* $t(x, n) \le t'(X, n)$ *for all* $x \in [-2^X, 2^X]$.

As we want to talk about general functions in $\mathcal{F}$, we extend the approach to more general functions. (for conciseness, when $\mathbf{x} = (x_1, \ldots, x_p)$, $\mathbf{X} = (X_1, \ldots, X_p)$, we write $\mathbf{x} \in [-2^{\mathbf{X}}, 2^{\mathbf{X}}]$ as a shortcut for $x_1 \in [-2^{X_1}, 2^{X_1}]$, $\ldots, x_p \in [-2^{X_p}, 2^{X_p}]$).

Definition 9 (Complexity for real functions: general case). *Consider a function* $f(x_1, \ldots, x_p, n_1, \ldots, n_q)$ *whose domain is* $\mathbb{R}^p \times \mathbb{N}^q$. *We say that the (non-uniform) time complexity of f is bounded by a function* $t' : \mathbb{N}^{p+q+1} \to \mathbb{N}$ *if the time complexity of* $f(\cdot, \ldots, \cdot, \ell(n_1), \ldots, \ell(n_q))$ *on* $[-2^{X_1}, 2^{X_1}] \times \ldots [-2^{X_p}, 2^{X_p}]$ *is bounded by a function* $t(\cdot, \ldots, \cdot, \ell(n_1), \ldots, \ell(n_q), \cdot) : \mathbb{N}^p \times \mathbb{N} \to \mathbb{N}$ *such that* $t(\mathbf{x}, \ell(n_1), \ldots, \ell(n_q), n) \le t'(\mathbf{X}, \ell(n_1), \ldots, \ell(n_q), n)$ *whenever* $\mathbf{x} \in [-2^{\mathbf{X}}, 2^{\mathbf{X}}]$. *We say that f is polynomial time computable if t' can be chosen as a polynomial. We say that a vectorial function is polynomial time computable iff all its components are.*

We do so that this measure of complexity extends the usual complexity for functions over the integers, where complexity of integers is measured with respects of their lengths, and over the reals, where complexity is measured with respect to their approximation. In particular, in the specific case of a function $f : \mathbb{N}^d \to \mathbb{R}^{d'}$, that basically means there is some polynomial $t' : \mathbb{N}^{d+1} \to \mathbb{N}$ so that the time complexity of producing some dyadic approximating $f(\mathbf{m})$ at precision 2^{-n} is bounded by $t'(\ell(m_1), \dots, \ell(m_d), n)$.

In other words, when considering that a function is polynomial time computable, it is in the length of all its integer arguments, as this is the usual convention. However, we need sometimes to consider also polynomial dependency directly in one of some specific integer argument, say n_i, and not on its length $\ell(n_i)$. We say that *the function is polynomial time computable,* with respect to the value of n_i when this holds (keeping possible other integer arguments n_j, $j \neq i$, measured by their length).

A well-known observation is the following.

Theorem 6. *Consider* $\mathbf{f}$ *as in Definition 9 computable in polynomial time. Then* $\mathbf{f}$ *has a polynomial modulus function of continuity, that is to say there is a polynomial function* $m_{\mathbf{f}} : \mathbb{N}^{p+q+1} \to \mathbb{N}$ *such that for all* $\mathbf{x}, \mathbf{y}$ *and all* $n > 0$, $\|\mathbf{x} - \mathbf{y}\| \leq 2^{-m_{\mathbf{f}}(\mathbf{X}, \ell(n_1), \dots, \ell(n_q), n)}$ *implies* $\|\mathbf{f}(\mathbf{x}, n_1, \dots, n_q) - \mathbf{f}(\mathbf{y}, n_1, \dots, n_q)\| \leq 2^{-n}$, *whenever* $\mathbf{x}, \mathbf{y} \in \left[-2^{\mathbf{X}}, 2^{\mathbf{X}}\right]$.

4   Functions from $\mathbb{LDL}^{\bullet}$ are in FPTIME

The following proposition can be proved by induction from standard arguments. The hardest part is to prove that the class of polynomial time computable functions is preserved by the linear length ODE schema: This is Lemma 3.

Proposition 1. *All functions of* $\mathbb{LDL}^{\bullet}$ *are computable (in the sense of computable analysis) in polynomial time.*

The following lemmas are proved in [5,6].

Lemma 1 (Alternative view, case of Length ODEs, from [5,6]). *Let* $f : \mathbb{N}^{p+1} \to \mathbb{Z}^d$, $\mathcal{L} : \mathbb{N}^{p+1} \to \mathbb{Z}$ *be some functions and assume that (1) holds considering* $\mathcal{L}(x, \mathbf{y}) = \ell(x)$. *Then* $\mathbf{f}(x, \mathbf{y})$ *is given by* $\mathbf{f}(x, \mathbf{y}) = \mathbf{F}(\ell(x), \mathbf{y})$ *where* $\mathbf{F}$ *is the solution of initial value problem*

$$\mathbf{F}(1, \mathbf{y}) = \mathbf{f}(0, \mathbf{y}),$$
$$\frac{\partial \mathbf{F}(t, \mathbf{y})}{\partial t} = \mathbf{h}(\mathbf{F}(t, \mathbf{y}), 2^t - 1, \mathbf{y}).$$

Lemma 2 (Solution of linear ODE, from [5,6]). *For matrices* $\mathbf{A}$ *and vectors* $\mathbf{B}$ *and* $\mathbf{G}$, *the solution of equation* $\mathbf{f}'(x, \mathbf{y}) = \mathbf{A}(\mathbf{f}(x, \mathbf{y}), \mathbf{h}(x, \mathbf{y}), x, \mathbf{y}) \cdot \mathbf{f}(x, \mathbf{y}) + \mathbf{B}(\mathbf{f}(x, \mathbf{y}), \mathbf{h}(x, \mathbf{y}), x, \mathbf{y})$ *with initial conditions* $\mathbf{f}(0, \mathbf{y}) = \mathbf{G}(\mathbf{y})$ *is*

$$\mathbf{f}(x, \mathbf{y}) = \left(\overline{2}^{\int_0^x \mathbf{A}(\mathbf{f}(t,\mathbf{y}), \mathbf{h}(t,\mathbf{y}), t, \mathbf{y}) \delta t} \right) \cdot \mathbf{G}(\mathbf{y})$$
$$+ \int_0^x \left(\overline{2}^{\int_{u+1}^x \mathbf{A}(\mathbf{f}(t,\mathbf{y}), \mathbf{h}(t,\mathbf{y}), t, \mathbf{y}) \delta t} \right) \cdot \mathbf{B}(\mathbf{f}(u, \mathbf{y}), \mathbf{h}(u, \mathbf{y}), u, \mathbf{y}) \delta u.$$

Remark 2. Notice, as in [5,6], that this can be rewritten as

$$\mathbf{f}(x,\mathbf{y}) = \sum_{u=-1}^{x-1} \left(\prod_{t=u+1}^{x-1} (1 + \mathbf{A}(\mathbf{f}(t,\mathbf{y}),\mathbf{h}(t,\mathbf{y}),t,\mathbf{y})) \right) \cdot \mathbf{B}(\mathbf{f}(u,\mathbf{y}),\mathbf{h}(u,\mathbf{y}),u,\mathbf{y}),$$

(3)

with the (not so usual) conventions that for any function $\kappa(\cdot)$, $\prod_x^{x-1} \kappa(x) = 1$ and $\mathbf{B}(-1,\mathbf{y}) = \mathbf{G}(\mathbf{y})$.

Lemma 3. *The class of polynomial time computable functions is preserved by the linear length ODE schema.*

We propose to write $\bar{x}$ for $2^x - 1$ for conciseness. We write $|\!|\!|\cdots|\!|\!|$ for the sup norm of integer part: given some matrix $\mathbf{A} = (A_{i,j})_{1\leq i\leq n, 1\leq j\leq m}$, $|\!|\!|\mathbf{A}|\!|\!| = \max_{i,j}\lceil A_{i,j} \rceil$. In particular, given a vector $\mathbf{x}$, it can be seen as a matrix with $m = 1$, and $|\!|\!|\mathbf{x}|\!|\!|$ is the sup norm of the integer part of its components.

Proof. Using Lemma 1, when the schema of Definition 4 holds, we can do a change of variable to consider $\mathbf{f}(x,\mathbf{y}) = \mathbf{F}(\ell(x),\mathbf{y})$, with $\mathbf{F}$ solution of a discrete ODE of the form $\frac{\partial \mathbf{F}(t,\mathbf{y})}{\partial t} = \mathbf{A}(\mathbf{F}(t,\mathbf{y}),\mathbf{h}(\vec{t},\mathbf{y}),\vec{t},\mathbf{y}) \cdot \mathbf{F}(t,\mathbf{y}) + \mathbf{B}(\mathbf{F}(t,\mathbf{y}),\mathbf{h}(\vec{t},\mathbf{y}),\vec{t},\mathbf{y})$, that is to say, of the form (4) below. It then follows from:

Lemma 4 (Fundamental observation). *Consider the ODE*

$$\mathbf{F}'(x,\mathbf{y}) = \mathbf{A}(\mathbf{F}(x,\mathbf{y}),\mathbf{h}(\vec{x},\mathbf{y}),\vec{x},\mathbf{y}) \cdot \mathbf{F}(x,\mathbf{y}) + \mathbf{B}(\mathbf{F}(x,\mathbf{y}),\mathbf{h}(\vec{x},\mathbf{y}),\vec{x},\mathbf{y}).$$

(4)

Assume:

1. *The initial condition $\mathbf{G}(\mathbf{y}) \stackrel{\text{def}}{=} \mathbf{F}(0,\mathbf{y})$, as well as $\mathbf{h}(\vec{x},\mathbf{y})$ are polynomial time computable with respect to the value of x.*
2. *$\mathbf{A}(\mathbf{F}(x,\mathbf{y}),\mathbf{h}(\vec{x},\mathbf{y}),\vec{x},\mathbf{y})$ and $\mathbf{B}(\mathbf{F}(x,\mathbf{y}),\mathbf{h}(\vec{x},\mathbf{y}),\vec{x},\mathbf{y})$ are sg-polynomial expressions essentially constant in $\mathbf{F}(x,\mathbf{y})$.*

Then, there exists a polynomial p such that $\ell(|\!|\!|\mathbf{F}(x,\mathbf{y})|\!|\!|) \leq p(x, \ell(|\!|\!|\mathbf{y}|\!|\!|))$ and $\mathbf{F}(x,\mathbf{y})$ is polynomial time computable with respect to the value of x.

Proof. The fact that there exists a polynomial p such that $\ell(|\!|\!|\mathbf{F}(x,\mathbf{y})|\!|\!|) \leq p(x, \ell(|\!|\!|\mathbf{y}|\!|\!|))$, follows from the fact that we can write some explicit formula for the solution of (4): This is Lemma 2 below repeated from [5,6]. Now, bounding the size of the right hand side of formula (3) provides the statement.

Now the fact that $\mathbf{F}(x,\mathbf{y})$ is polynomial time computable, follows from a reasoning similar to the one of following lemma (the lemma below restricts the form of the recurrence by lack of space, but the more general recurrence of (4) would basically not lead to any difficulty): The fact that the modulus of continuity of a linear expression of the form of the right hand side of (4) is necessarily affine in its first argument follows from the hypotheses and from previous paragraph, using the fact that $\overline{\text{cond}}()$ has a linear modulus of convergence.

Lemma 5. *Suppose that function the* $\mathbf{f} : \mathbb{N} \times \mathbb{R}^d \to \mathbb{R}^{d'}$ *is such that for all* $x, \mathbf{y}$,

$$\mathbf{f}(0, \mathbf{y}) = \mathbf{g}(\mathbf{y}) \quad and \quad \mathbf{f}(x+1, \mathbf{y}) = \mathbf{h}(\mathbf{f}(x, \mathbf{y}), x, \mathbf{y})$$

for some functions $\mathbf{g} : \mathbb{R}^d \to \mathbb{R}^{d'}$ *and* $\mathbf{h} : \mathbb{R}^{d'} \times \mathbb{R} \times \mathbb{R}^d \to \mathbb{R}^{d'}$ *both computable in polynomial time with respect to the value of* x. *Suppose that the modulus* m_h *of continuity of* $\mathbf{h}$ *is affine in its first argument: For all functions* $\mathbf{f}, \mathbf{f}'$ *defined in* $[-2^{\mathbf{F}}, 2^{\mathbf{F}}]$, $\mathbf{y} \in [-2^{\mathbf{Y}}, 2^{\mathbf{Y}}]$, $\|\mathbf{f} - \mathbf{f}'\| \le 2^{-m_h(\mathbf{F}, \ell(x), \mathbf{Y}, n)}$ *implies* $|\mathbf{h}(\mathbf{f}, x, \mathbf{y}) - \mathbf{h}(\mathbf{f}', x, \mathbf{y})| \le 2^{-n}$ *with* $m_h(\mathbf{F}, \ell(x), \mathbf{Y}, n) = \alpha n + p_h(\mathbf{F}, \ell(x), \mathbf{Y})$ *for some* α. *Suppose there exists a polynomial* p *such that* $\ell(\|\|\mathbf{f}(x, \mathbf{y})\|\|) \le p(x, \ell(\|\|\mathbf{y}\|\|))$.

Then $\mathbf{f}(x, \mathbf{y})$ *is computable in polynomial time with respect to the value of* x.

Proof. The point is that we can compute $\mathbf{f}(n, \mathbf{y})$ by $\mathbf{z}_0 = \mathbf{f}(0, \mathbf{y}) = \mathbf{g}(\mathbf{y})$, then $\mathbf{z}_1 = \mathbf{f}(1, \mathbf{y}) = \mathbf{h}(\mathbf{z}_0, 0, \mathbf{y})$, then $\mathbf{z}_2 = \mathbf{f}(2, \mathbf{y}) = \mathbf{h}(\mathbf{z}_1, 1, \mathbf{y})$, then $\ldots$, then $\mathbf{z}_m = \mathbf{f}(m, \mathbf{y}) = \mathbf{h}(\mathbf{z}_{m-1}, m-1, \mathbf{y})$. One needs to do so with some sufficient precision so that the result given by $\mathbf{f}(l, \mathbf{y})$ is correct, and so that the whole computation can be done in polynomial time.

Given $\mathbf{y}$, we can determine $\mathbf{Y}$ such that $\mathbf{y} \in [-2^{\mathbf{Y}}, 2^{\mathbf{Y}}]$. Assume for now that for all m,

$$z_m \in [-2^{Z_m}, 2^{Z_m}] \tag{5}$$

For $i = 0, 1, \ldots l$, consider $p(i) = \alpha^{l-i} n + \sum_{k=i}^{l-1} \alpha^{k-i} p_h(\mathbf{Z}_k, \ell(k), \mathbf{Y})$.

Using the fact that $\mathbf{g}$ is computable, approximate $\mathbf{z}_0 = \mathbf{g}(\mathbf{y})$ with precision $2^{-p(0)}$. This is doable polynomial time with respect to the value of $p(0)$.

Then for $i = 0, 1, \ldots, l$, using the approximation of $\mathbf{z}_i$ with precision $2^{-p(i)}$, compute an approximation of $\mathbf{z}_{i+1}$ with precision $2^{-p(i+1)}$: this is feasible to get precision $2^{-p(i+1)}$ of $\mathbf{z}_{i+1}$, as $\mathbf{z}_{i+1} = \mathbf{f}(i+1, \mathbf{y}) = \mathbf{h}(\mathbf{z}_i, i, \mathbf{y})$, it is sufficient to consider precision $m_h(\mathbf{Z}_i, \ell(i), \mathbf{Y}, p(i+1)) = \alpha p(i+1) + p_h(\mathbf{Z}_i, \ell(i), \mathbf{Y}) = \alpha^{l-i-1+1} n + \sum_{k=i+1}^{l-1} \alpha^{k-i-1+1} p_h(\mathbf{Z}_k, \ell(k), \mathbf{Y}) + p_h(\mathbf{Z}_i, \ell(i), \mathbf{Y}) = p(i)$. Observing that $p(l) = n$, we get z_l with precision 2^{-n}. All of this is is indeed feasible in polynomial time with respect to the value of l, under the condition that all the Z_i remain of size polynomial, that is to say, that we have indeed (5). But this follows from our hypothesis on $\ell(\|\|\mathbf{f}(x, \mathbf{y})\|\|)$.

5   Functions from FPTIME are in $\mathbb{LDL}^\bullet$

This section is devoted to prove a kind of reverse implication of Proposition 1: For any polynomial time computable function $\mathbf{f} : \mathbb{N}^d \to \mathbb{R}^{d'}$, we can construct some function $\tilde{\mathbf{f}} \in \mathbb{LDL}^\bullet$ that simulates the computation of f. This basically requires to be able to simulate the computation of a Turing machine using some functions from $\mathbb{LDL}^\bullet$.

Consider without loss of generality some Turing machine

$$M = (Q, \{0, 1\}, q_{init}, \delta, F)$$

using the symbols $0, 1, 3$, where $B = 0$ is the blank symbol. The reason of the choice of symbols 1 and 3 will be made clear later. We assume $Q = \{0, 1, \ldots, |Q| - 1\}$. Let

$$\ldots l_{-k} l_{-k+1} \ldots l_{-1} l_0 r_0 r_1 \ldots r_n \ldots.$$

denote the content of the tape of the Turing machine M. In this representation, the head is in front of symbol r_0, and $l_i, r_i \in \{0, 1, 3\}$ for all i. Such a configuration C can be denoted by $C = (q, l, r)$, where $l, r \in \Sigma^\omega$ are (possibly infinite, if we consider that the tape can be seen as a non finite word, in the case there is no blank on it) words over alphabet $\Sigma = \{1, 3\}$ and $q \in Q$ denotes the internal state of M.

The idea is that such a configuration C can also be encoded by some element $\gamma_{config}(C) = (q, \bar{l}, \bar{r}) \in \mathbb{N} \times \mathbb{R}^2$, by considering

$$\bar{r} = r_0 4^{-1} + r_1 4^{-2} + \cdots + r_n 4^{-(n+1)} + \ldots,$$
$$\bar{l} = l_0 4^{-1} + l_{-1} 4^{-2} + \cdots + l_{-k} 4^{-(k+1)} + \ldots$$

Basically, in other words, we encode the configuration of bi-infinite tape Turing machine M by real numbers using their radix 4 encoding, but using only digits 1,3. If we write: $\gamma_{word} : \Sigma^\omega \to \mathbb{R}$ for the function that maps word $w = w_0 w_1 w_2 \ldots$ to $\gamma_{word}(w) = w_0 4^{-1} + w_1 4^{-2} + \cdots + w_n 4^{-(n+1)} + \ldots$, we can also write $\gamma_{config}(C) = \gamma_{config}(q, l, r) = (q, \gamma_{word}(l), \gamma_{word}(r))$.

Notice that this lives in $Q \times [0, 1]^2$. Actually, if we denote the image of $\gamma_{word} : \Sigma^\omega \to \mathbb{R}$ by $\mathcal{I}$, this even lives in $Q \times \mathcal{I}^2$.

Lemma 6. *We can construct some function $\overline{Next}$ in $\mathbb{LDL}^\bullet$ that simulates one step of M, i.e. that computes the Next function sending a configuration C of Turing machine M to the next one. This function is essentially linear.*

Proof. We can write $l = l_0 l^\bullet$ and $r = r_0 r^\bullet$, where $l^\bullet$ and $r^\bullet$ corresponding to (possibly infinite) word $l_{-1} l_{-2} \ldots$ and $r_1 r_2 \ldots$ respectively.

$$\underbrace{\ldots \; l^\bullet \; \big| \; l_0 \; \big| \; r_0 \; \big| \; r^\bullet \; \ldots}_{\;\;\;\;\underbrace{}_{l} \;\; \underbrace{}_{r}}$$

The function $Next$ is basically of the form

$$\begin{aligned} Next(q, l, r) = Next(q, l^\bullet l_0, r_0 r^\bullet) &= (q', l', r') \\ &= (q', l^\bullet l_0 x, r^\bullet) \text{ whenever } \delta(q, r_0) = (q', x, \rightarrow) \\ &\quad (q', l^\bullet, l_0 x r^\bullet) \text{ whenever } \delta(q, r_0) = (q', x, \leftarrow) \\ &\quad \ldots \end{aligned}$$

where the dots is a list of lines of similar types for the various values of q and $\overline{r_0}$. This rewrites as a function $\overline{Next}$ which is similar, working over the representation of the configurations as reals:

$$\overline{Next}(q, \overline{l}, \overline{r}) = \overline{Next}(q, \overline{l^{\bullet}l_0}, \overline{r_0r^{\bullet}}) = (q', \overline{l'}, \overline{r'})$$
$$= (q', \overline{l^{\bullet}l_0x}, \overline{r^{\bullet}}) \ whenever \ \delta(q, r_0) = (q', x, \rightarrow)$$
$$(q', \overline{l^{\bullet}}, \overline{l_0xr^{\bullet}}) \ whenever \ \delta(q, r_0) = (q', x, \leftarrow)$$

$$\cdots$$

where $r_0 = \lfloor 4\overline{r} \rfloor$ and
- in the first case "$\rightarrow$" : $\overline{l'} = 4^{-1}\overline{l} + 4^{-1}x$ and $\overline{r'} = \overline{r^{\bullet}} = \{4\overline{r}\}$ (6)
- in the second case "$\leftarrow$" : $\overline{l'} = \overline{l^{\bullet}} = \{4\overline{l}\}$ and $\overline{r'} = 4^{-2}\overline{r^{\bullet}} + 4^{-2}x + \lfloor 4\overline{l} \rfloor$

Here $\{.\}$ stands for fractional part.

The problem about such expressions is that we cannot expect the integer part and the fractional part function to be in $\mathbb{LDL}^{\bullet}$ (as functions of this class are computable, and hence continuous, unlike the fractional part). But, a key point is that from our trick of using only symbols 1 and 3, we are sure that in an expression like $\lfloor \overline{r} \rfloor$, either it values 0 (this is the specific case where there remain only blanks in r), or that $4\overline{r}$ lives in interval $[1, 1+1)$ or in interval $[3, 3+1)$. That means that we could replace $\{4\overline{r}\}$ by $\sigma(4\overline{r})$ where σ is some (piecewise affine) function obtained by composing in a suitable way the basic functions of $\mathbb{LDL}^{\bullet}$. Namely, define $If(b, T, E)$ as a synonym for $\overline{cond}(b) \times T + (1 - \overline{cond}(b)) \times E$. Then, considering $i(x) = If(x, 0, If(x - 1, 1, 3))$, $\sigma(x) = x - i(x)$, then $i(4\overline{r})$ would be the same as $\lfloor 4\overline{r} \rfloor$, and $\sigma(4\overline{r})$ would be the same as $\{4\overline{r}\}$ in our context in above expressions. In other words, we could replace the paragraph (6) above by:

where $r_0 = i(4\overline{r})$
- in the first case "$\rightarrow$" : $\overline{l'} = 4^{-1}\overline{l} + 4^{-1}x$ and $\overline{r'} = \overline{r^{\bullet}} = \sigma(4\overline{r})$
- in the second case "$\leftarrow$" : $\overline{l'} = \overline{l^{\bullet}} = \sigma(4\overline{l})$ and $\overline{r'} = 4^{-2}\overline{r^{\bullet}} + 4^{-1}x + i(4\overline{l})$

and get something that would be still work exactly, but using only functions from $\mathbb{LDL}^{\bullet}$. Notice that these imbrications of If rewrite to an essentially constant expression.

We can then write:

$$q' = If(q-0, nextq^0, If(q-1, nextq^1, \cdots, If(q-|Q-2|, nextq^{|Q|-2}, nextq^{|Q|-1})))$$

where

$$nextq^q = If(v - 0, nextq_0^q, If(v - 1, nextq_1^q, nextq_3^q))$$

and where $nextq_v^q = q'$ if $\delta(q, v) = (q', x, m)$ for $m \in \{\leftarrow, \rightarrow\}$, for $v \in \{0, 1, 3\}$. Similarly, we can write

$$r' = If(q-0, nextr^0, If(q-1, nextr^1, \cdots, If(q-|Q-2|, nextr^{|Q|-2}, nextr^{|Q|-1})))$$

where $nextr^q = If(v - 0, nextr_0^q, If(v - 1, nextr_1^q, nextr_3^q))$ and where $nextr_v^q$ that corresponds to the corresponding expression in the item above according to the value of $\delta(q, v)$. We can clearly write a similar expression for l'. These imbrications of *If* rewrite to some essentially linear expressions.

Once we have one step, we can simulate some arbitrary computation of a Turing machine, using some linear length ODE:

Proposition 2. *Consider some Turing machine M that computes some function $f : \Sigma^* \to \Sigma^*$ in some time $T(\ell(\omega))$ on input ω. One can construct some function $\tilde{\mathbf{f}} : \mathbb{N} \times \mathbb{R} \to \mathbb{R}$ in $\mathbb{LDL}^\bullet$ that does the same, with respect to the previous encoding: $\tilde{\mathbf{f}}(2^{T(\ell(\omega))}, \gamma_{word}(\omega))$ provides $f(\omega)$.*

Proof. The idea is to define the function $\overline{Exec}$ that maps some time 2^t and some initial configuration C to the configuration number at time t. This can be obtained using some linear length ODE using Lemma 6.

$$\overline{Exec}(0, C) = C \quad and \quad \frac{\partial \overline{Exec}}{\partial \ell}(t, C) = \overline{Next}(\overline{Exec}(t, C))$$

We can then get the value of the computation as $\overline{Exec}(2^{T(\ell(\omega))}, C_{init})$ on input ω, considering $C_{init} = (q_0, 0, \gamma_{word}(\omega))$. By applying some projection, we get the following function $\tilde{\mathbf{f}}(x, y) = \pi_3^3(\overline{Exec}(x, q_0, 0, y))$ that satisfies the property.

6   Towards Functions from Integers to the Reals

The purpose of this section is to prove Theorem 3. The reverse implication of Theorem 3 mostly follows from Proposition 1 and arguments from computable analysis. By lack of space, details are in appendix.

For the direct implication of Theorem 3, the difficulty is that we know from the previous section how to simulate Turing machines working over $\mathcal{I}$, while we want functions that work directly over the integers and over the reals. A key is to be able to convert from integers/reals to representations using only symbols 1 and 3, that is to say, to map integers to $\mathcal{I}$, and $\mathcal{I}$ to reals.

Lemma 7 (From $\mathcal{I}$ to $\mathbb{R}$). *We can construct some function $Encode : \mathbb{N} \times [0, 1] \to \mathbb{R}$ in $\mathbb{LDL}^\bullet$ that maps $\gamma_{word}(\overline{d})$ with $\overline{d} \in \{1, 3\}^*$ to some real d. It is surjective over the dyadic, in the sense that for any dyadic $d \in \mathbb{D}$, there is some (easily computable) such $\overline{d}$ with $Encode(2^{\ell(\overline{d})}, \overline{d}) = d$.*

Proof. Consider the following transformation: Every digit in the binary expansion of d is encoded by a pair of symbols in the radix 4 encoding of $\overline{d} \in [0, 1]$: digit 0 (respectively: 1) is encoded by 11 (respectively 13) if before the "decimal" point in d, and digit 0 (respectively: 1) is encoded by 31 (respectively 33) if after. For example, for $d = 101.1$ in base 2, $\overline{d} = 0.13111333$ in base 4.

The transformation from $\overline{d}$ to d can be done by considering a function $F :$ $[0,1]^2 \to [0,1]^2$ that satisfies

$$
F(\overline{r_1}, \overline{l_2}) = \begin{cases} (\sigma(16\overline{r_1}), 2\overline{l_2} + 0) & \text{whenever } i(16\overline{r_1}) = 5 \\ (\sigma(16\overline{r_1}), 2\overline{l_2} + 1) & \text{whenever } i(16\overline{r_1}) = 7 \\ (\sigma(16\overline{r_1}), (\overline{l_2} + 0)/2) & \text{whenever } i(16\overline{r_1}) = 13 \\ (\sigma(16\overline{r_1}), (\overline{l_2} + 1)/2) & \text{whenever } i(16\overline{r_1}) = 15 \end{cases}
$$

A natural candidate for this is an expression such as $If\,(i(16\overline{r_1}) - 0, (\sigma(16\overline{r_1}), 2\overline{l_2} + 0), If\,(i(16\overline{r_1}) - 7, (\sigma(16\overline{r_1}), 2\overline{l_2} + 1), If\,(i(16\overline{r_1}) - 13, (\sigma(16\overline{r_1}), (\overline{l_2} + 0)/2), (\sigma(16\overline{r_1}), (\overline{l_2} + 1)/2))))$ with σ and i constructed as suitable approximation of the fractional and integer part as in previous section.

We then just need to apply $\ell(d)$ times F on $(\overline{d}, 0)$, and then project on the second component to get a function $Encode$ that does the job. That is $Encode(x, y) = \pi_3^3(G(x, y))$ with

$$
G(0, y) = (\overline{d}, 0) \quad and \quad \frac{\partial G}{\partial \ell}(t, \overline{d}, \overline{l}) = F(G(t, \overline{d}, \overline{l})).
$$

Lemma 8 (From $\mathbb{N}$ to $\mathcal{I}$). *We can construct some function $Decode : \mathbb{N}^d \to \mathbb{R}$ in $\mathbb{LDL}^\bullet$ that maps $n \in \mathbb{N}$ to some (easily computable) encoding of n in $\mathcal{I}$.*

Proof. We discuss only the case $d = 1$ by lack of space. Let div_2 (respectively: mod_2) denote integer (respectively remainder of) division by 2: As these functions are from $\mathbb{N} \to \mathbb{N}$, from Theorem 1 from [5,6], they belongs to $\mathbb{LDL}$. Their expression in $\mathbb{LDL}$, replacing sg() by $\overline{cond}()$, provides some extensions $\overline{div_2}$ and $\overline{mod2}$ in $\mathbb{LDL}^\bullet$. We then do something similar as in the previous lemma but now with function

$$
F(\overline{r_1}, \overline{l_2}) = \begin{cases} (\overline{div_2}(\overline{r_1}), (\overline{l_2} + 0)/2) & \text{whenever } \overline{mod_2}(\overline{r_1}) = 0 \\ (\overline{div_2}(\overline{r_1}), (\overline{l_2} + 1)/2) & \text{whenever } \overline{mod_2}(\overline{r_1}) = 1. \end{cases}
$$

We can now prove the direct direction of Theorem 3: Assume that $\mathbf{f} : \mathbb{N}^d \to \mathbb{R}^{d'}$ is computable in polynomial time. That means that each of its components are, thus, we can consider without loss of generality that $d' = 1$. We assume also that $d = 1$ (otherwise consider either multi-tape Turing machines, or some suitable alternative encoding in $Encode$). That means that we know that there is a TM polynomial time computable functions $d : \mathbb{N}^{d+1} \to \{1, 3\}^*$ so that on $\mathbf{m}, n$ it provides the encoding of some dyadic $\phi(\mathbf{m}, n)$ with $\|\phi(\mathbf{m}, n) - \mathbf{f}(\mathbf{m})\| \le 2^{-n}$ for all $\mathbf{m}$.

From Proposition 2, we can construct $\tilde{d}$ with $\tilde{d}(2^{p(max(\mathbf{m},n))}, Decode(n, \mathbf{m})) = d(\mathbf{m}, n)$ for some polynomial p corresponding to the time required to compute d.

Both functions $\ell(\mathbf{x}) = \ell(x_1) + \ldots + \ell(x_p)$ and $B(\mathbf{x}) = 2^{\ell(\mathbf{x}) \cdot \ell(\mathbf{x})}$ are in $\mathbb{LDL}$ (see [5,6]). It is easily seen that : $\ell(\mathbf{x})^c \le B^{(c)}(\ell(\mathbf{x}))$ where $B^{(c)}$ is the c-fold composition of function B.

Then $\tilde{\mathbf{f}}(\mathbf{m}, n) = Encode(\tilde{d}(B^{(c)}(max(\mathbf{m}, n)), Decode(n, \mathbf{m})))$ provides a solution such that $\|\tilde{\mathbf{f}}(\mathbf{m}, 2^n) - \mathbf{f}(\mathbf{m})\| \le 2^{-n}$.

7   Proving Theorems 4 and 5

Clearly Theorem 5 follows from the case where $d = 1$ and $d' = 1$ from Theorem 4. Hence, there only remain to prove Theorem 4. The direct direction is immediate from Theorem 3. For the reverse direction, by induction, the only thing to prove is that the class of functions from the integers to the reals computable in polynomial time is preserved by the operation $ELim$. Take such a function $\tilde{\mathbf{f}}$. By definition, given $\mathbf{m}$, we can compute $\tilde{f}(\mathbf{m}, 2^n)$ with precision 2^{-n} in time polynomial in n. This must be by definition of $ELim$ schema some approximation of $\mathbf{f}(\mathbf{m})$, and hence $\mathbf{f}$ is computable in polynomial time.

8   Generalizations

Recall that a function $M : \mathbb{N} \to \mathbb{N}$ is a modulus of convergence of $g : \mathbb{N} \to \mathbb{R}$, with $g(n)$ converging toward 0 when n goes to ∞, if and only if for all $i > M(n)$, we have $\|g(i)\| \le 2^{-n}$. A function $M : \mathbb{N} \to \mathbb{N}$ is a uniform modulus of convergence of a sequence $g : \mathbb{N}^{d+1} \to \mathbb{R}$, with $g(\mathbf{m}, n)$ converging toward 0 when n goes to ∞ if and only if for all $i > M(n)$, we have $\|g(\mathbf{m}, i)\| \le 2^{-n}$. Intuitively, the modulus of convergence gives the speed of convergence of a sequence.

Definition 10 (Operation $E_2 Lim$). *Given $\tilde{\mathbf{f}} : \mathbb{N}^{d+1} \to \mathbb{R} \in \mathbb{LDL}^{\bullet}$, $g : \mathbb{N}^{d+1} \to \mathbb{R}$ such that for all $\mathbf{m} \in \mathbb{N}^d$, $n \in \mathbb{N}$, $\|\tilde{\mathbf{f}}(\mathbf{m}, 2^n) - \mathbf{f}(\mathbf{m})\| \le g(\mathbf{m}, n)$ under the condition that $0 \le g(\mathbf{m}, n)$ is decreasing to 0, with $\|g(\mathbf{m}, p(n))\| \le 2^{-n}$ for some polynomial $p(n)$ then $E_2 Lim(\tilde{\mathbf{f}}, g)$ is the (clearly uniquely defined) corresponding function $\mathbf{f} : \mathbb{N}^d \to \mathbb{R}^e$.*

Theorem 7. *We could replace $ELim$ by $E_2 Lim$ in the statements of Theorems 4 and 5.*

This is equivalent to prove the following, and observe from the proof that we can replace in above statement "$g(\mathbf{m}, n)$ going to 0" by "decreasing to 0", and last condition by $\|g(\mathbf{m}, p(n))\| \le 2^{-n}$.

Theorem 8. $\mathbf{F} : \mathbb{N}^d \to \mathbb{R}^{d'}$ *is computable in polynomial time iff there exists* $\mathbf{f} : \mathbb{N}^{d+1} \to \mathbb{Q}^{d'}$*, with $\mathbf{f}(\mathbf{m}, n)$ computable in polynomial time with respect to the value of n, and $g : \mathbb{N}^{d+1} \to \mathbb{Q}$ such that*

- $\|\mathbf{f}(\mathbf{m}, n) - \mathbf{F}(\mathbf{m})\| \le g(\mathbf{m}, n)$
- $0 \le g(\mathbf{m}, n)$ *and $g(\mathbf{m}, n)$ converging to 0 when n goes to $+\infty$,*
- *with a uniform polynomial modulus of convergence $p(n)$.*

From the proofs we also get a normal form theorem. In particular,

Theorem 9 (Normal form theorem). *Any function $f : \mathbb{N}^d \to \mathbb{R}^{d'}$ can be obtained from the class $\overline{\mathbb{LDL}^{\bullet}}$ using only one schema $ELim$ (or $E_2 Lim$).*

9   Conclusion and Future Work

In this article, we characterized the set of functions from the integer to the reals. As we already said, our aim in a future work is to characterize $\textbf{FPTIME} \cap \mathbb{R}^{\mathbb{R}}$ and not only $\textbf{FPTIME} \cap \mathbb{R}^{\mathbb{N}}$. This is clearly a harder task. In particular, a natural approach would be to consider some function $Encode$ from $\mathbb{R}$ to $\mathcal{I}$. Unfortunately, such a function $decode$ is necessarily discontinuous, and is hence not-computable, and cannot be in the class. The approach of $mixing$ of [4] might provide a solution, even if the constructions there, based on (classical) continuous ODEs use deeply some closure properties of these functions that are not true for discrete ODEs.

10   Thanks

We would like to thank warmly Arnaud Durand, for several very helpful discussions, and comments about this work as well as very relevant questions and suggestions who influenced strongly the way some of our results are formulated.

References

1. Arnold, V.I.: Ordinary Differential Equations. MIT Press, Cambridge (1978)
2. Bellantoni, S., Cook, S.: A new recursion-theoretic characterization of the polytime functions. Comput. Complex. **2**, 97–110 (1992)
3. Birkhoff, G., Rota, G.C.: Ordinary Differential Equations, 4th edn. Wiley, Hoboken (1989)
4. Bournez, O., Campagnolo, M.L., Graça, D.S., Hainry, E.: Polynomial differential equations compute all real computable functions on computable compact intervals. J. Complex. **23**(3), 317–335 (2007)
5. Bournez, O., Durand, A.: Recursion schemes, discrete differential equations and characterization of polynomial time computation. Technical report (2018, Submitted). A preliminary version coauthored with Sabrina Ouazzani. https://arxiv.org/abs/1810.02241
6. Bournez, O., Durand, A.: Recursion schemes, discrete differential equations and characterization of polynomial time computation. In: Rossmanith, P., Heggernes, P., Katoen, J. (eds.) 44th International Symposium on Mathematical Foundations of Computer Science, MFCS. LIPIcs, vol. 138, pp. 23:1–23:14. Schloss Dagstuhl - Leibniz-Zentrum für Informatik (2019)
7. Bournez, O., Pouly, A.: A survey on analog models of computation. In: Handbook of Computability and Complexity in Analysis. TAC, pp. 173–226. Springer, Cham (2021). https://doi.org/10.1007/978-3-030-59234-9_6
8. Brattka, V.: Recursive characterization of computable real-valued functions and relations. Theoret. Comput. Sci. **162**(1), 45–77 (1996)
9. Brattka, V., Hertling, P., Weihrauch, K.: A tutorial on computable analysis. In: Cooper, S.B., Löwe, B., Sorbi, A. (eds.) New Computational Paradigms, pp. 425–491. Springer, New York (2008). https://doi.org/10.1007/978-0-387-68546-5_18
10. Clote, P.: Computational models and function algebras. In: Griffor, E.R. (ed.) Handbook of Computability Theory, Amsterdam, North-Holland, pp. 589–681 (1998)

11. Clote, P., Kranakis, E.: Boolean Functions and Computation Models. Springer, Cham (2013)
12. Cobham, A.: The intrinsic computational difficulty of functions. In: Bar-Hillel, Y. (ed.) Proceedings of the International Conference on Logic, Methodology, and Philosophy of Science, North-Holland, Amsterdam, pp. 24–30 (1962)
13. Coddington, E.A., Levinson, N.: Theory of Ordinary Differential Equations. Mc-Graw-Hill, New York (1955)
14. Gelfond, A.: Calculus of Finite Differences (1971)
15. Gleich, D.: Finite calculus: a tutorial for solving nasty sums. Stanford University (2005)
16. Graham, R.L., Knuth, D.E., Patashnik, O., Liu, S.: Concrete mathematics: a foundation for computer science. Comput. Phys. **3**(5), 106–107 (1989)
17. Izadi, F., Aliev, N., Bagirov, G.: Discrete Calculus by Analogy. Bentham Science Publishers, Sharjah (2009)
18. Ko, K.I.: Complexity Theory of Real Functions. Progress in Theoretical Computer Science, Birkhaüser, Boston (1991)
19. Lau, G.: http://www.acm.ciens.ucv.ve/main/entrenamiento/material/ DiscreteCalculus.pdf. Course notes for the course "Discrete calculus". http:// gustavolau.com
20. Leivant, D.: Intrinsic theories and computational complexity. In: Leivant, D. (ed.) LCC 1994. LNCS, vol. 960, pp. 177–194. Springer, Heidelberg (1995). https://doi. org/10.1007/3-540-60178-3_84
21. Leivant, D.: Predicative recurrence and computational complexity I: word recurrence and poly-time. In: Clote, P., Remmel, J. (eds.) Feasible Mathematics II, pp. 320–343. Birkhäuser (1994)
22. Leivant, D., Marion, J.Y.: Lambda calculus characterizations of Poly-Time. Fundamenta Informatica **19**(1,2), 167–184 (1993)
23. Leivant, D., Marion, J.-Y.: Ramified recurrence and computational complexity II: substitution and poly-space. In: Pacholski, L., Tiuryn, J. (eds.) CSL 1994. LNCS, vol. 933, pp. 486–500. Springer, Heidelberg (1995). https://doi.org/10.1007/ BFb0022277
24. Ng, K.M., Tavana, N.R., Yang, Y.: A recursion theoretic foundation of computation over real numbers. J. Logic Comput. **31**(7), 1660–1689 (2021)
25. Siegelmann, H.T.: Neural Networks and Analog Computation - Beyond the Turing Limit. Birkauser, Basel (1999)
26. Siegelmann, H.T., Sontag, E.D.: On the computational power of neural nets. J. Comput. Syst. Sci. **50**(1), 132–150 (1995)
27. Weihrauch, K.: Computable Analysis: An Introduction. Springer, Cham (2000)

Languages of Distributed Reaction Systems

Lucie Ciencialová[1], Luděk Cienciala[1], and Erzsébet Csuhaj-Varjú[2(✉)]

[1] Institute of Computer Science and Research Institute of the IT4Innovations Centre of Excellence, Silesian University in Opava, Opava, Czech Republic
{lucie.ciencialova,ludek.cienciala}@fpf.slu.cz
[2] Department of Algorithms and Their Applications, Faculty of Informatics, ELTE Eötvös Loránd University, Pázmány Péter sétány 1/c, 1117 Budapest, Hungary
csuhaj@inf.elte.hu

Abstract. Reaction systems are a formal model of interactions between biochemical reactions. The motivation for the concept of a reaction system was to model the behavior of biological systems in which a large number of individual reactions interact with each other. A reaction system consists of a finite set of objects that represent chemicals and a finite set of triplets (reactants, inhibitors, products) that represent chemical reactions; the reactions may facilitate or inhibit each other. An extension of the concept of the reaction system is the distributed reaction system which model was inspired by multi-agent systems, agents (represented by reaction systems) interact with their environment (context provided by a context automaton). In this paper, we assign languages to distributed reaction systems and provide representations of some well-known language classes by these systems.

Keywords: reaction systems · distributed reaction systems · right-linear simple matrix language · recursively enumerable language

1 Introduction

Reaction systems were introduced by A. Ehrenfeucht and G. Rozenberg in 2004 as a formal concept for modeling the behavior of biological systems in which a large number of individual reactions interact with each other [7]. Since then the topic has become a recognized area in natural computing.

A reaction system consists of a finite set of objects that represent chemicals and a finite set of triplets that represent chemical reactions. The three components of the reactions are the set of reactants, the set of inhibitors, and the set of products, each of them is a nonempty set. The set of reactants and the set of inhibitors are disjoint. Let T be a set of reactants. A reaction is enabled for a set of reactants T if all of its reactants are present in T and none of its inhibitors are present in T. Every reaction enabled for T can be performed on T. When a reaction is performed, then the set of its reactants is replaced by the set of

J. Durand-Lose and G. Vasil (Eds.): MCU 2022, LNCS 13419, pp. 75–90, 2022.
https://doi.org/10.1007/978-3-031-13502-6_5

its products. All enabled reactions are applied in parallel. Reaction systems are qualitative models, since the concept focuses on the presence or absence of the chemical species, but not their amounts. Multiple reactions that have common reactants do not interfere. All the reactions that are enabled at a given step are performed simultaneously. Another important feature of reaction systems is the lack of permanency; those reactants that are not involved in any reaction disappear from the system. For further details, the reader is referred to [8].

Reaction systems have been studied in detail over the last almost twenty years. One of the main directions of investigations is the study of the mathematical properties of reaction systems: functions defined by reaction systems, state sequences, the effect of bounded resources, cycles, and connections to propositional logic. For details, consult [6,16,17]. One other important research direction aims at studying reaction systems as a modeling framework, model checking for reaction systems. For example, a temporal logic was introduced in [13] for checking temporal properties of reaction systems. Biologically inspired properties of reaction systems are of interest as well, they were defined and studied in [1–3].

An interesting research area is the theory of networks of reaction systems [4] and communicating reaction systems with direct communication [5]. These systems are virtual graphs with a reaction system in each node. The reaction systems work in a synchronized manner and interact with each other using distribution and communication protocols. The set of products of each reaction system in the network forms a part of the environment of the network.

A related topic is the notion of a distributed reaction system, motivated by multi-agent systems, where agents (represented by reaction systems) are in interaction with their environment (context provided by an extended context automaton) [12]. The concept was introduced by A. Meski, M. Koutny, and W. Penczek in 2017 and it is also suitable for modeling both distributed systems and different synchronization schemes for concurrent systems. Related notions are dP systems and dP automata in membrane computing [14,15].

In this paper, we present a slightly modified version of distributed reaction systems. Such a system consists of n reaction systems over a common background set (alphabet), which work synchronously. In each step, a so-called context automaton provides sets of reactants (contexts) for the reaction systems. These contexts are added to the current reactant sets (states) of the reaction systems. Then the reactions will be performed on the new reactant sets obtained in this way, and the procedure will be repeated. This interactive process is terminating if it is finite and the distributed reaction system enters a so-called finite state.

In this paper, we assign languages to distributed reaction systems and provide representations of some well-known language classes by these systems. Thus, we open a new aspect of investigations. We show that languages of (extended) distributed reaction systems correspond the simple right-linear matrix languages and vice versa, and present a representation of the recursively enumerable language class by extended distributed reaction systems and morphisms.

The paper is organized as follows. In Sect. 2, we present the basic notions concerning reaction systems and distributed reaction systems and we define the notion of languages assigned to the latter constructs. In Sect. 3, we provide representations of some language classes by extended distributed reaction systems and mappings. We close the paper with conclusions and provide a few suggestions for further research.

2   Basic Notions and Notations

2.1   Formal Language Theory Prerequisites

Throughout the paper we assume the reader to be familiar with the basics of formal language theory; for more details consult [10].

An alphabet V is a finite nonempty set. For an alphabet V, V^* denotes the set of words (strings) over V, including the empty word, λ. A language L is a subset of V^*. For a finite set V, $card(V)$ denotes the number of elements of V; if V is the emptyset, then $card(V) = 0$.

A generative grammar is denoted by $G = (N, T, P, S)$ where N and T denote the set of nonterminals and the set of terminals, P is the set of productions, and S is the startsymbol. For details on regular, linear, and context-free grammars consult [10]. The family of regular languages is denoted by REG and the family of recursively enumerable languages is denoted by RE.

A right-linear simple matrix grammar, [11], of degree n is an $(n+3)$-tuple of the form $G = (N_1, \ldots, N_n, T, S, M)$ where $N_1, \ldots, N_n$ and T are pairwise disjoint alphabets, $S \notin (T \cup N)$, where $N = \bigcup_{i=1}^{n} N_i$, and M consists of matrices of the following forms:

1. $(S \to x)$, $x \in T^*$.
2. $(S \to A_1 \ldots A_n)$, $A_i \in N_i$, $1 \leq i \leq n$.
3. $(A_1 \to x_1 B_1, \ldots, A_n \to x_n B_n)$, $A_i, B_i \in N_i$, $x_i \in T^*$, $1 \leq i \leq n$.
4. $(A_1 \to x_1, \ldots, A_n \to x_n)$, $A_i \in N_i$, $x_i \in T^*$, $1 \leq i \leq n$.

Let $V = N \cup T \cup \{S\}$. For $u, v \in V^*$ we write $u \Longrightarrow v$ if one of the following cases holds: (1) $u = S$ and $(S \to v) \in M$, (2) $u = x_1 A_1 \ldots x_n A_n$, $v = x_1 w_1 B_1 \ldots x_n w_n B_n$ where $(A_1 \to w_1 B_1, \ldots, A_n \to w_n B_n) \in M$, (3) $u = x_1 A_1 \ldots x_n A_n$, $v = x_1 w_1 \ldots x_n w_n$ where $(A_1 \to w_1, \ldots, A_n \to w_n) \in M$, $A_i, B_i \in N_i$, v, $x_i, w_i \in T^*$.

The language generated by G is $L(G) = \{z \in T^* \mid S \Longrightarrow^* z\}$, where $\Longrightarrow^*$ denotes the reflexive transitive closure of $\Longrightarrow$.

For right-linear simple matrix grammars (with erasing rules) the following normal form is known: matrix of type (1) can be omitted, in matrices of type (3) we have $x_i \in T \cup \{\lambda\}$, $1 \leq i \leq n$, and in matrices of type (4) we have $x_i = \lambda$, $1 \leq i \leq n$.

RSM_n denotes the family of languages $L(G)$ for right-linear simple matrix grammars G of degree at most n, $n \geq 1$. The union of language families RSM_n, for all $n \geq 1$ is denoted by RSM_*.

It is known that $RSM_n \subset RSM_{n+1}$, $n \geq 1$. Furthermore, $REG \subset RSM_*$, and RSM_* and CF are incomparable [11].

In this paper, we will refer to the Extended Post Correspondence, a tool for representing recursively enumerable languages [9]. Let $V = \{a_1, a_2, \ldots, a_l\}$ be an alphabet, $l \geq 1$. An Extended Post Correspondence (an EPC) is a pair $\mathcal{E} = (\{(u_1, v_1), \ldots, (u_m, v_m)\}, (z_{a_1}, \ldots, z_{a_l}))$, where $m \geq 1$, $u_i, v_i, z_{a_j} \in \{0, 1\}^*$ for $1 \leq i \leq m$ and $1 \leq j \leq l$.

The language represented by $\mathcal{E}$ in V, written as $L(\mathcal{E})$, is the following set:
$$L(\mathcal{E}) = \{x_1 \ldots x_n \in V^* \mid \exists s_1 s_2 \ldots s_r \in \{1, 2, \ldots, m\}^r \text{ such that } r \geq 1 \text{ and }$$
$u_{s_1} u_{s_2} \ldots u_{s_r} = v_{s_1} v_{s_2} \ldots v_{s_r} z_{x_1} z_{x_2} \ldots z_{x_n}\}$.

It is shown that for every recursively enumerable language $L \subseteq V^*$, there exists an Extended Post Correspondence $\mathcal{E}$ such that $L(\mathcal{E}) = L$ [9].

2.2   Distributed Reaction Systems

We first recall the notion of a reaction system [7,8] and then we define the concept of a distributed reaction system based on [12].

A reaction system is a pair $\mathcal{A} = (S, A)$ where S is a finite nonempty set, called the background set of $\mathcal{A}$, and A is a finite set of reactions over S.

Every reaction of A is a triplet $b = (R_b, I_b, P_b)$ where R_b, I_b, P_b are nonempty subsets of S with $R_b \cap I_b = \emptyset$. Sets R_b, I_b, P_b are called the set of reactants, the set of inhibitors, and the set of products of b.

A reaction $b \in A$ is enabled for $T \subseteq S$, denoted by $en_b(T)$, if $R_b \subseteq T$ and $I_b \cap T = \emptyset$. The result of b on T, denoted by $res_b(T)$, is equal to P_b if b is enabled on T and it is equal to the empty set otherwise. The result of A on T is $res_A(T) = \bigcup_{b \in A} res_b(T)$.

The dynamic behavior of the reaction systems is captured through the notion of an interactive process defined as follows.

Let $\mathcal{A} = (S, A)$ be a reaction system. An interactive process in $\mathcal{A}$ is a pair $\pi = (\gamma, \varphi)$ of finite sequences such that $\gamma = c_0, c_1, \ldots, c_{n-1}, \varphi = d_1, \ldots, d_n$ with $n \geq 1$, where $c_0, \ldots, c_{n-1}, d_1, \ldots, d_n \subseteq S$, $d_1 = res_A(c_0)$, and $d_i = res_A(d_{i-1} \cup c_{i-1})$ for $2 \leq i \leq n$.

The sequences $c_0, \ldots, c_{n-1}$ and $d_1, \ldots, d_n$ are the context and result sequences of π, respectively. Context c_0 represents the initial state of π (the state in which the interactive process is initiated), and the contexts $c_1, \ldots, c_{n-1}$ represent the influence of the environment to the computation.

In the following, we define the concept of a distributed reaction system, with slight modifications of the notion and notations introduced in [12].

Definition 1. *A distributed reaction system (a DRS, for short) is a pair $\Delta = (S, \mathcal{A})$ where S is a finite nonempty set, called the background set of Δ, and $\mathcal{A} = \{A_1, \ldots, A_n\}$. A_i, $1 \leq i \leq n$, is a finite nonempty set of reactions over S, called the ith component of Δ.*

Notice that (S, A_i) is a reaction system; if no confusion arises, then A_i can also be called the ith reaction system of Δ.

Reaction systems in the DRS interact with the environment, which provides contexts for them, i.e., sets of reactants that influence their behavior.

Now, we present the notion of a context automaton (or context provider). This concept is a slightly modified variant of the notion of a context automaton in [12].

Definition 2. *Let* $\Delta = \{S, \mathcal{A}\}$ *with* $\mathcal{A} = (A_1, \ldots, A_n)$, $n \geq 1$, *be a distributed reaction system. A 5-tuple* $M = (Q, C, R, q_0, F)$ *is called a context automaton (or a context provider) for* Δ *if the following conditions are met:*

- Q *is a finite set, called the set of states of* M,
- $C \subseteq \{(c_1, \ldots, c_n) \mid c_i \subseteq S, 1 \leq i \leq n\}$ *is the finite set of n-tuples of contexts provided for components* $A_1, \ldots, A_n$,
- $R \subseteq \{(q, (c_1, \ldots, c_n), r) \mid q, r \in Q, (c_1, \ldots, c_n) \in C\}$, *called the set of transitions of* M,
- $q_0 \in Q$, *the initial state of* M,
- $F \subseteq Q$, *the set of final states of* M.

In the following, we extend the notion of a distributed reaction system to a distributed reaction system interacting with its environment, called an extended distributed reaction system. In the extended distributed reaction system each component maintains its local state, which is a subset of S. A global state of Δ is an n-tuple of the local states of the components. The distributed reaction system is in interaction with its environment, i.e., at each transition from one global state to the next, the environment provides each component of the distributed reaction system with a context. The context is a finite, possibly empty set of elements of S.

Definition 3. *An extended distributed reaction system (an EDRS, for short) is a triplet* $\Gamma = (\Delta, M, \sigma_0)$, *where*

- $\Delta = (S, \mathcal{A})$ *with* $\mathcal{A} = (A_1, \ldots, A_n)$, $n \geq 1$, *is a distributed reaction system over* S,
- $M = (Q, C, R, q_0, F)$ *is a context automaton for* Δ,
- $\sigma_0 = (q_0, (c_{1,0}, \ldots, c_{n,0}), (d_{1,0}, \ldots, d_{n,0}))$ *is the initial state of* Δ, *where*
- $(d_{1,0}, \ldots, d_{n,0})$ *with* $d_{i,0} \neq \emptyset$, $1 \leq i \leq n$; $d_{i,0}$ *is called the initial state of* A_i,
- $(c_{1,0}, \ldots, c_{n,0}) \in C$ *and there exists* j, $1 \leq j \leq n$, *such that* $c_{j,0} \neq \emptyset$. *Set* $c_{i,0}$ *is called the initial context for* A_i.

We now define the state of a distributed reaction system.

Definition 4. *Let* $\Gamma = (\Delta, M, \sigma_0)$ *be an extended distributed reaction system, where* $\Delta = (S, \mathcal{A})$, $\mathcal{A} = (A_1, \ldots, A_n)$, $n \geq 1$, $M = (Q, C, R, q_0, F)$, $\sigma_0 = (q_0, (c_{1,0}, \ldots, c_{n,0}), (d_{1,0}, \ldots, d_{n,0}))$.

A triplet $\sigma = (q, (c_1, \ldots, c_n), (d_1, \ldots, d_n))$ *is called a state of* Γ *if* $q \in Q$, $(c_1, \ldots, c_n) \in C$, *and for* $(d_1, \ldots, d_n)$ *it holds that* $d_i \subseteq S$, $1 \leq i \leq n$.

Each state $\sigma_f = (q_f, (c_1, \ldots, c_n), (d_1, \ldots, d_n))$ *where* $\sigma_f \in F$ *is called a final state of* Γ.

We present the notion of a direct transition in an EDRS.

Definition 5. *Let $\Gamma = (\Delta, M, \sigma_0)$ be an extended distributed reaction system, where $\Delta = (S, \mathcal{A})$, $\mathcal{A} = (A_1, \ldots, A_n)$, $n \geq 1$, $M = (Q, C, R, q_0, F)$ is the context automaton for Γ, and σ_0 is the initial state of Γ.*

Let σ_1 and σ_2 be two states of Γ, where $\sigma_1 = (q, (c_1, \ldots, c_n), (d_1, \ldots, d_n))$ and $\sigma_2 = (r, (c'_1, \ldots, c'_n), (d'_1, \ldots, d'_n))$.

- *We say that there is a direct transition from σ_1 to σ_2 in Γ, denoted by $\sigma_1 \Longrightarrow \sigma_2$, if the following conditions are met:*
- *$(q, (c_1, \ldots, c_n), r) \in R$,*
- *$(c'_1, \ldots, c'_n) \in C$,*
- *$d'_i = res_{A_i}(c_i \cup d_i)$, $1 \leq i \leq n$.*

The transitive reflexive closure of relation $\Longrightarrow$ is denoted by $\Longrightarrow^*$.

Next, we define the notion of a finite interactive process in an extended distributed reaction system.

Definition 6. *Let $\Gamma = (\Delta, M, \sigma_0)$ be an extended distributed reaction system.*

A finite sequence of states $\sigma_0, \ldots, \sigma_m$ of Γ is said to be a finite interactive process in Γ if $\sigma_0 \Longrightarrow_t \sigma_1 \Longrightarrow \ldots \Longrightarrow \sigma_{m-1} \Longrightarrow \sigma_m$, $m \geq 1$ holds.

The finite interactive process is called terminating if σ_m is a final state of Γ. The set of all terminating finite interactive processes of Γ is denoted by Π_Γ.

Notice that if $\sigma_0 \Longrightarrow \sigma_1 \Longrightarrow \ldots \Longrightarrow \sigma_{m-1} \Longrightarrow \sigma_m$, $m \geq 1$, is a terminating interactive process, then $\sigma_0 \Longrightarrow \sigma_1 \Longrightarrow \ldots \Longrightarrow \sigma_{m-1} \Longrightarrow \sigma_m \Longrightarrow \sigma_{m+1} \Longrightarrow \ldots \Longrightarrow \sigma_{m+k}$, $k \geq 1$, can also be a terminating interactive process if σ_{m+k} is a final state of Γ.

We present a simple example for extended distributed reaction systems.

Example 1. Let $\Gamma = (\Delta, M, \sigma_0)$ be an extended distributed reaction system, where

- $\Delta = (S, A_1, A_2, A_3)$ where $S = \{x, y, z\}$,
  $A_1 = \{(\{x, y\}, \{z\}, \{x\})\}$, $A_2 = \{(\{y, z\}, \{x\}, \{y\})\}$,
  $A_3 = \{(\{z, x\}, \{y\}, \{z\})\}$.
- Let $M = (Q, C, R, q_0, F)$ where $Q = \{q_0, q_1, q_2\}$,
- $C = \{\bar{c}_1, \bar{c}_2\}$ with $\bar{c}_1 = (\{y\}, \{z\}, \{x\})$, and $\bar{c}_2 = (\{y\}, \emptyset, \{x\})\}$.
  (To help the easier reading, we simplified the notation).
- Let $R = \{r_1, r_2, r_3, r_4, r_5\}$ with
  $r_1 = (q_0, (\{y\}, \{z\}, \{x\}), q_0)$, $r_4 = (q_0, (\{y\}, \emptyset, \{x\}), q_2)$,
  $r_2 = (q_0, (\{y\}, \{z\}, \{x\}), q_1)$, $r_5 = (q_2, (\{y\}, \emptyset, \{x\}), q_2)$.
  $r_3 = (q_1, (\{y\}, \{z\}, \{x\}), q_1)$,
- Let q_0 be the initial state of M, and let $F = \{q_1\}$.
- Let $\sigma_0 = (q_0, (\{y\}, \{z\}, \{x\}), (\{x\}, \{y\}, \{z\}))$.

We briefly explain how Γ works. At the initial state, component A_1 has single-ton state $\{x\}$, A_2 has singleton state $\{y\}$, and the state of the third component, A_3, is $\{z\}$. The initial state of context automaton M is q_0 and the contexts, the set of reactants added to the states of components A_1, A_2, A_3 are $\{y\}, \{z\}, \{x\}$, respectively. Then, the components perform their reactions (each component has only one reaction) and they obtain $\{x\}, \{y\}, \{z\}$, the same states as they had at the beginning.

$$\text{initial state of } \Gamma\colon \sigma_0 = (q_0, (\{y\}, \{z\}, \{x\}) , (\{x\}, \{y\}, \{z\}))$$

	state	environment	transition / reaction
Context provider M	q_0		$(q_0, (\{y\}, \{z\}, \{x\}) , q_0)$
EDRS Γ	A_1 $\{x\} \longleftarrow \{y\}$		$(\{x, y\}, \{z\}, \{x\})$
	A_2 $\{y\} \longleftarrow \{z\}$		$(\{y, z\}, \{x\}, \{y\})$
	A_3 $\{z\} \longleftarrow \{x\}$		$(\{z, x\}, \{y\}, \{z\})$

$$\text{new state of } \Gamma\colon \sigma_1 = (q_0, (\{y\}, \{z\}, \{x\}) , (\{x\}, \{y\}, \{z\}))$$

or

$$\text{new state of } \Gamma\colon \sigma_1' = (q_0, (\{y\}, \emptyset, \{x\}) , (\{x\}, \{y\}, \{z\}))$$

After that, the context automaton may enter either state q_0 or q_1. As long as transition r_1 of M is repeated, the states of the components remain unchanged. When transition r_2 is performed after r_1, then the next state of Γ, obtained by transition r_3, is a final state. Thus, the interactive process is terminating. If transition r_4 of M is performed after r_1, then the interactive process of Γ will never be terminating. The only possible transition after r_4 is transition r_5 that can be repeated arbitrarily many times. Transition r_4 results in states $\{x\}, \emptyset, \{z\}$ of components A_1, A_2, A_3, respectively, and these states remain unchanged in the subsequent steps. Since q_2 in transition r_5 is not a final state, the interactive process is not a terminating one.

In the following, we assign languages to extended distributed reaction systems. We first assign symbols of an alphabet Σ to states of components of Δ, the distributed reaction system of EDRS Γ, then we assign (finite) words in Σ^* to terminating interactive processes of Γ. We then define the language of Γ over Σ. We consider only such an alphabet Σ which has $card(2^S) - 1$ elements, that is, we can give a bijective mapping between Σ and the set of nonempty subsets of S (S is the background set of Δ). Notice that the notion can also be defined for alphabets Σ where 2^S can injectively be mapped into Σ^*. For technical reasons, we do not consider this type of extension.

Definition 7. Let $\Gamma = (\Delta, M, \sigma_0)$ be an extended distributed reaction system, where $\Delta = (S, \mathcal{A})$, $\mathcal{A} = (A_1, \ldots, A_n)$, $n \geq 1$, is a distributed reaction system over S, $M = (Q, C, R, q_0, F)$ is the context automaton for Γ, and σ_0 is the initial state of Γ. Let Q_Γ be the set of all states of Γ. We define mappings ρ, ϕ, ϕ_i as follows.

1. Let Σ be an alphabet such that $card(\Sigma) = card(2^S) - 1$. We define a bijective mapping $\rho : 2^S \to \Sigma \cup \{\lambda\}$ such that $\rho(d) = \lambda$ if and only if $d = \emptyset$.
2. Mapping $\phi : Q_\Gamma \to \underbrace{\Sigma^* \times \cdots \times \Sigma^*}_{n \text{ times}}$ is defined as follows:
   for each state $\sigma = (q, (c_1, \ldots, c_n), (d_1, \ldots, d_n))$, let $\phi(\sigma) = (\rho(d_1), \ldots, \rho(d_n))$.
3. Mapping $\phi_i : Q_\Gamma \to \Sigma^*$, $1 \le i \le n$, is defined as follows:
   for each state $\sigma = (q, (c_1, \ldots, c_n), (d_1, \ldots, d_n))$, let $\phi_i(\sigma) = \rho(d_i)$.

We present some more details on mapping ρ. It is easy to see that Σ has as many elements as the number of nonempty subsets of S and ρ orders to any nonempty subset of S a letter of Σ. Since ρ is a bijective mapping, there is no letter in Σ that is the map of two different nonempty subsets of S, and vice versa. One possible variant of such a mapping ρ can be based on the powerset enumeration.

Definition 8. *Let $\Gamma = (\Delta, M, \sigma_0)$ be an extended distributed reaction system, where $\Delta = (S, \mathcal{A})$, $\mathcal{A} = (A_1, \ldots, A_n)$, $n \ge 1$, is the distributed reaction system of Γ, $M = (Q, C, R, q_0, F)$ is the context automaton, σ_0 is the initial state of Γ. Let alphabet Σ and mappings ρ, ϕ, ϕ_i, $1 \le i \le n$ be defined as in Definition 7.*

Let $\pi : \sigma_0 \Longrightarrow \ldots \Longrightarrow \sigma_m$, $m \ge 1$, be a terminating finite interactive process of Γ, where $\sigma_j = (q_j, (c_{j,1}, \ldots, c_{j,n}), (d_{j,1}, \ldots, d_{j,n}))$, $1 \le j \le m$, is a state of Γ. We define $H(\pi) = (\phi_1(\sigma_0) \ldots \phi_1(\sigma_m)), \ldots, (\phi_n(\sigma_0) \ldots \phi_n(\sigma_m))$.
The language of Γ over Σ is defined as follows:

$$L(\Gamma, \Sigma) = \{\phi_1(\sigma_0) \ldots \phi_1(\sigma_m) \ldots \phi_n(\sigma_0) \ldots \phi_n(\sigma_m) \mid$$
$$\pi : \sigma_0 \Longrightarrow \ldots \Longrightarrow \sigma_m \in \Pi_\Gamma, m \ge 1\}.$$

The language of A_i over Σ, $1 \le i \le n$, is

$$L(A_i, \Sigma) = \{\phi_i(\sigma_0) \ldots \phi_i(\sigma_m) \mid \pi : \sigma_0 \Longrightarrow \ldots \Longrightarrow \sigma_m \in \Pi_\Gamma, m \ge 1\}.$$

Note that the definition of the language assigned to the EDRS can also be based on a different concatenation order. These variants would describe the successive transitions from different perspectives.

We present an example for languages assigned to extended distributed reaction systems.

Example 2. Let us consider the EDRS of Example 1 with slight modifications.
Let $\Gamma = (\Delta, M, \sigma_0)$ be an extended distributed reaction system, where

- $\Delta = (S, A_1, A_2, A_3)$ where $S = \{x, y, z\}$,
  $A_1 = \{(\{x, y\}, \{z\}, \{x, y\})\}$, $A_2 = \{(\{y, z\}, \{x\}, \{y\})\}$,
  $A_3 = \{(\{z, x\}, \{y\}, \{z\})\}$.
- Let $M = (Q, C, R, q_0, F)$ where $Q = \{q_0, q_1, q_2\}$,
- $C = \{c_1, c_2\}$ with $c_1 = (\{y\}, \{z\}, \{x\})$, and $c_2 = (\{y\}, \emptyset, \{x\})$.
- Let $R = \{r_1, r_2, r_3, r_4, r_5\}$ with
  $r_1 = (q_0, (\{y\}, \{z\}, \{x\}), q_0)$, $r_4 = (q_0, (\{y\}, \emptyset, \{x\}), q_2)$,
  $r_2 = (q_0, (\{y\}, \{z\}, \{x\}), q_1)$, $r_5 = (q_2, (\{y\}, \emptyset, \{x\}), q_2)$.
  $r_3 = (q_1, (\{y\}, \{z\}, \{x\}), q_1)$,

– Let q_0 be the initial state of M, and let $q_1, q_2 \in F$.
– Let $\sigma_0 = (q_0, (\{x,y\}, \{z\}, \{x\}), (\{x\}, \{y\}, \{z\}))$.

We changed A_1 to $\{((\{x,y\}\{z\}), \{x,y\})\}$, i.e., the set of products of the only reaction of A_1 is $\{x,y\}$, and we added q_2 to F.

Notice that $S = \{x, y, z\}$ has seven nonempty subsets ($2^3 - 1$), i.e., $\{x\}, \{y\}, \{z\}, \{x,y\}, \{y,z\}, \{x,z\}, \{x,y,z\}$.

Let $\Sigma = \{a_k \mid 1 \leq k \leq 7\}$. We define $\rho : 2^S \to \Sigma \cup \{\lambda\}$ as follows.

$\rho(\{x\}) = a_1, \rho(\{y\}) = a_2, \rho(\{z\}) = a_3, \rho(\{x,y\}) = a_4, \rho(\{y,z\}) = a_5,$
$\rho(\{z,x\}) = a_6, \rho(\{x,y,z\}) = a_7, \rho(\emptyset) = \lambda.$

We now will consider two terminating interactive processes.

Let $\pi_1 : \sigma_0 \Longrightarrow \sigma_1 \Longrightarrow \sigma_2 \Longrightarrow \sigma_3 \Longrightarrow \sigma_4$, where

$\sigma_0 = (q_0, (\{y\}, \{z\}, \{x\}), (\{x,y\}, \{y\}, \{z\}))$
$\sigma_i = (q_0, (\{y\}, \{z\}, \{x\}), (\{x,y\}, \{y\}, \{z\})), \ i = 1, 2, 3$
$\sigma_4 = (q_1, (\{y\}, \{z\}, \{x\}), (\{x,y\}, \{y\}, \{z\})).$

The reader may easily see that the transitions of M performed in π_1 are r_1, r_1, r_2, r_3. Then we obtain

$$H(\pi_1) = ((\phi_1(\sigma_0) \ldots \phi_1(\sigma_4)), \ (\phi_2(\sigma_0) \ldots \phi_2(\sigma_4), \ (\phi_3(\sigma_0) \ldots \phi_3(\sigma_4)),$$

where for j, $0 \leq j \leq 4$,

$$\phi_1(\sigma_j) = \rho(\{x,y\}) = a_4, \ \phi_2(\sigma_j) = \rho(\{y\}) = a_2, \ \phi_3(\sigma_j) = \rho(\{z\}) = a_3.$$

Thus, the word $w \in L(\Gamma, \Sigma)$ obtained by π_1 is $w = a_4^5 a_2^5 a_3^5$.

We now consider another terminating interactive process. Let $\pi_2 : \sigma_0 \Longrightarrow \sigma_1' \Longrightarrow \sigma_2' \Longrightarrow \sigma_3' \Longrightarrow \sigma_4'$, where

$\sigma_0 = (q_0, (\{x,y\}, \{z\}, \{x\}), (\{x,y\}, \{y\}, \{z\})),$
$\sigma_1' = (q_0, (\{x,y\}, \{z\}, \{x\}), (\{x,y\}, \{y\}, \{z\})),$
$\sigma_2' = (q_0, (\{x,y\}, \{z\}, \{x\}), (\{x,y\}, \{y\}, \{z\})),$
$\sigma_3' = (q_2, (\{x,y\}, \emptyset, \{x\}), (\{x,y\}, \emptyset, \{z\})),$
$\sigma_4' = (q_2, (\{x,y\}, \emptyset, \{x\}), (\{x,y\}, \emptyset, \{z\})).$

It can be seen that the transitions of M performed in π_2 are r_1, r_1, r_4, r_5. Then we obtain

$$H(\pi_2) = ((\phi_1(\sigma_0) \ldots \phi_1(\sigma_4')), \ (\phi_2(\sigma_0) \ldots \phi_2(\sigma_4'), \ (\phi_3(\sigma_0) \ldots \phi_3(\sigma_4')),$$

where for j, $0 \leq j \leq 4$,

$\phi_1(\sigma_j) = \rho(\{x,y\}) = a_4, \ \phi_3(\sigma_j) = \rho(\{z\}) = a_3,$
$\phi_2(\sigma_k) = \rho(\{y\}) = a_2, \ 0 \leq k \leq 2$ and $\phi_2(\sigma_l) = \rho(\emptyset) = \lambda, \ 3 \leq l \leq 4.$

The word $w \in L(\Gamma, \Sigma)$ obtained by π_2 is $w = a_4^5 a_2^3 a_3^5$.

The language we obtain is $L(\Gamma, \Sigma) = \{a_4^n a_2^k a_3^n \mid n \geq k, k \geq 1\}$. We leave the proof to the reader.

3   Languages of Extended Distributed Reaction Systems

Although the interest in studying distributed reaction systems is primarily focused on their behavior, these constructs can also be considered language-generating devices. In the following, we provide representations of some well-known language classes by extended distributed reaction systems.

Theorem 1. *Let $\Gamma = (\Delta, M, \sigma_0)$ be an extended distributed reaction system and let Σ be an alphabet such that Σ and Γ satisfy the condition given in Definition 7, item 1. Then $L(\Gamma, \Sigma)$ is a right-linear simple matrix language.*

Proof. Let $\Gamma = (\Delta, M, \sigma_0)$ be of degree n, $n \geq 1$, i.e., let $\Delta = (S, \mathcal{A})$, $\mathcal{A} = (A_1, \ldots, A_n)$, $M = (Q, C, R, q_0, F)$, $\sigma_0 = (q_0, (c_{0,1}, \ldots, c_{0,n}), (d_{0,1}, \ldots, d_{0,n}))$.

Furthermore, let ρ_i, $1 \leq i \leq n$, be mappings that satisfy the conditions of Definition 7.

We construct a right-linear simple matrix grammar $G = (N, \Sigma, A_0, \mathcal{M})$ such that $L(\Gamma, \Sigma) = L(G)$ holds. (To avoid confusion, the startsymbol of G is denoted by A_0, and the set of matrices by $\mathcal{M}$.) Let Q_Γ be the set of states of Γ.

We define the components of G.

Let $N = \bigcup_{i=0}^{n} N_i$, where $N_0 = \{A_0\} \bigcup_{j=0}^{r} A_{\sigma_j}$ and $N_k = \{X_k\}$, $1 \leq k \leq n$, such that $N_i \cap N_j = \emptyset$ for $i \neq j$, $0 \leq i, j \leq n$.

The set of matrices of G is given as follows.

Let $m_0 : (A_0 \rightarrow A_{\sigma_0} X_1 \ldots X_n)$ be the only initial matrix of G.

We add matrix m_{0,σ_0} to $\mathcal{M}$ where m_{0,σ_0} : $(A_0 \rightarrow A_{\sigma_0}, X_1 \rightarrow \rho(d_{0,1})X_1, \ldots, X_n \rightarrow \rho(d_{0,n})X_n)$ and $\sigma_0 = (q_0, (c_{0,1}, \ldots, c_{0,n}), (d_{0,1}, \ldots, d_{0,n}))$ is the initial state of Γ.

For every direct transition

$$\sigma_i = (q_i, (c_{i,1}, \ldots, c_{i,n}), (d_{i,1}, \ldots d_{i,n})) \Longrightarrow (q_j, (c_{j,1}, \ldots, c_{j,n}), (d_{j,1}, \ldots d_{j,n})) = \sigma_j,$$

$0 \leq i, j \leq r$, in Γ, we define a matrix m_{σ_i, σ_j} as follows: m_{σ_i, σ_j} : $(A_{\sigma_i} \rightarrow A_{\sigma_j}, X_1 \rightarrow \rho(d_{j,1})X_1, \ldots, X_n \rightarrow \rho(d_{j,n})X_n)$ where $\rho(d_{j,k})$, $1 \leq j \leq n$, are elements of $\Sigma \cup \{\lambda\}$.

Finally, for every state $\sigma_f = (q_f, (c_{f,1}, \ldots, c_{f,n}), (d_{f,1}, \ldots d_{f,n}))$ where $q_f \in F$, we add matrix m_f to $\mathcal{M}$ where m_f : $(A_{\sigma_f} \rightarrow \lambda, X_1 \rightarrow \lambda, \ldots, X_n \rightarrow \lambda)$. There are no more matrices in $\mathcal{M}$.

To prove that $L(\Gamma, \Sigma) = L(G)$, we first show that for every terminating finite interactive process $\sigma_0 \Longrightarrow \sigma_1 \Longrightarrow \ldots \Longrightarrow \sigma_t$ with the associated word $w = \phi_1(\sigma_0) \ldots \phi_1(\sigma_t) \ldots \phi_n(\sigma_0) \ldots \phi_n(\sigma_t)$, where σ_t is a final state of Δ, there is a derivation in $L(G)$ resulting in w. Notice that mapping $\phi_i : Q_\Gamma \rightarrow \Sigma^*$, $1 \leq i \leq n$, is given as follows: $\phi_i(\sigma) = \rho(d_i)$ for each state $\sigma = (q, (c_1, \ldots, c_n), (d_1, \ldots d_n))$. This implies that $w = \rho(d_{0,1})\rho(d_{1,1}) \ldots \rho(d_{t,1}) \ldots \rho(d_{0,n})\rho(d_{1,n}) \ldots \rho(d_{t,n})$.

By definition of matrices in $\mathcal{M}$, if we start from A_0 and we apply matrices in the following order $m_0, m_{0,\sigma_0}, m_{\sigma_0,\sigma_1}, \ldots, m_{\sigma_{t-1},\sigma_t}, m_{\sigma_f}$, then we obtain the same word $w = \rho(d_{0,1})\rho(d_{1,1}) \ldots \rho(d_{t,1}) \ldots \rho(d_{0,n})\rho(d_{1,n}) \ldots \rho(d_{t,n})$ as before.

Thus, $L(G) \subseteq L(\Gamma, \Sigma)$ holds. Next, we show that the reverse inclusion holds, too. Suppose that the application of the matrix sequence

$$m_0, m_{0,\sigma_0}, m_{\sigma_0,\sigma_1}, \ldots, m_{\sigma_{t-1},\sigma_t}, m_{\sigma_f}$$

in G corresponds to a terminating derivation in G and it results in

$$w = \rho(d_{0,1})\rho(d_{1,1}) \ldots \rho(d_{t,1}) \ldots \rho(d_{0,n})\rho(d_{1,n}) \ldots \rho(d_{t,n}).$$

By the definition of matrices in $\mathcal{M}$, if matrix $m_{i,j}$, $0 \leq i, j \leq t-1$ can be applied, then there exists a direct transition

$$\sigma_i = (q_i, (c_{i,1}, \ldots, c_{i,n}), (d_{i,1}, \ldots d_{i,n})) \implies (q_j, (c_{j,1}, \ldots, c_{j,n}), (d_{j,1}, \ldots d_{j,n})) = \sigma_j,$$

$0 \leq i, j \leq r$, in Γ. It can also be observed that matrices m_0 and m_{0,σ_0} correspond to the initialization of Γ, i.e. they simulate establishing the initial state σ_0. Finally, matrix m_{σ_f} indicates the end of the generating process; notice that it may appear only if $\sigma = (q_f, (c_1, \ldots, c_n), (d_1, \ldots, d_n))$ is a final state of Γ. Thus, it can be seen that if w can be generated in G, then there exists a terminating finite interactive process $\sigma_0 \implies \sigma_1 \implies \ldots \implies \sigma_t$ in Γ such that $w \in L(\Gamma, \Sigma)$ holds. Hence $L(G) = L(\Gamma, \Sigma)$ holds.

As a consequence of the previous result, we obtain the following statement.

Theorem 2. *Let $\Gamma = (\Delta, M, \sigma_0)$ be an extended distributed reaction system where $\Delta = (S, \mathcal{A})$, $\mathcal{A} = (A_1, \ldots, A_n)$, $n \geq 1$. Let Σ be an alphabet such that Σ and Γ satisfy the condition given in Definition 7, item 1. Then $L(A_k, \Sigma)$, $1 \leq k \leq n$, is a right-linear (regular) language.*

We provide only the basic idea of the proof; it is similar to the proof of Theorem 1. Let $M = (Q, C, R, q_0, F)$ be the context automaton and σ_0 be the initial state of Γ. For every k, $1 \leq k \leq n$, a regular (right-linear) grammar $G_k = (N_k, \Sigma, P_k, A_0)$ can be constructed such that $L(A_k, \Sigma) = L(G_k)$ holds. Let Q_Γ be the set of states of Γ. We define the components of G_k. Let $N_k = \{A_0\} \bigcup_{j=0}^r A_{\sigma_j}$. Elements of P_k are defined as follows. P_k contains an initial rule $p_{0,\sigma_0} : A_0 \to A_{\sigma_0}$. For every direct transition

$$\sigma_i = (q_i, (c_{i,1}, \ldots, c_{i,n}), (d_{i,1}, \ldots d_{i,n})) \implies (q_j, (c_{j,1}, \ldots, c_{j,n}), (d_{j,1}, \ldots d_{j,n})) = \sigma_j,$$

$0 \leq i, j \leq r$, in Γ, G_k has a production $p_{\sigma_i,\sigma_j} : A_{\sigma_i} \to \rho(d_{j,k})A_{\sigma_j}$ in P_k where $\rho(d_{j,k})$, $1 \leq j \leq n$ is an element of $\Sigma \cup \{\lambda\}$. Finally, for every state $\sigma_f = (q_f, (c_{f,1}, \ldots, c_{f,n}), (d_{f,1}, \ldots d_{f,n}))$ of Γ, where $q_f \in F$, we add a production $p_f : A_{\sigma_f} \to \lambda$ to P_k. By similar considerations that are used in the proof of Theorem 1, it can be shown that $L(A_k, \Sigma) = L(G_k)$ holds.

Theorem 3. *For every right-linear simple matrix language $L \subseteq T^*$ we can give an extended distributed reaction system $\Gamma = (\Delta, M, \sigma_0)$ and an alphabet Σ satisfying conditions of Definition 7, and a projection $h : \Sigma \to T$ such that $= h(L(\Gamma, \Sigma))$ holds.*

Proof. Let $G = (N, T \cup \{\#, \$, X\}, A_0, \mathcal{M})$ be a right-linear simple matrix grammar of degree n, where $n \geq 1$ that generates L. (Notice that $N = \bigcup_{0=1}^{n} N_i$, where $N_0 = \{A_0\}$ and N_j and N_k are pairwise disjoint sets of nonterminals for j, k, $0 \leq j, k \leq n$.) Let $\#$, $\$$, X be auxiliary symbols, terminals that are not in $(N \cup T)$. Without loss of generality we may assume that G is in normal form and G has only one initial matrix.

We construct $\Gamma = (\Delta, M, \sigma_0)$, where $\Delta = (S, A_1, \ldots, A_n)$, $M = (Q, C, R, q_0, F)$, and σ_0 is the inital state of Γ.

We first define the context automaton of Γ. We start with the set of transitions R of M; the other components can be inferred from R.

For the initial matrix $m_0 = A_0 \to A_1 \ldots A_n$ in G, M has transitions

$(q_0, (\{\#\}, \ldots, \{\#\}), q_{0,l})$ and $(q_{0,l}(\{x_1\}, \ldots, \{x_n\}), q_j)$, where $m_l : (A_1 \to x_1 B_1, \ldots A_n \to x_n B_n)$, $A_i, B_i \in N_i$, $x_i \in T \cup \{\lambda\}$, $1 \leq i \leq n$, and m_l, $1 \leq l \leq n$ is directly applicable after m_0.

For every pair of matrices m_k, m_l, $0 \leq k, l \leq card(\mathcal{M}) - 1$, where $m_k : (A_1 \to x_1 B_1, \ldots, A_n \to x_n B_n)$, $A_i, B_i \in N_i$, $x_i \in (T \cup \{\lambda\}$, $1 \leq i \leq n$, and $m_l : (B_1 \to y_1 E_1, \ldots, B_n \to y_n E_n)$, $B_i, E_i \in N_i$, $y_i \in T \cup \{\lambda\}$, $1 \leq i \leq n$, i.e., m_l is directly applicable after performing m_k, context automaton M has a transition $(q_k, (z_1, \ldots, z_n), q_l)$, where q_k and q_l are states of the M and z_i is the context added to the current state of A_i; $z_i = \{m_k, x_i\}$ if $x_i \in \Sigma$ and $z_i = \{m_k\}$ if $x_i = \lambda$.

For every matrix of the form $m_f : (A_1 \to \lambda, \ldots, A_n \to \lambda)$, $A_i \in N_i$, $1 \leq i \leq n$, M has a transition $(q_f, (\#, \ldots, \#), q_{halt})$, where $g_f, q_{halt} \in F$ and there is no transition starting from q_{halt}.

Next, we define components A_k, $1 \leq k \leq n$. For every matrix $m : (A_1 \to x_1 B_1, \ldots, A_n \to x_n B_n) \in \mathcal{M}$, $A_i, B_i \in N_i$, $x_i \in T \cup \{\lambda\}$, $1 \leq i \leq n$, A_k has a reaction $(\{m, x_k, z\}, \{X\}, \{x_k\})$ if $x_k \in T$. Furthermore, it also has a reaction $(\{\#\}, \{X\}, \{\#\})$. X is an auxiliary symbol that ensures the non-emptiness of the inhibitor set. Based on the above considerations, we can construct transitions $\sigma_k = (q_k, (x_1, \ldots, x_n), (z_1, \ldots, z_n))$ of Γ.

The initial state of Δ is $\sigma_0 = (q_0, (\{\#\}, \ldots, \{\#\}), (\{\#\}, \ldots, \{\#\}))$. By the construction of the transitions of M and the components of Γ, it can be seen that if $m_0, m_{i_1}, \ldots, m_{i_j}, \ldots m_{i_l}, m_f$ is a terminating derivation in G, then there exists a terminating finite interactive process $\sigma_0, \sigma_{i_1}, \ldots, \sigma_{i_j}, \ldots \sigma_{i_l}, \sigma_f$ in Γ and vice versa. Let Σ be an alphabet and ρ be a mapping satisfying the conditions of Definition 7 such that $T \subseteq \Sigma$ and $\rho(\{x\}) = x$ for any $x \in T$. Furthermore, let h be a projection such that $h(y) = y$ for $y \in T \cap \Sigma$ and $h(z) = \lambda$ otherwise. Then $L(G) = h(L(\Gamma, \Sigma))$ holds.

In the following, we provide a representation of recursively enumerable languages with extended distributed reaction systems and morphisms. The proof of the statement is based on a variant of the Geffert normal forms [9].

Theorem 4. *For every recursively enumerable language L, $L \subseteq T^*$ there exists a distributed reaction system Γ and an alphabet Σ such that Γ and Σ satisfy the conditions of Definition 7, $T \subseteq \Sigma$, and there exist two morphism h and*

h', and a right-linear simple matrix language L' over $(T \cup \{1,0\})^*$ such that $L = h(L(\Gamma, \Sigma)) \cap h'(L')$. Furthermore, Γ has only two components.

Proof. Let L be defined over alphabet $T = \{a_1, \ldots, a_n\}$ and represented by an Extended Post Correspondence $\mathcal{E} = (\{(u_1, v_1), \ldots, (u_m, v_m)\}, (z_{a_1}, \ldots, z_{a_n}))$, where $m \geq 1$, $u_i, v_i, z_{a_j} \in \{0,1\}^*$ for $1 \leq i \leq m$ and $1 \leq j \leq n$. That is, let $L = L(\mathcal{E}) = \{x_1 \ldots x_l \in T^* \mid \exists s_1 s_2 \ldots s_r \in \{1, 2, \ldots, m\}^r\}$ such that $r \geq 1$ and $u_{s_1} u_{s_2} \ldots u_{s_r} = v_{s_1} v_{s_2} \ldots v_{s_r} z_{x_1} z_{x_2} \ldots z_{x_l}\}$.

The reader can easily observe that we can decide whether a word w is in L by the following three phases of generation of w, according to $\mathcal{E}$. In the first phase, we construct two words, $u = u_{s_1} \ldots u_{s_r}$ and $v = v_{s_1} \ldots v_{s_r}$, by appending elements of pairs (u_{s_k}, v_{s_k}), $1 \leq k \leq r$, to the current strings in generation. In the second phase, using pairs $(a_{i_j}, z_{a_{i_j}})$, $1 \leq i \leq l$, we append strings $w = a_{i_1} \ldots a_{i_l}$ and $z_w = z_{a_{i_1}} \ldots z_{a_{i_l}}$ to the corresponding words in generation. Thus we obtain two strings uw and vz_w. In the third phase, we check whether or not $u = vz_w$ holds. If this is the case, then w can be successfully generated by $\mathcal{E}$.

We construct an extended distributed reaction system $\Gamma = (\Delta, M, \sigma_0)$ such that any terminating finite interactive process in Γ corresponds to a successful generation in $\mathcal{E}$.

Let the background set of Δ, S, be given by $S = \{a_1, \ldots, a_n, Z_{a_1}, \ldots, Z_{a_n}, U_1, \ldots, U_m, V_1, \ldots, V_m, \bar{a}_1, \ldots, \bar{a}_n, \bar{Z}_{a_1}, \ldots, \bar{Z}_{a_n}, \bar{U}_1, \ldots, \bar{U}_m, \bar{V}_1, \ldots, \bar{V}_m, \#, X\}$, where n and m are given as in $\mathcal{E}$.

To help the easier reading, we first define the context automaton $M = (Q, C, R, q_0, F)$ of Γ.

Let $Q = \{q_0, q_1, \ldots, q_n, q_{n+1}, \ldots, q_{n+m}, q_f, q_h\}$, where n and m are given as in $\mathcal{E}$, Let $F = \{q_f, q_h\}$ be the set of final states of M such that no transition of M starts from q_h. Furthermore, let $C = \{(\{\#\}, \{\#\})\} \cup \{(\{\bar{a}_i\}, \{\bar{Z}_{a_i}\}) \mid 1 \leq i \leq n\} \cup \{(\{\bar{U}_j\}, \{\bar{V}_j\}) \mid n+1 \leq l \leq m\}$.

For technical reasons, let $\bar{U} = \{U_1, \ldots, U_m\}$ and let $\bar{V} = \{V_1, \ldots, V_m\}$.

We define R as follows. Let

$$
\begin{aligned}
R = \{&(q_0, (\{\#\}, \{\#\}), q_l) \mid n+1 \leq l \leq n+m\} \cup \\
&\{(q_{n+k}, (\{\bar{U}_k\}, \{\bar{V}_k\}), q_l) \mid 1 \leq k \leq m, n+1 \leq l \leq n+m\} \cup \\
&\{(q_{n+l}, (\{\bar{U}_l\}, \{\bar{V}_l\}), q_f) \mid 1 \leq l \leq m\} \cup \\
&\{(q_{n+l}, (\{\bar{U}_l\}, \{\bar{V}_l\}), q_i) \mid 1 \leq l \leq m, 1 \leq i \leq n\} \cup \\
&\{(q_i, (\{\bar{a}_i\}, \{\bar{Z}_{a_i}\}), q_j) \mid 1 \leq i, j \leq n\} \cup \\
&\{(q_i, (\{\bar{a}_i\}, \{\bar{Z}_{a_i}\}), q_f) \mid 1 \leq i \leq n\} \cup \\
&\{(q_f, (\{\#\}, \{\#\}), q_h)\}.
\end{aligned}
$$

We continue with the other elements of Δ. Let

$$
\begin{aligned}
A_1 = \{&(\{\#\}, \{X\}, \{\#\})\} \cup \\
&\{(\{\bar{U}_k\}, \{X\} \cup \bar{U}, \{U_k\}) \mid 1 \leq k \leq m\} \cup \\
&\{(\{\bar{U}_i, U_k\}, \{X\}, \{U_i\}) \mid 1 \leq i, k \leq m\} \cup \\
&\{(\{\bar{a}_i, U_k\}, \{X\}, \{a_i\}) \mid 1 \leq i \leq n, 1 \leq k \leq m\} \cup \\
&\{(\{\bar{a}_i, a_k\}, \{X\}, \{a_i\}) \mid 1 \leq i, k \leq n\}
\end{aligned}
$$

and let

$$A_2 = \{((\{\#\}, \{X\}, \{\#\}))\} \cup$$
$$\{(\{\bar{V}_k\}, \{X\} \cup \bar{V}, \{V_k\}) \mid 1 \leq k \leq m\} \cup$$
$$\{(\{\bar{V}_i, V_k\}, \{X\}, \{V_i\}) \mid n + 1 \leq i, k \leq m\} \cup$$
$$\{(\{\bar{Z}_{a_i}, V_k\}, \{X\}, \{Z_{a_i}\}) \mid 1 \leq i \leq n, n + 1 \leq k \leq m\} \cup$$
$$\{(\{\bar{Z}_{a,i}, Z_{a_k}\}, \{X\}, \{Z_{a_i}\}) \mid 1 \leq i, k \leq n\}.$$

The initial state of Γ is $\sigma_0 = (q_0, (\{\#\}, \{\#\}), (\{\#\}, \{\#\})$.

In the following, we show that every terminating finite interactive process in Γ corresponds to a generation in EPC $\mathcal{E}$, and vice versa, every generation in $\mathcal{E}$ corresponds to a terminating finite interactive process in Γ.

Notice that for every pair (u_j, v_j), $1 \leq j \leq m$, M has a transition $(q_{n+j}, (\{\bar{U}_j\}, \{\bar{V}_j\}), q_l)$, where q_i, q_l are states of M and q_{n+j} refers to that the appending of the pair (u_j, v_j) is simulated. Analogously, for every pair (a_i, Z_{a_i}), M has transitions $(q_i, (\bar{a}_i, \bar{Z}_{a_i}), q_j)$, where q_i, q_j are states of M and q_i refers to that the appending of the pair (a_i, Z_{a_i}) is simulated. When transition $(q_k, (\{\bar{U}_k\}, \{\bar{V}_k\}), q_l)$ is performed, then the current state of A_1 is changed to $\{U_k, \#\}$ and the current state of A_2 is changed to $\{V_k, \#\}$. When transition $(q_i, (\bar{a}_i, \bar{Z}_{a_i}), q_j)$ of M is performed, then the current state of A_1 is changed to $\{a_i, \#\}$ and the current state of A_2 is changed to $\{Z_{a_i}, \#\}$, due to the definition of their reactions. These actions correspond to appending pairs (u_j, v_j) and (a_i, z_{a_i}) to the words in generation.

Suppose that $u_{j_1} \ldots u_{j_r} a_{i_1} \ldots a_{i_l}$ and $v_{j_1} \ldots v_{j_r} z_{a_{i_1}} \ldots z_{a_{i_l}}$ are two strings obtained by EPC $\mathcal{E}$.

Then there exists a terminating finite interactive process π in Γ, where $\pi : \sigma_0 \Longrightarrow \sigma_{j_1} \Longrightarrow \sigma_{j,r} \Longrightarrow \sigma_{i_1} \Longrightarrow \sigma_{i_l} \Longrightarrow \sigma_f$ such that the state sequence of A_1 according to π is $\{\#\}, \{U_{j_1}, \#\}, \ldots, \{U_{j_r}, \#\}, \{a_{i_1}, \#\}, \ldots, \{a_{i_l}, \#\}$, $\{\#\}$, and the state sequence of A_2 is $\{\#\}, \{V_{j_1}, \#\}, \ldots, \{V_{j_r}, \#\}, \{Z_{a_{i_1}}, \#\}, \ldots, \{Z_{a_{i_l}}, \#\}, \{\#\}$.

We note that any terminating finite interactive process in Γ is similar to π, i.e., the interactive process has an initial step, after that it continues with a sequence of transitions which simulates the appending of pairs (u_j, v_j)- Then, a sequence of transitions follows, which transitions simulate the appending of pairs (a_i, z_{a_i}). After that, the transitions of the ending phase are performed.

If $\lambda \in L$, then the terminating finite interactive process is of the form $\pi' : \sigma_0 \Longrightarrow \sigma_{j_1} \Longrightarrow \sigma_{j,r} \Longrightarrow \sigma_f$ where the state sequence of A_1 according to π' is $\{\#\}, \{U_{j_1}, \#\}, \ldots, \{U_{j_r}, \#\}, \{\#\}$, and the state sequence of A_2 is $\{\#\}, \{V_{j_1}, \#\}, \ldots, \{V_{j_r}, \#\}, \#\}, \{\#\}$. This case can be treated analogously to the previous case.

Let Σ be an alphabet defined to Γ such that Σ satisfies the conditions of Definition 7 and the following holds: $\rho(\{a_i\}) = a_i$, $\rho(\{Z_{a_i}\}) = Z_{a_i}$, $1 \leq i \leq n$, and $\rho(\{U_j\}) = U_j$, $\rho(\{V_j\}) = V_j$, $1 \leq j \leq m$, $\rho(\{\#\}) = \#$. It can easily be seen that the word in Σ^* which belongs to A_1 is of the form uw, where $w \in \{a_1, \ldots, a_n\}^*$ and $u \in \{U_1, \ldots, U_r\}^*$. The word that belongs to A_2 is of the form vz_w, where $v \in \{V_1, \ldots, V_r\}^*$ and $z_w \in \{Z_{a_1}, \ldots, Z\}^*$. This means that

$uwvz_w$ is in $L(\Gamma, \Sigma)$. Let us define a homomorphism h as follows: $h(a_i) = a_i$, $h(Z_{a_i}) = z_{a_i}$, $h(U_j) = u_j$ and $h(V_j) = v_j$ and $h(\#) = \lambda$. Notice that $w \in L$ if and only if $h(u) = h(vz)$ holds.

Let us define a right-linear simple matrix grammar $G' = (N', T', S', M)$ as follows. Let $N' = \{S', S_1, S_2, S'_1, S'_2\}$, $T' = T \cup \{1, 0\}$, and $M = \{(S' \to S_1 S'_1), (S_1 \to 1S_1, S'_1 \to 1S'_1), (S_1 \to 0S_1, S'_1 \to 0S'_1), (S_1 \to 1S_2, S'_1 \to 1S'_2), (S_1 \to 0S_2, S'_1 \to 0S'_2)\} \cup \{(S_2 \to a_i S_2, S'_2 \to S'_2) \mid a_i \in T, 1 \le i \le n\} \cup \{(S_2 \to \lambda, S'_2 \to \lambda)\}$. It is easy to see that any word w in $L(G')$ is of the form xwx, where $x \in \{0, 1\}^*$ and $w \in T^*$. Let us define a homomorphism h' as follows: $h'(a_i) = a_i$, $h'(1) = \lambda$, and $h'(0) = \lambda$.

Then, it is easy to see that $w \in L$ if and only if $h(L(\Gamma, \Sigma)) \cap h'(L')$ holds.

4   Conclusions

We assigned languages to extended distributed reaction systems and provided representations of some well-known language classes by these constructs. The new approach to distributed reaction systems raises several open problems: for example the effect of further restrictions concerning the context automaton, or the study of other variants of context providers. We plan investigations on these topics in the future.

Acknowledgements. The authors thank the reviewers for their the valuable comments and suggestions.

The work by E. Csuhaj-Varjú was supported by the National Research, Development, and Innovation Office - NKFIH, Hungary, Grant no. K 120558. The work by L. Ciencialová and L. Cienciala was supported by the project no. CZ.02.2.69/0.0/0.0/18_054/0014696, "Development of R&D capacities of the Silesian University in Opava", co-funded by the European Union.

References

1. Azimi, S.: Steady states of constrained reaction systems. Theor. Comput. Sci. **701**, 20–26 (2017). https://doi.org/10.1016/j.tcs.2017.03.047
2. Azimi, S., Gratie, C., Ivanov, S., Manzoni, L., Petre, I., Porreca, A.E.: Complexity of model checking for reaction systems. Theor. Comput. Sci. **623**, 103–113 (2016). https://doi.org/10.1016/j.tcs.2015.11.040
3. Azimi, S., Iancu, B., Petre, I.: Reaction system models for the heat shock response. Fundam. Informaticae **131**(3–4), 299–312 (2014). https://doi.org/10.3233/FI-2014-1016
4. Bottoni, P., Labella, A., Rozenberg, G.: Networks of reaction systems. Int. J. Found. Comput. Sci. **31**(1), 53–71 (2020)
5. Csuhaj-Varjú, E., Sethy, P.K.: Communicating reaction systems with direct communication. In: Freund, R., Ishdorj, T.-O., Rozenberg, G., Salomaa, A., Zandron, C. (eds.) CMC 2020. LNCS, vol. 12687, pp. 17–30. Springer, Cham (2021). https://doi.org/10.1007/978-3-030-77102-7_2

6. Ehrenfeucht, A., Main, M.G., Rozenberg, G.: Functions defined by reaction systems. Int. J. Found. Comput. Sci. **22**(1), 167–178 (2011). https://doi.org/10.1142/S0129054111007927
7. Ehrenfeucht, A., Rozenberg, G.: Basic notions of reaction systems. In: Calude, C.S., Calude, E., Dinneen, M.J. (eds.) DLT 2004. LNCS, vol. 3340, pp. 27–29. Springer, Heidelberg (2004). https://doi.org/10.1007/978-3-540-30550-7_3
8. Ehrenfeucht, A., Rozenberg, G.: Reaction systems. Fundam. Informaticae **75**(1–4), 263–280 (2007)
9. Geffert, V.: Normal forms for phrase-structure grammars. RAIRO Theor. Inform. Appl. **25**, 473–496 (1991). https://doi.org/10.1051/ita/1991250504731
10. Hopcroft, J.E., Motwani, R., Ullman, J.D.: Introduction to Automata Theory, Languages, and Computation, 3rd edn. Pearson International Edition. Addison-Wesley (2007)
11. Ibarra, O.H.: Simple matrix languages. Inf. Control **17**(4), 359–394 (1970). https://doi.org/10.1016/S0019-9958(70)80034-1
12. Meski, A., Koutny, M., Penczek, W.: Model checking for temporal-epistemic properties of distributed reaction systems. Technical report Series CS-TR-1526, Newcastle University, April 2019
13. Meski, A., Penczek, W., Rozenberg, G.: Model checking temporal properties of reaction systems. Inf. Sci. **313**, 22–42 (2015). https://doi.org/10.1016/j.ins.2015.03.048
14. Păun, Gh., Pérez-Jiménez, M.J.: dP automata versus right-linear simple matrix grammars. In: Dinneen, M.J., Khoussainov, B., Nies, A. (eds.) WTCS 2012. LNCS, vol. 7160, pp. 376–387. Springer, Heidelberg (2012). https://doi.org/10.1007/978-3-642-27654-5_29
15. Păun, Gh., Pérez-Jiménez, M.J.: An infinite hierarchy of languages defined by dP systems. Theor. Comput. Sci. **431**, 4–12 (2012). https://doi.org/10.1016/j.tcs.2011.12.053
16. Salomaa, A.: Functions and sequences generated by reaction systems. Theor. Comput. Sci. **466**, 87–96 (2012). https://doi.org/10.1016/j.tcs.2012.07.022
17. Salomaa, A.: Functional constructions between reaction systems and propositional logic. Int. J. Found. Comput. Sci. **24**(1), 147–160 (2013)

PSPACE-Completeness of Reversible Deterministic Systems

Erik D. Demaine[1], Robert A. Hearn[3], Dylan Hendrickson[1],
and Jayson Lynch[2(✉)]

[1] MIT Computer Science and Artificial Intelligence Laboratory, 32 Vassar Street,
Cambridge, MA 02139, USA
{edemaine,dylanhen}@mit.edu
[2] Cheriton School of Computer Science, University of Waterloo,
Waterloo, ON, Canada
jayson.lynch@uwaterloo.ca
[3] Cambridge, USA
bob@hearn.to

Abstract. We prove PSPACE-completeness of several reversible, fully
deterministic systems. At the core, we develop a framework for such
proofs (building on a result of Tsukiji and Hagiwara and a framework
for motion planning through gadgets), showing that any system that
can implement three basic gadgets is PSPACE-complete. We then apply
this framework to four different systems, showing its versatility. First,
we prove that Deterministic Constraint Logic is PSPACE-complete, fix-
ing an error in a previous argument from 2008. Second, we give a new
PSPACE-hardness proof for the reversible 'billiard ball' model of Fredkin
and Toffoli from 40 years ago, newly establishing hardness when only two
balls move at once. Third, we prove PSPACE-completeness of zero-player
motion planning with any reversible deterministic interacting k-tunnel
gadget and a 'rotate clockwise' gadget (a zero-player analog of branching
hallways). Fourth, we give simpler proofs that zero-player motion planning is PSPACE-complete with just a single gadget, the 3-spinner. These
results should in turn make it even easier to prove PSPACE-hardness of
other reversible deterministic systems.

1 Introduction

Reversible deterministic systems arise in various situations, some of the most
important of which come from physics because fundamental existing physical
theories are reversible and deterministic[1]. In particular, due to the thermody-
namics of information, reversible computation can potentially use significantly
less energy than irreversible computation because Landauer's Principle requires
physical systems expend $k_B T \ln 2$ energy per bit of information lost.[2] Thus

---

[1] The time evolution of the wave-function in the Standard Model is deterministic even
if the observation of macroscopic phenomena is probabilistic.

[2] Here $k_B \approx 1.4 \cdot 10{-}23$ is the Boltzmann constant and T is the temperature in kelvins.
At room temperature, this comes to about $2.8 \cdot 10^{-21}$ joules per bit. Current chips
are rapidly approaching this limit; see [5,6].

© The Author(s), under exclusive license to Springer Nature Switzerland AG 2022
J. Durand-Lose and G. Vaszil (Eds.): MCU 2022, LNCS 13419, pp. 91–108, 2022.
https://doi.org/10.1007/978-3-031-13502-6_7

understanding how reversible systems can solve computationally difficult problems may help in designing general-purpose reversible computing hardware.

More precisely, a system is *deterministic* if its configuration at each time in the future is entirely determined by its current configuration. A system is *reversible* if, in addition, its configuration at each time in the past is entirely determined by its current configuration. The systems we consider all satisfy, or nearly satisfy, the stronger property of *time-reversal symmetry*: evolution forward in time and backward in time obey the same rules, so by looking at a sequence of configurations it is not possible to determine whether time is moving forwards or backwards. To reverse time, we simply need to reverse the direction of motion of each moving part in each of the systems we consider. In one system, we use a slightly more general symmetry by replacing each 'rotate clockwise' gadget with a 'rotate counterclockwise' gadget, and vice-versa. A physicist might call this parity–time (PT) symmetry; see, e.g., [10].

In this paper (Sect. 2), we develop a framework for proving PSPACE-completeness of reversible deterministic systems. Our framework extracts and simplifies a framework implicit in the work of Tsukiji and Hagiwara [11], who proved PSPACE-hardness for Langton's reversible 'ant' model of artificial life in two geometries, the square and hexagonal grids. Their hardness reductions construct five core gadgets in each grid, and show that these gadgets suffice for PSPACE-hardness by a reduction from satisfiability in Quantified Boolean Formulas (QBF). Our framework decreases the number of required gadgets to just three, showing that some of the previous gadgets are unnecessary (essentially, redundant) and others can be simplified. The framework also guarantees that the gadgets are connected together without crossings, making it well suited to reducing to planar systems (which all of our applications are).

We then apply our framework to analyzing the complexity of four reversible deterministic systems:

1. We prove in Sect. 3 that Deterministic Constraint Logic is PSPACE-complete. While this result was already claimed 14 years ago [3,8], we describe in Sect. 3.1 an error in the previous reduction. Luckily the new framework enables a correct proof of the same result.
2. We develop in Sect. 4 a new PSPACE-hardness proof for the 'billiard ball' reversible model of computation, introduced and analyzed by Fredkin and Toffoli in 1982 [7]. In this model, unit-radius 2D balls move without friction and collide elastically with pinned or movable objects, according to classical physics. Unlike the previous proof, our PSPACE-hardness result works even in the case when only two balls ever move at once (and the rest are stationary), which results in a substantially simpler proof (no longer needing complex timing arguments to guarantee simultaneity).
3. We prove in the full version of the paper that zero-player motion planning through gadgets is PSPACE-complete when the gadgets include *any* reversible deterministic interacting k-tunnel gadget and a 'rotate clockwise' gadget (a 1-state 3-location gadget where an entering signal simply exits along the clockwise-next location). This result can be thought of as extend-

ing Table 1 in the motion-planning-through-gadgets framework [2,4] to add a 'zero-player' column in the unbounded row, analogous to zero-player Deterministic Constraint Logic [8]. Our proof indeed uses the same simulations as for motion planning with a positive number of players [4] to reduce to one core case—locking 2-toggles and rotate clockwise—and then shows that case is PSPACE-complete.

4. We prove in the full version of the paper that zero-player motion planning with one very simple gadget called a '3-spinner' is PSPACE-complete. Specifically, a *3-spinner* has two states—'clockwise' and 'counterclockwise'—and three locations at which the signal can enter; after entering, the gadget flips its state and the signal exits in the next port in the order given by the state. This result is weaker than Tsukiji and Hagiwara's PSPACE-hardness of 'ant' on a hexagonal lattice [11], because the vertices in the lattice act exactly as 3-spinners. We effectively translate this result into the motion-planning-through-gadgets framework of Demaine et al. [4], and simplify it significantly.

All of the systems we consider can straightforwardly be simulated using polynomial space, so the decision problems are in PSPACE.

2   The Framework

Our framework for proving PSPACE-hardness, which is a modest simplification of one due to Tsukiji and Hagiwara [11], can be understood in terms of the motion-planning gadgets framework of Demaine et al. [4]. In particular, it is closely related to, and can be described in terms of, the 'input/output gadgets' of Ani et al. [1]. We will describe it independently.

The framework may apply to any setting with a single *signal* deterministically navigating a planar *network* of *gadgets* with the following properties. Each gadget has some designated *ports*. When the signal enters the gadget at one of its ports, it then exits the same gadget at one of its port, which is determined by the entrance port and any previous traversals of that gadget. The network links gadgets by connecting the ports of the gadgets in disjoint pairs: when the signal exits at a port, it enters at the paired port.

To describe the "behavior" of a gadget, we define a *traversal* to be of the form $a \to b$ for any two ports a and b of the gadget. A gadget *implements* a sequence $[a_1 \to b_1, \ldots, a_k \to b_k]$ of traversals if, when the sequence of the signal's entrance ports to the gadget is $[a_1, \ldots, a_k]$, the sequence of exit ports from the gadget is $[b_1, \ldots, b_k]$. Note that a gadget implements any prefix of a sequence it implements.

All of the gadgets we consider in this section are *symmetric under time-reversal*, meaning if we perform a sequence of traversals followed by its time-reverse, the gadget is returned to its original state. Formally, if a gadget implements two sequences $X = [a_1 \to b_1, \ldots, a_k \to b_k]$ and $Y = [c_1 \to d_1, \ldots c_\ell \to d_\ell]$, then it also implements

$$XX^{-1}Y = [a_1 \to b_1, \ldots, a_k \to b_k, b_k \to a_k, \ldots, b_1 \to a_1, c_1 \to d_1, \ldots, c_\ell \to d_\ell].$$

In the language of Hendrickson [9], our gadgets can be modeled as 'prefix-closed gizmos', and time-reversal symmetry means they satisfy the 'implication property' $X, Y \implies XX^{-1}Y$.

If every gadget in a network is symmetric under time-reversal, then the entire network is as well: if we reverse the direction of the signal by returning it to the just-exited port instead of the port paired to just-exited port, it will retrace its steps in reverse, eventually returning to the initial configuration. This is a special case of a result applying to implication properties in general [9].

2.1 Required Gadgets

We are now ready to describe the gadgets which we will show suffice for PSPACE-hardness.

We describe each gadget by specifying some sequences it implements. The gadgets then also implement all prefixes of implemented sequences, and all sequences required for time-reversal symmetry. We don't fully specify the behavior of the gadgets: they are allowed to do anything if the signal arrives in an unspecified sequence, and this does not affect our PSPACE-hardness result because it never happens in the networks created by the reduction. The required behavior of our gadgets is summarized in Table 1. In addition, for each gadget G described below, we also allow our network to include the gadget G after $[\alpha_1 \rightarrow \beta_1, \ldots, \alpha_i \rightarrow \beta_i]$, which behaves like G would after having performed the traversals $\alpha_1 \rightarrow \beta_1, \ldots, \alpha_i \rightarrow \beta_i$ in that order. That is, if G implements $[\alpha_1 \rightarrow \beta_1, \ldots, \alpha_i \rightarrow \beta_i, a_1 \rightarrow b_1, \ldots, a_k \rightarrow b_k]$, then G after $[\alpha_1 \rightarrow \beta_1, \ldots, \alpha_i \rightarrow \beta_i]$ implements $[a_1 \rightarrow b_1, \ldots, a_k \rightarrow b_k]$.

Our first, and most complicated gadget, is the *Switch*. This corresponds to three of Tsukiji and Hagiwara's gadgets, the 'Switch & Pass', 'Switch & Turn', and 'Pseudo-Crossing', which are all equivalent except for the cyclic order of ports in the planar embedding, and that Switch & Turn merges the ports we call Set and Out. The Switch has 5 ports, called 'Set', 'Out', 'Test', 'T-Out', and 'F-Out'. It implements [Set → Out, Test → T-Out] and [Test → F-Out]. Intuitively, it has an internal state which is initially False, and is set to True by the traversal Set → Out. Entering Test reveals the current state. Time-reversal symmetry implies that the Switch is reusable: for instance, it must also implement

[Set → Out, Test → T-Out, T-Out → Test, Out → Set, Test → F-Out].

There are really 12 different Switch gadgets (up to rotation and reflection), based on the cyclic order of the ports. We allow any cyclic order of the ports; our PSPACE-hardness applies to any individual order.

Our next gadget is the *Reversible Fan-in*. Tsukiji and Hagiwara call this gadget 'CONJ'. It has three ports a, b, and c, and implements $[a \rightarrow c]$ and $[b \rightarrow c]$. Intuitively, it is a fan-in that sends both a and b to c, but—as required by time-reversal symmetry—remembers which entrance was taken so that when the signal returns to c, it exits the port it originally entered.

Our final gadget is the *A/BA Crossover*. The A/BA Crossover has four ports A, B, a, and b in cyclic order, and implements $[A \rightarrow a]$ and $[B \rightarrow b, A \rightarrow a]$. Tsukiji and Hagiwara build a slightly more powerful crossover they call 'CROSS', which also implements $[A \rightarrow a, B \rightarrow b]$. However, this is not necessary for PSPACE-hardness, and the A/BA Crossover can easily be constructed using Tsukiji and Hagiwara's Pseudo-Crossing (which is a particular planar embedding of a Switch) and CONJ.

Table 1. Summary of time-reversal-symmetric gadgets required for PSPACE-hardness. Each gadget implements all sequences generated from those under Implements by prefixes and time-reversal symmetry $(X, Y \implies XX^{-1}Y)$.

Gadget	Ports	Cyclic Order	Implements
Switch	Set Out Test T-Out F-Out	Any order	$[\text{Set} \rightarrow \text{Out}, \text{Test} \rightarrow \text{T-Out}]$ $[\text{Test} \rightarrow \text{F-Out}]$
Reversible Fan-in	a b c	(Only one possible)	$[a \rightarrow c]$ $[b \rightarrow c]$
A/BA Crossover	A B a b	A, B, a, b	$[A \rightarrow a]$ $[B \rightarrow b, A \rightarrow a]$

2.2 PSPACE-Hardness

We now prove PSPACE-hardness for the natural decision problem concerning these gadgets: given a planar network containing Switches, Reversible Fan-ins, and A/BA Crossovers (including these gadgets after some traversals), a starting port which the signal enters first, and a target port, does the signal ever reach the target port? We reduce from QBF, still following Tsukiji and Hagiwara [11] with some simplification and slightly different abstractions.

We first ignore the requirement of planarity, showing PSPACE-hardness for general networks containing just Switches and Reversible Fan-ins. Then we argue that A/BA Crossovers suffice for all required crossings in a planar embedding of the networks we construct.

Given a quantified formula $Q_1 x_1 : \cdots Q_n x_n : \phi(x_1, \ldots, x_n)$ where ϕ is a 3-CNF formula, we construct a network of Switches and Reversible Fan-ins. At a high level, the network consists of a series of 'quantifier gadgets', ending in 'CNF evaluation'. When the signal arrives at a quantifier gadget, the quantifier gadget sets the variable it controls, and then queries the next quantifier. Depending on the response, it may perform a second query with the other setting of its variable, and then it sends a response to the previous quantifier. The final quantifier Q_n instead queries the CNF evaluation, which computes the value of ϕ under the current variable assignment. The structure of the reduction is shown in Fig. 1.

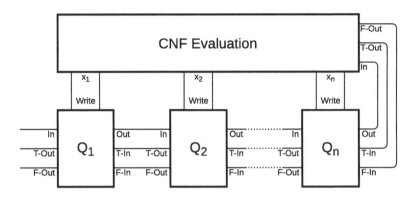

Fig. 1. The high-level structure of the network produced by our reduction. The signal begins at In on Q_1, evaluates the formula, and eventually arrives at T-Out or F-Out on Q_1 depending on its truth value.

Because we are working with gadgets which are symmetric under time-reversal, we need our quantifier gadgets have this symmetry as well. Quantifiers need to be used multiple times, so we will reset them in the way suggested by time-reversal symmetry: the signal needs to backtrack across its entire path through each quantifier gadget before returning to the previous quantifier. We will describe the desired behavior of quantifier gadgets which are symmetric under time-reversal, and later show how to build them using Switches and Reversible Fan-ins.

We specifically discuss universal quantifiers; existential quantifiers require only a minor modification. A universal quantifier gadget Q_i has eight locations, named in cyclic order 'F-Out', 'T-Out', 'In', 'Write-Out', 'Write-In', 'Out', 'T-In', and 'F-In'.[3] The gadget is activated when the signal arrives at In, and the signal proceeds to Out to query the next quantifier; the variable x_i is currently set to False.

Eventually, the signal returns at either T-In or F-In, indicating the truth value of the remainder of the formula with the current variable assignment up to x_i. If it enters at F-In, the universally quantified formula is false, so it passes this along to Q_{i-1} by exiting at F-Out. If it enters at T-In, we need to try the other assignment, which means we need to reset the quantifiers after Q_i by backtracking through them. So the quantifier gadget 'remembers' that it received one True signal, and sends the signal back out T-In. Due to reversibility, the signal eventually returns to Out, at which point it is sent to Write-Out to set

---

[3] Tsukiji and Hagiwara call these '$OUT_{i,FALSE}$', '$OUT_{i,TRUE}$', 'IN_i', 'I_{x_i}', 'O_{x_i}', 'IN_{i+1}', '$OUT_{i+1,TRUE}$', and '$OUT_{i+1,FALSE}$', respectively.

x_i to True. The signal goes through a series of Switches in the CNF evaluation, and then returns at Write-In. Now Q_i sends the signal to Out, this time with the other setting of x_i. Eventually the signal returns again at either T-In or F-In, and it is sent straight to T-Out or F-Out to answer the query from Q_{i-1}.

Once Q_{i-1} has dealt with the response, the signal returns to Q_i at the same one of T-Out or F-Out it exited, at which point everything is reversed, ending with the signal exiting at In with x_i set to False, and Q_i and all later quantifiers in their initial configuration.

Formally, we need a universal quantifier to implement these sequences (and those implied by time-reversal symmetry), corresponding to the first query to Q_{i+1} returning False, the first query returning True but the second returning False, and both queries returning True, respectively:

$$[\text{In} \to \text{Out}, \text{F-In} \to \text{F-Out}]$$

$$[\text{In} \to \text{Out}, \text{T-In} \to \text{T-In}, \text{Out} \to \text{Write-Out}, \text{Write-In} \to \text{Out}, \text{F-In} \to \text{F-Out}]$$

$$[\text{In} \to \text{Out}, \text{T-In} \to \text{T-In}, \text{Out} \to \text{Write-Out}, \text{Write-In} \to \text{Out}, \text{T-In} \to \text{T-Out}]$$

An existential quantifier gadget is constructed by swapping T-In with F-In and T-Out with F-Out on a universal quantifier gadget.

The signal starts at In on Q_1, which queries the truth value of the whole formula. It eventually arrives at either T-Out or F-Out depending on the answer; we make T-Out on Q_1 the target port. If we connect In, T-Out, and F-Out to themselves, then after evaluating the formula the signal will backtrack all the way to the beginning, and repeat this cycle.

The final quantifier Q_k interfaces directly with the CNF evaluation instead of another quantifier. The CNF evaluation maintains the current variable assignment, initially with all variables False. It has a path for each variable x_i which is connected to Write-Out and Write-In on Q_i; traversing this path forwards sets x_i True, and then traversing it backwards returns x_i to False. The CNF evaluation has three additional ports In, T-Out, and F-Out, analogous to those on a quantifier gadget. When the signal arrives at In, it exits at either T-Out or F-Out depending on the truth value of the formula under the current variable assignment. These ports are connected to Out, T-In, and T-Out on Q_k in the same way as other quantifiers.

By the designed behavior of quantifier gadgets and CNF evaluation, the signal arrives at T-Out on Q_1 if and only if the quantified formula is true. We still need to fill in the details: how do we build quantifier gadgets and CNF evaluation and of Switches and Reversible Fan-ins, and how do we handle crossings?

CNF Evaluation. Our CNF evaluation is the same as Tsukiji and Hagiwara's, and is shown in Fig. 2. There is a switch for each literal in ϕ. For each variable x_i, there is a path that goes through all switches corresponding to instances of x_i (or $\neg x_i$) in ϕ, and traversing this path sets x_i to True. When the signal enters In, it checks each clause in series. For each clause, it goes through the switches corresponding to literals in the clause, and emerges in one of two locations depending on whether the clause is satisfied. If it is not satisfied, the signal exits at F-Out, and otherwise it proceeds to the next clause, exiting at T-Out once it has passed every clause. Later, it will return to either T-Out or F-Out and reverse its path back to In; the Reversible Fan-ins remember the path taken and necessarily send it back along the same path.

Quantifier Gadgets. Our quantifier gadgets are essentially the same as Tsukiji and Hagiwara's, the only differences are due to planar arrangement and that we must build their Switch & Turn gadget out of a Switch and a Reversible Fan-in. The universal quantifier gadget is shown in Fig. 3. The existential quantifier gadget is constructed by exchanging the roles of T-In with F-In and T-Out with F-Out, so there is a direct path from T-In to T-Out which crosses some edges linking F-In and F-Out to the other ports. This similarity is sensible: for existential quantifiers if the formula is false we need to try again with the other value, but for universal quantifiers if the formula is true we are allowed to attempt the other required value for the variable.

We must check that the universal quantifier gadget correctly implements the behavior described above. Recall that the signal will first arrive at In. It proceeds to the upper left switch, taking [F-Out → Test] and leaving the Switch in its default state. Then signal takes [a → c] in the upper right Fan-in and leaves at Out. If it now enters F-In, it goes directly to F-Out. If instead it enters T-In, it goes from Test to F-Out on the bottom switch, goes along edge 8 to the Reversible Fan-In (which is after [a → c]), and traverses [c → a]. Then the signal traverses Set → Out on the top switch, and returns to the bottom switch via the Reversible Fan-in, leaving both the Switch and Reversible Fan-in in different states than before. The signal then backtracks from F-Out to Test on the bottom Switch, and exits T-In, where it just entered. Now if the signal enters Out, the Reversible Fan-in sends it back to Test on the top Switch along edge 2. But the top Switch has been activated, so the signal exits the Switch at T-Out and exits the quantifier at Write-Out. It next enters Write-In, at which point it traverses Set → Out on the bottom Switch, and exits Out. Finally, if the signal now enters F-In, it is still sent to F-Out, and if it enters T-In then it goes from Test to T-Out on the bottom switch (which has now been activated) and exits the quantifier at T-Out.

Planarity. Finally, we argue that we can use A/BA Crossovers to avoid crossings in the network produced by this reduction.

Note that each edge in the network is directed, in the sense that the first traversal across the edge is in a predetermined direction which we call *forwards*, and all future traversals alternate direction—we never traverse an edge twice consecutively in the same direction. At any time while running the system, we say an edge is *used* if it has been traversed forwards more recently than backwards. Initially no edges are used, and they are used and unused throughout the process. For two edges x and y which cross, an A/BA Crossover suffices for their crossing

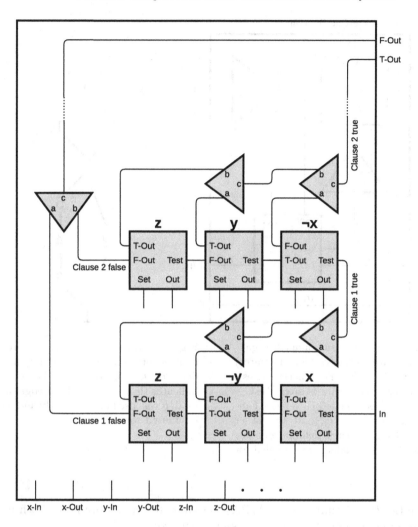

Fig. 2. Our CNF evaluation. Each clause consists of three Switches corresponding to the literals in the clause, with Reversible Fan-ins to merge paths. A variable and its negation differ in the positions of T-Out and F-Out on the corresponding Switch. When the signal enters In, if any literal in the first clause is true it will take the edge labeled "Clause 1 true" and otherwise will take the edge labeled "Clause 1 false". All the exits for false clauses merge and lead to F-Out. If all clauses are true, the signal will traverse them in series and then exit T-Out. For each variable x_i, there is also a path from x_i-In to x_i-Out which goes through Set → Out on the switch corresponding to each instance of x_i or $\neg x_i$.

provided that whenever both x and y are used, always the same edge—say x— was traversed forwards more recently, and also x will be traversed backwards sooner in the future. In this case, we can set x to be the $A \rightarrow a$ tunnel and y

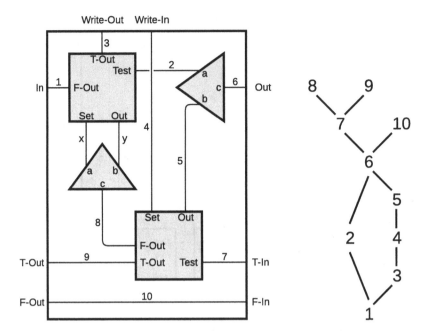

Fig. 3. The universal quantifier gadget built from two Switches (squares) and two Reversible Fan-ins (triangles). The top Switch begins is after [Test → F-Out], the bottom left Reversible Fanin is after [a → c], and the other two gadgets are their default versions. Edges between gadgets are labeled for later use.

Fig. 4. A Hasse diagram of the order relation on used edges in our quantifier gadgets (Fig. 3). That a is above b indicates that whenever both edges are used, a was used more recently and will be unused sooner.

to be the $B \to b$ tunnel of an A/BA Crossover. If x and y are never both used, either orientation of the A/BA Crossover will work.

So we just need to argue that there is a consistent order edges (other than the few we showed can avoid crossings) are used. There are no crossings outside the CNF evaluation and quantifier gadgets, so we need only check those gadgets. For the CNF evaluation, this is straightforward:

- For $i < j$, the path to set x_i is used before the path to set x_j.
- Within the path to set x_i, the edges are used in order.
- All paths for setting variables are used before edges involved in testing the current value.
- The edges involved in testing the current value are used in order. Specifically, there is a partial order on these edges based on when it is possible to traverse one and then another on the way from In to T-Out or F-Out. We arbitrarily extend this partial order to a total order, or equivalently, for two edges which

can't both be used, we arbitrarily choose which is A and which is B in the A/BA Crossover.

For quantifier gadgets, the numbering listed in Fig. 3 works as an order for all edges other than x and y. More generally, a Hasse diagram of the "is sometimes used after" partial order on these edges is shown in Fig. 4, and positioning A/BA Crossovers to respect this order suffices for all crossings between these edges. It is straightforward to verify this partial order by considering the behavior of our quantifier gadgets.

For crossings inside a quantifier gadget which involve edge x or y, we need a different approach: for instance, if edge 2 crosses x, then the signal will sometimes traverse 2, then x, then 2 backwards, which isn't supported by the default A/BA Crossover. When x or y is involved in crossing, we use an A/BA crossover as follows:

- If x crosses y, make x the $B \to b$ tunnel since it is always used first.[4]
- If x or y crosses 1, make 1 the $B \to b$ tunnel since it is always used first.
- If x or y crosses 3, 4, 5, 9, or 10, make x or y the $B \to b$ tunnel since they are always used first.
- If x or y crosses 2, 6, 7, or 8, use an A/BA Crossover after $A \to a$, and make the numbered tunnel $a \to A$. By time-reversal symmetry, the A/BA Crossover after $A \to a$ implements $[a \to A, B \to b, A \to a]$, which corresponds for instance to traversing 2 forwards, x backwards, and then 2 backwards, which is what is needed.

To carefully check that this arrangement of A/BA Crossovers works for the quantifier gadget, we can consider the possible sequences of edge traversals. Using $\cdot^{-1}$ for backwards traversals, these are (generated by time-reversal symmetry from)

- $[1, 2, 6, 10]$
- $[1, 2, 6, 7, 8, x, y, 8^{-1}, 7^{-1}, 6^{-1}, 2^{-1}, 3, 4, 5, 6, 10]$
- $[1, 2, 6, 7, 8, x, y, 8^{-1}, 7^{-1}, 6^{-1}, 2^{-1}, 3, 4, 5, 6, 7, 9]$

which correspond to the sequences the quantifier gadget was built to implement. It is straightforward to verify, for each pair of edges, that an A/BA Crossover as described supports all of the ways that pair of tunnels is used. For instance, the possible sequences for just 2 and x are $[2]$ and $[2, x, 2^{-1}]$, which are $[a \to A]$ and $[a \to A, B \to b, A \to a]$ on the A/BA Crossover involved, and both of these are implemented by an A/BA Crossover after $A \to a$. It suffices to check just the sequences listed, since taking the closure under time-reversal symmetry does not give rise to any new intermediate configurations.

Hence we have the main result of this section:

Theorem 1. *Given a planar network of Switches, Reversible Fan-ins, A/BA Crossovers, and these gadgets after some traversals, a starting location, and*

---

[4] Alternatively, avoid this crossing by adjusting the Reversible Fan-in connecting x and y.

a target location, it is PSPACE-complete to determine whether the signal ever reaches the target location from the starting location. This result holds even when all Switches have any particular cyclic order of ports.

To apply this framework to a specific problem, we simply need to describe the signal and how it moves along wires, and then construct a Switch (with ports in any order), Reversible Fan-in, and A/BA Crossover.

3   Deterministic Constraint Logic

Constraint Logic is a problem about graph orientation reconfiguration introduced by Hearn and Demaine [3, 8] as a tool for proving hardness results. A *constraint graph* is a directed planar graph where each edge has *weight* 1 or 2, which are colored red and blue, respectively.[5] Each vertex in a constraint graph is either an AND vertex, which has two red and one blue edge, or an OR vertex, which has three blue edges. Each vertex is required to have at least 2 total weight in edges pointing towards it. Edges change orientation, while maintaining this constraint. Hearn and Demaine show how to 'tie up' loose edges, allowing the use of degree-2 vertices with any combination of colors, for which the required weight is only 1 (so a single red edge satisfies it).

In this paper, we are specifically interested in *Deterministic Constraint Logic (DCL)*, in which edges flip according to the following deterministic rule. Each time step, an edge flips if it didn't flip in the previous time step and it can flip without violating the in-weight constraint of the vertex it is currently directed towards, or it did flip in the previous time step but no other edge pointing towards the vertex it is now directed towards can flip this time step.

Here are the basic behaviors that result from the deterministic rule:

- Begin with a path of edges of any color, all pointing to the left. If the leftmost edge flips, all the edges in the path will flip, one in each time step.
- If a blue edge flips to point towards an OR vertex, in the next time step the blue edge which was already pointing towards the OR vertex will flip.
- If a blue edge flips to point towards an AND vertex, in the next time step both red edges pointing towards that vertex will flip.
- If both red edges flip to point towards an AND vertex in the same time step, in the next time step the blue edge will flip.
- If one red edge but not the other flips to point towards an AND vertex, in the next time step the same red edge will flip again.

The decision problem in Deterministic Constraint Logic is whether some specified edge will eventually flip, given a constraint graph and the set of edges that are considered to have flipped in time step 0.

---

[5] In grayscale, blue edges are darker than red edges. Figures also draw blue edges thicker than red edges.

3.1 Issue with Existing Proof

Hearn and Demaine's proof of PSPACE-hardness for Deterministic Constraint Logic [8] has a subtle issue. When their universal quantifier receives a 'satisfied in' signal, it records this fact, much like our universal quantifier gadget. When it receives a second 'satisfied in' signal (assuming the signal did not enter 'try out' in between), it erases the record of the first one; this is by design, to reset the gadget for the next variable assignment.

The existential quantifier tries assigning its variable False, then True, and then False again, and passes every 'satisfied in' signal it gets to 'satisfied out' to inform the previous quantifier. If the existential quantifier is satisfied when its variable is False but not True, it sends two such signals instead of one. This is the problem: if the previous quantifier is universal, the second signal cancels the first one, and that quantifier behaves as though there was no signal. The simplest formula for which the reduction fails is $\forall x \exists y : \neg y$. Modifying the existential quantifier to test each assignment exactly once does not fix the problem, because then if the quantifier is satisfied by both values for its variable, it sends two signals to the previous quantifier. In particular, $\forall x \exists y : y \vee \neg y$ would fail.

The proof may be fixable by modifying the existential quantifier gadget to ensure it only ever sends one signal; it would likely be about as complicated as the universal quantifier. The approach our framework takes is different: it adds an additional query return line, so instead of just 'satisfied in' we have both T-in and F-in, and quantifier gadgets are guaranteed to receive exactly one response for each query.

3.2 PSPACE-Hardness

Our PSPACE-hardness proof for Deterministic Constraint Logic uses many of the same elements as Hearn and Demaine's. The signal is a flipping edge, which propagates along paths in the direction opposite the orientation of the edges in the path. Like Hearn and Demaine, our gadgets will sometimes contain 'bouncing' edges which flip in a periodic way, and we ensure the length of each path through a gadget is a multiple of this period—for us, the period is 2, though Hearn and Demaine used a period of 4. The ports of our gadgets are always blue edges, which are connected by joining them with a degree-2 vertex. The target edge is the edge corresponding to the target port, and it flips if and only if the signal reaches the target port.

While DCL itself is symmetric under time reversal, it is possible to build a DCL gadget which is not, by including periodically bouncing edges calibrated such that the signal enters out of phase with when it exits. Some of Hearn and Demaine's gadgets [8] behave this way. However, all of our gadgets will be symmetric under time reversal in all of their relevant behavior, as is required for the framework we are using.

We simply need to build valid Switch, Reversible Fan-in, and A/BA Crossover gadgets. A Reversible Fan-in is simply an OR vertex, which always takes 2 time steps to traverse. We use Hearn and Demaine's A/BA crossover, which we reproduce in Fig. 5. This A/BA crossover always takes an even number of time steps to traverse, and contains bouncing edges with period 2.

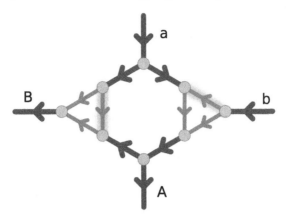

Fig. 5. An A/BA Crossover for Deterministic Constraint Logic, from Hearn and Demaine [8]. Glowing auras indicate edges that flip every time step—the state shown is the state immediately before the signal enters the gadget, so that when the signal enters, the blue edge at the entered port and all glowing edges simultaneously flip from the shown configuration.

Our Switch gadget is a bit more complicated, and is shown in Fig. 6. If the signal arrives at Set, it exits at Out and reflects the configuration by flipping the bottom four edges and setting the left red edge bouncing instead of the right red edge. If the signal arrives at Test, at exists either F-Out or T-Out based on which red edge is currently bouncing, and sets one of the top red edges bouncing. Every traversal through this gadget takes four time steps.

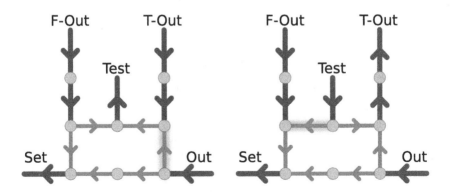

Fig. 6. A Switch for Deterministic Constraint Logic. Left: the initial configuration. Right: the configuration after the traversal Test → T-Out.

4 Billiard Balls

Our final application is the billiard ball model, which was introduced by Fredkin and Toffoli [7] and is one of the best known reversible models of computation. In the billiard ball model, there are circular *balls* colliding elastically with each other and with fixed *mirrors*. For simplicity, all balls have the same size and mass, and will only move at a single nonzero speed. This model is based on classical physics, and in fact exactly matches the classical kinetic theory of perfect gasses.

The decision problem we consider is whether a ball ever reaches a particular position, given a configuration of mirrors and initial positions and velocities of balls. Fredkin and Toffoli [7] proved that this model can perform arbitrary computation by showing how to build and string together Fredkin gates; it follows that the decision problem is PSPACE-complete.

We present a new proof of PSPACE-hardness using our framework. The primary advantage this proof has over Fredkin and Toffoli's is that only a constant number—in particular, two—of balls will be moving at any time, and the two moving balls will always be in close proximity. This means there are fewer details to work out relating to issues like timing; Fredkin and Toffoli had to ensure that signals from disparate parts of the construction arrive at a logic gate simultaneously.

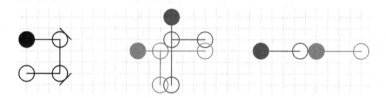

Fig. 7. The billiard ball model. Filled circles depict initial positions of balls, and empty circles depict intermediate or final positions. Diagonal lines are mirrors, and horizontal or vertical lines are paths taken by balls. Left: a ball bounces off of mirrors. Middle: two moving balls collide. If only one ball arrives, it goes straight through, but if both balls arrive simultaneously, they bounce off each other. Right: A moving blue ball collides with a stationary red ball, transferring its momentum and leaving the blue ball not grid-aligned. (Color figure online)

The balls in our construction all have a radius of $\frac{1}{\sqrt{2}}$, and will move only horizontally or vertically. The types of collisions that will occur are shown in Fig. 7. One can think of a head-on collision with a stationary ball as moving the stationary ball backwards by the ball diameter, and teleporting the moving ball forwards by the same amount.

The signal will be represented by two balls moving along parallel paths $2\sqrt{2}$ (i.e. twice the diameter) apart. This signal is easy to route, as demonstrated by Fig. 8. We will always have the two balls aligned with each other when the signal enters a gadget. Full crossovers, and in particular A/BA crossovers, are trivial:

simply have two paths the signal might take cross each other. For simplicity, our diagrams show the paths separated by 3 units, rather than the actual distance $2\sqrt{2} \approx 2.8$.

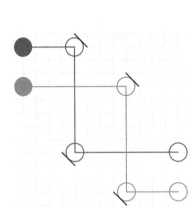

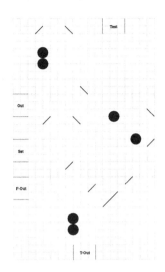

Fig. 8. A signal consisting of two billiard balls is sent from the top left to the bottom right. The paths of the two balls have the same length.

Fig. 9. The Switch for the billiard ball model. Each port is marked with a pair of green lines, along which the two balls of the signal may enter or exit. (Color figure online)

All that remains is constructing the Switch and Reversible Fan-In. Our Switch is shown in its initial state Fig. 9. The key idea is that stationary balls inside the gadget might (depending on the state) be in the way of one of the balls in the signal entering at Test, effectively making that ball arrive slightly earlier. This change in timing affects whether that ball collides with the other ball in the signal, resulting in two possible places for the signal to end up.

The three relevant traversals are shown in Fig. 10. Since the model has time-reversal symmetry, any gadget built in it also has time-reversal symmetry, so we only need to check that the sequences listed in Table 1 are implemented correctly.

Finally, our Reversible Fan-in is shown in Fig. 11. It works in a very similar way to Switch, but in reverse, and essentially combining the Set traversal with one of the Test traversals. If the signal enters at a, the balls collide and arrive at c. If the signal enters at b, the signal balls do not collide, and arrive at c with a slightly different timing. To correct the timing, we have the signal entering at b first remove two balls from the path near c.

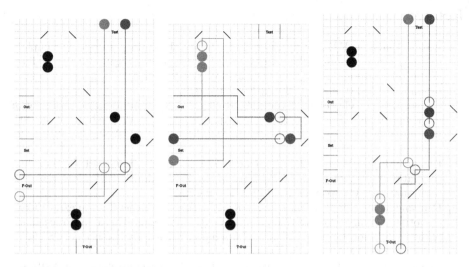

Fig. 10. The ways a signal moves through the switch. Left: in the initial state, the signal bounces from Test to F-Out. The two balls don't collide where there paths cross. Middle: the blue ball hits the green, which hits the purple, leaving two balls in the path of the Test port. The red ball's path is extended north so that two balls exit at Out simultaneously; the two red balls in its path save the same amount of time as the two balls in the blue ball's path. Right: with the purple and green balls in the way of the signal entering Test, the green ball arrives soon enough to collide with the red ball, resulting in the signal exiting at F-Out. The two additional red balls are to help synchronize the exit signal. (Color figure online)

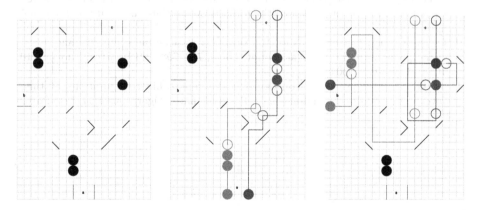

Fig. 11. The Reversible Fan-in for the billiard ball model. Left: the gadget in its initial state. Middle: the signal enters at a. The signal balls ricochet off each other, and then exit at c. They each collide with two stationary balls, so the balls exiting c get there at the same time. Right: The signal enters at b. The blue ball knocks the green ball, which knocks the purple ball, clearing the vertical path to c. The red ball and the purple ball then exit at c without colliding. The red zigzag to the north and two additional red balls are to make the timing correct. (Color figure online)

References

1. Ani, J., Demaine, E.D., Hendrickson, D.H., Lynch, J.: Trains, games, and complexity: 0/1/2-player motion planning through input/output gadgets. In: Proceedings of the 16th International Conference and Workshops on Algorithms and Computation (WALCOM 2022) (2022). arXiv:2005.03192
2. Demaine, E.D., Grosof, I., Lynch, J., Rudoy, M.: Computational complexity of motion planning of a robot through simple gadgets. In: Proceedings of the 9th International Conference on Fun with Algorithms (FUN 2018), pp. 18:1–18:21 (2018)
3. Demaine, E.D., Hearn, R.A.: Constraint logic: a uniform framework for modeling computation as games. In: Proceedings of the 23rd Annual IEEE Conference on Computational Complexity, pp. 149–162, June 2008
4. Demaine, E.D., Hendrickson, D.H., Lynch, J.: Toward a general complexity theory of motion planning: characterizing which gadgets make games hard. In: Proceedings of the 11th Innovations in Theoretical Computer Science Conference (ITCS 2020), pp. 62:1–62:42 (2020)
5. Demaine, E.D., Lynch, J., Mirano, G.J., Tyagi, N.: Energy-efficient algorithms. In: Proceedings of the 7th Annual ACM Conference on Innovations in Theoretical Computer Science (ITCS 2016), Cambridge, Massachusetts, pp. 321–332, 14–16 January 2016
6. Frank, M.P.: Fundamental physics of reversible computing-an introduction. Technical report, Sandia National Lab. (SNL-NM), Albuquerque, NM, USA (2020)
7. Fredkin, E., Toffoli, T.: Conservative logic. Int. J. Theor. Phys. **21**(3), 219–253 (1982)
8. Hearn, R.A., Demaine, E.D.: Games, Puzzles, and Computation. CRC Press, Boca Raton (2009)
9. Hendrickson, D.: Gadgets and Uizmos: a formal model of simulation in the gadget framework for motion planning. Ph.D. thesis, Massachusetts Institute of Technology (2021)
10. Özdemir, Ş.K., Rotter, S., Nori, F., Yang, L.: Parity-time symmetry and exceptional points in photonics. Nat. Mater. **18**(8), 783–798 (2019). https://doi.org/10.1038/s41563-019-0304-9
11. Tsukiji, T., Hagiwara, T.: Recognizing the repeatable configurations of time-reversible generalized Langton's ant is PSPACE-hard. Algorithms **4**(1), 1–15 (2011)

From Finite Automata to Fractal Automata – The Power of Recursion

Benedek Nagy[✉]

Department of Mathematics, Faculty of Arts and Sciences,
Eastern Mediterranean University, Famagusta, North Cyprus, Mersin-10, Turkey
nbenedek.inf@gmail.com

Abstract. In procedural programming languages the order of executing the statements may follow a regular pattern, including sequence of statements, conditional and branching statements and loops. On the other hand, regular languages can be represented by finite state acceptors (finite automata), by regular expressions and by (special form of) railroad diagrams (syntax diagrams) allowing alternatives, option, concatenation and iteration. Context-free languages can also be described by (the general form of) railroad diagrams allowing also recursion. Based on the analogy of finite automata and railroad diagrams, special infinite state automata, namely the fractal automata are established to characterize the class of context-free languages. A transformation between the pushdown automata and fractal automata is also shown. The proposed model gives some new insight and a new view of context-free languages.

Keywords: railroad diagrams · context-free languages · infinite state automata · fractals · recursion

1   Introduction

In (sequential) algorithms and in computer programming the steps/instructions are executed one after the other. There are various types of classical procedural programming languages and programs including straight-line programs (e.g., to compute the solution of an equation), branching programs, and programs with loops (cycles) [13]. These are frequently used programming techniques. Another, we may say, more advanced technique is by recursion. In a usual high-level programming language, the programmer has the right to choose among various possibilities that could give equivalent result but usually with various complexities (including time and space complexities as well as the length of the code).

There are various well-known ways developed to describe the syntax of programming languages, and in fact, these methods including Backus-Naur form (BNF), hybrid notation, extended BNF and also railroad diagrams, are equivalent to context-free grammars (and behind the scene the computers usually use grammars and compilers based on them) [3, 14].

© The Author(s), under exclusive license to Springer Nature Switzerland AG 2022
J. Durand-Lose and G. Vaszil (Eds.): MCU 2022, LNCS 13419, pp. 109–125, 2022.
https://doi.org/10.1007/978-3-031-13502-6_8

On the other hand, graphical representations of various theoretical notions are useful for several reasons. First, they help to capture the ideas and establish connections of various concepts. Second, if they are defined in mathematical precision, then they can also be used to prove results in a visual, easily understandable way. Further, graphical representations can be used in various ways in teaching, in research, etc.

In this paper, we deal with some basic concepts of (theoretical) computer science, like, regular and context-free languages, finite and pushdown automata. They are well-known from the middle of the last century. Regular languages are used in lexical analysis, in text processing, etc. Their wide-spread use is based on the fact that they have very nice properties, finite state acceptors accept them and it is easy to deal with them in a visual way. However, there are several places where regular languages are not enough, more complex languages, e.g., context-free languages are needed. We analyze the context-free languages from diagrammatic representations point of view, and investigate the fractal automata as a special infinite-state automata model (this model was already coined up in [9,10]).

The structure of the paper is as follows. In the next sections we recall formally the basic definitions that are needed to understand the paper, then we present the case of regular languages, as an analogy, by showing (visual graph) transformations from one visual representation to the other one and vice versa. In Sect. 4, we present our main results on context-free languages. Starting from the well-known description of context-free languages by railroad diagrams (syntax diagrams), by using the same type of transformation as earlier we arrive to the concept of fractal automata. In Sect. 5 some properties of this new automata model are described and they are compared to pushdown automata. The paper is closed by some concluding remarks.

2   Basic Definitions

Here we recall some necessary concepts about the classes of regular and context-free languages and also fix our notations [4–6,11,12].

For a finite non-empty set of symbols Σ, called an alphabet, Σ^* denotes the set of all strings (also called words) over Σ including the empty string ε. The length a word is the number of its symbols (with multiplicities), consequently the length of ε is 0. Further, Σ^k denotes the set of all words with length k from Σ^* for any natural number k. A *language* over Σ is any subset of Σ^*. We denote the size of a set F by $|F|$ and its powerset by 2^F.

A *regular expression* describes a language over an alphabet Σ and it is defined inductively as follows:

- $\emptyset$, ε, and a, for a in Σ, are regular expressions referring to the empty language $\{\}$, the unit language $\{\varepsilon\}$ and to the singleton language $\{a\}$, respectively.
- If r and t are regular expressions and L_r and L_t are the languages described by them, respectively, then
  - $(r + t)$ is also a regular expression and it describes the language $L_r \cup L_t$;

- $(r \cdot t)$ is also a regular expression, it describes the language $L_r \cdot L_t$ and
- r^* is also a regular expression describing the language L_r^*.

In practice the sign $\cdot$ is usually omitted, and some of the brackets can also be omitted based on some equivalences (e.g., associativity laws) and a widely used precedence relation among the operations. The operations concatenation $\cdot$, union $+$ and Kleene-star iteration * are called regular operations (for languages). In some descriptions, the Kleene-plus $^+$ abbreviating $r^+ = r \cdot r^*$ can also be used.

As an analogy, one may think the Σ as the set of possible statements in a programming language. Then concatenation refers to execute another code after the first code. The union refers to conditional statements, i.e., with a then and an else branch. The Kleene closures describe loops, iterative executions of the statements in the body. This analogy could be helpful to see a relation between programs and regular expressions, but it is only an analogy, as our computer programs are deterministic, but the determinism is not really connected to regular expressions (as they describe all the possibilities).

A language L is regular if there exists a regular expression describing L.

A *(nondeterministic) finite automaton* (fa) is a quintuple $M = (Q, \Sigma, \delta, s, F)$, where Q is a finite, non-empty set of states, Σ is an input alphabet, $s \in Q$ is the initial state, $F \subseteq Q$ is the set of accepting (also called final) states, and δ is the transition function that maps $Q \times (\Sigma \cup \{\varepsilon\})$ into 2^Q.

Finite automata are usually represented in a graphical way. In the graph of an automaton the states are the vertices drawn by circles (the name of the state can be included inside the circle). The transitions are drawn as directed edges of the graph. These edges are labeled: an arrow from state p to state q labeled by a represents the transition $q \in \delta(p, a)$ (where $p, q \in Q, a \in \Sigma \cup \{\varepsilon\}$). In this way the input alphabet is implicitly given by labels of the edges. Further, the initial state is marked by an in-arrow (without label), while each accepting state is marked by an out-arrow (without label).

A computation by the automaton M on input w is starting from the state s, and each step is done according to the transition function. Actually (using the graphical representation of the automaton), it is a walk of the graph of the automaton M, starting from the initial state s such that the labels of edges of the walk gives w, where a walk is an alternating sequence of vertices and edges such that every edge (p, q) of the walk connects the states p and q in the given order, where p is the element of the sequence preceding (p, q) and q is the element following that edge. If such a walk ends in an accepting state, then this is an accepting computation of the automaton. A word is accepted by the fa M if there is (at least one) accepting computation/walk for it. The language *accepted* by fa M is $L(M) = \{w \in \Sigma^* \mid$ there is an accepting computation for w in $M\}$.

It is well-known (by the Kleene-theorem) that the class of finite automata accepts exactly the class of the regular languages.

Context-free languages are defined by context-free grammars [2]: formally a *context-free grammar* is a quadruple $G = (N, \Sigma, S, D)$, where N and Σ are two disjoint alphabets, namely the nonterminal and terminal alphabets; $S \in N$ is the startsymbol (or sentence symbol) and D is a finite set of productions (derivation rules), where a production is a pair written in the form $A \rightarrow u$ with $A \in N$, $u \in (N \cup \Sigma)^*$. The derivation starts with the startsymbol S. We say that u can directly be derived from v, $v \Rightarrow u$, if $v = xAy$, $u = xzy$ (with some $x, y, z \in (N \cup \Sigma)^*$ and $A \in N$) and $A \rightarrow z \in D$. The reflexive and transitive closure of the direct derivation gives the derivation relation (denoted by $\Rightarrow^*$). Further the *generated* language of grammar G contains every terminal word that can be derived in G, i.e., $L(G) = \{w \in \Sigma^* \mid S \Rightarrow^* w\}$. A language is context-free if there is a context-free grammar that generates it.

The class of context-free languages is one of the main classes of the Chomsky hierarchy. It is well-known that the class of context-free languages properly includes the class of regular languages. Moreover, context-free languages play very important role in compiler technologies for programming languages. Since context-free languages and programming languages are related to each other, starting from the 1950's till the beginning of 1970's there were various techniques and technologies that developed to represent (describe) context-free (and programming) languages. Such technologies are the Backus-Naur form (shortly BNF, based on the work of J. Backus at IBM describing the syntax of the programming language Algol 58 [1] and P. Naur describing Algol 60), the Cobol-type description (used to describe the programming languages Cobol and PL/1), the hybrid notation (having a mixture of the previous descriptions, it was frequently used for syntactical descriptions and definitions in 1990's), the extended BNF (that form is very similar to the context-free grammars) and a visual representation technique, the railroad diagrams (used in the description of the Pascal language [15]). Railroad diagrams are more readily understood by most people. For the sake of simplicity (and by the lack of space) here we recall only the concept of the latter ones, the railroad diagrams. They are also called syntax diagrams (syntax graphs or flow charts).

Railroad diagrams (rd) can be defined iteratively as follows (see also Fig. 1). The basic elements are the arrows and the terminals and nonterminals (as vertices):

- nothing (empty language), it is not used, since in practice only languages containing words are described, every other diagram has exactly one starting arrow and finishing arrow (these arrows may also be called entry point and end point; and the diagram is between them);
- an arrow (representing the empty word ε) (being the starting and finishing arrow at the same time),
- a terminal is an ellipse (or a circle), and the terminal itself is written inside the ellipse,
- a nonterminal is represented by a (rectangular) box, the name of the nonterminal is written inside the box.

Using these bases of the iteration the following iteration steps can be used:

- concatenation: two diagrams are joined one after the other by having the finishing arrow of the first one be the starting arrow of the second one (it is similar to the serial wiring),

- alternatives: two or more diagrams can be joined together (in the same way as parallel wiring): having a common entry point and having a common end point,
- option: it is actually alternatives of a diagram and an arrow (representing ε),
- iteration: a diagram having an additional arrow from its end point to its entry point.

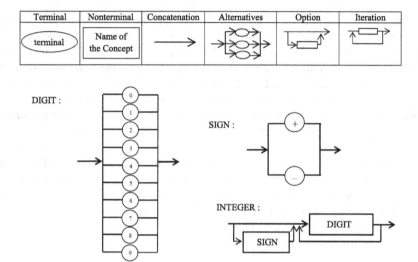

Fig. 1. The parts of the railroad diagrams and an example (INTEGER). (Note that in a programming language, it is always optional to use the sign + for an integer.)

Actually, each nonterminal (there is a finite number of them) is defined by a railroad diagram. Each diagram is understood to define a set of full paths from its entry point (starting arrow) to its end point (finishing arrow). When a nonterminal is reached in a path, then a word described by the diagram defining that nonterminal must be substituted there. In this way, recursion can be used, e.g., using the nonterminal itself in the description. There is a main diagram (for the concept itself that we want to describe by our language), it defines the *described* language.

Pictorially these diagrams look like railroad maps and thus the name railroad diagrams matches for them. More generally, one may consider a railroad diagram as the (directed) rail network between 2 cities (from the entry/start city to the end city), where there are various junctions, where some rail lines are merged and/or branching. The terminals and nonterminals may be seen as stations, but only the terminals represent 'normal' stations. At a nonterminal a "subtravel" starts on the other diagram, and we may continue our travel only when this subtravel is finished. By reading all the 'normal' stations during our travel, we got the description of our journey, a word of the specified language.

It can be proven in a constructive way that exactly the context-free languages can be described by railroad diagrams. Thus a context-free grammar can be represented by a finite set of railroad diagrams.

Notice that most of the used operations are highly related to the regular operations. The concatenation is the same in regular expressions and in railroad diagrams, they both represent concatenation of languages. The alternatives in railroad diagrams represent nondeterministic choices. They have the same role as union has at languages/regular expressions. Option refers for a special union, where one of the languages is the (unit)language $\{\varepsilon\}$. The iteration is equivalent to the positive Kleene closure, i.e., the Kleene-plus. By a combination of option and iteration one can also define a structure that is equivalent to the Kleene-star operation (for languages/regular expressions). It can also be easily proven that the same class of languages can be described if instead of the original iteration (equivalent to Kleene-plus) we use the following alternative form of the iteration (that is equivalent to Kleene-star): there is an arrow (direct connection) from the entry point to the end point of the diagram and additionally, from the end point there is the starting arrow of the original diagram and its finishing arrow goes to the entry point of the new diagram. Thus, the iterations equivalent to r^* can also be drawn (see Fig. 2) and used in railroad diagrams (see also [8], where regular languages in union-normal form [7] were described).

Fig. 2. The alternative form of iteration in railroad diagrams equivalent to Kleene-star.

Railroad diagrams are used to describe the syntax of the Pascal programming language, therefore they are also called syntax diagrams. Their visuality and thus simplicity was one of the main reasons of the widespread use of the programming language Pascal. Till the present date, it (or one of its modern versions, e.g., TurboPascal) is one of the first programming languages that pupils can learn in various schools and also it is the base of one of the most usual pseudo-code descriptions of various algorithms in universities and (text)books.

While context-free grammars are widely used generating devices for context-free languages, the railroad diagrams are used to analyze the described context-free languages. We also recall a third way to define context-free languages, they can be accepted by a well-known type of automata.

Pushdown automata are automata equipped with an auxiliary pushdown storage. Formally, a *pushdown automaton* (pda) is a septuple $P = (Q, \Sigma, \Gamma, \delta, s, B, F)$, where Q, Σ, s and F are the same as at the finite automata; Γ is the (finite, nonempty) stack alphabet, $B \notin \Gamma$ is the non-erasable bottom marker that is initially in the stack, δ is the transition function that maps $Q \times \Gamma \times (\Sigma \cup \{\varepsilon\})$ into the finite subsets of $2^{Q \times \Gamma^*}$ and $Q \times \{B\} \times (\Sigma \cup \{\varepsilon\})$ into the finite subsets of $2^{Q \times (B \cdot \Gamma^*)}$.

A computation by the automaton P on input w is starting from the state s with the stack containing only the symbol B, and each step is done according to the transition function. A computation on input w is an accepting computation if the whole input is processed and the pda P reaches an accepting state in the end. The language *accepted* by pda P is the set of strings
$L(P) = \{w \in \Sigma^* \mid$ there is an accepting computation for w in $P\}$.

There is another way to define the accepted language and it is done by empty stack: the input $w \in \Sigma^*$ is accepted, if there is a computation such that the input is fully processed and the stack is empty (contains only the bottom marker B). It is also usual to define the accepted language of pushdown automata by final state and empty stack (such that accepting computations end in a final state with empty stack).

It is well-known in formal language theory that the expressive power of context-free grammars and the (nondeterministic) pushdown automata coincide (even if the latter, more restricted version of pda is used).

In this paper, we consider regular and context-free languages from a diagrammatic point of view and based on some analogies we investigate the fractal automata for context-free languages.

3   Regular Languages

There is a way to represent regular expressions by special railroad diagrams. As it is mentioned, for instance, in [8], the described language is regular if it can be described by a railroad diagram without nonterminals.

Now, we have two types of visual descriptions of the regular languages (see Fig. 3). Let us see what is the relation between them.

First, let us observe that in finite automata the terminals are written on transitions (labels of the edges) and we have got the recognized/accepted word by reading these labels in an accepting walk. In the railroad diagrams the circles are referring for terminals, and thus a word of the described language is obtained by reading these labels of a full path. Actually, a railroad diagram can be seen as a kind of dual graph of an automaton. The (labeled) edges of the automaton play the role of labeled nodes, while instead of the states of the automaton in the railroad diagram there are some arrows and junctions, i.e., edges instead of the vertices of the graph of the automaton. This is a kind of duality relation between these concepts (analogously to state-transition Petri nets, where the dual is obtained by switching the role of places and transitions).

In the following part of this section we show an algorithm, Algorithm 1, that transfers a railroad diagram without nonterminals to a finite automaton that corresponds to the same regular language.

Visual representations of the transformation from railroad diagrams to finite automata, i.e., the work of Algorithm 1 can be seen, for our previous example, as it is shown in Fig. 4. (Note that using the algorithm the number of states could be much larger than in the automaton shown in the figure and usually the resulting automaton contains several ε-transitions.)

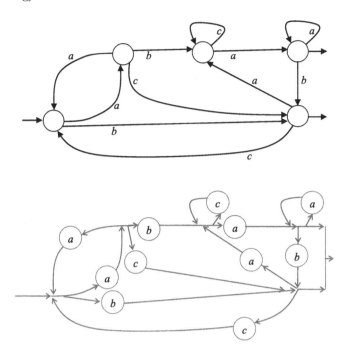

Fig. 3. Representations of a regular language: a finite automaton (up) and a railroad diagram (down).

Algorithm 1.

Input: a railroad diagram.

1. Let a state (a circle) be assigned to each junction.

2. Let also be a state between two terminals when they are directly connected by an arrow (without having any junctions between them).

3. Further let the initial state be given at the starting arrow of the diagram.

4. Let there be only one final state, and let it be placed on the finishing arrow of the diagram.

5. Finally, if there is a terminal a in the railroad from state p to state q, then let the transition $q \in d(p, a)$ be given in the automaton, and, if there is not any terminal at the railroad connecting state p to state q, then let $q \in d(p, \varepsilon)$ be in the automaton.

We note here that the obtained automaton is usually not optimal in any sense, it can often be simplified (by merging some states etc.), but it is not a task of this paper to detail these options.

We show also that a related algorithm, Algorithm 2, can transform any finite automaton to a syntax diagram that describes the same language.

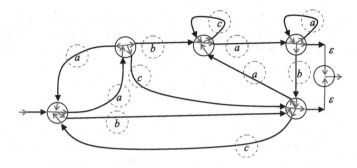

Fig. 4. An example for transforming a railroad diagram without nonterminals to a finite automaton and/or vice-versa.

Algorithm 2.

Input: a finite automaton.

1. The incoming arrow into the initial state without any label is set to the starting arrow of the diagram.

2. The outgoing arrows from the final/accepting states is joined together to have only one outgoing arrow that will be the finishing arrow of the diagram (in a similar way every finite automaton can be transformed to an equivalent automaton having only one accepting state, i.e., by adding a new accepting state with ε-transitions from the old accepting states).

3. We draw arrows (parts of the arrows) inside the state circles as follows: each incoming arrow at a state is gathered in a junction and then each outgoing arrows are drawn from another junction that follows the previous gathering junction, in this way allowing to continue the path with any outgoing arrow after any incoming arrow; then the states of the automaton (the circles of the graph) are deleted (only the new arrows and junctions inside them are kept).

4. Further each label of the arrows that differ from ε must be circled to form a terminal (station) breaking the labeled arrow to two parts. (The labels ε are deleted, only their arrows are kept.)

The resulting graph is the railroad diagram of the regular language that the original finite automaton accepts.

Now, in the next section, we show how we can deal with non-terminals in our transformation.

4   The Context-Free Case

If one considers a railroad diagram representing the statements of a program (with our analogy), then the nonterminals refer to subprograms, i.e., to function calls.

Analogously to the regular case, let us start from the syntax diagrams of a context-free grammar, i.e., the description of a context-free language by a (set of) railroad diagram(s).

The syntax diagrams describing regular languages were analyzed in [8], where it is shown that if the railroad maps can be ordered in such a way that in every diagram only those nonterminals can be used that were already defined (not allowing to use the nonterminal being currently defined by this railroad), then the described language is regular. This condition is exactly the necessary and sufficient condition to exclude arbitrary deep recursions. Thus, the described language is regular if and only if its description is possible by using only finite recursions. Actually, if this condition is fulfilled, then by drawing the railroad diagram of the nonterminals instead of their boxes, the language is described by a railroad diagram without nonterminals, and thus it is regular.

Now let us assume that our language is non-regular and thus, we have (a possible infinite) recursion.

Let a finite set of rail-road diagrams be given that defines a context-free language. Now, let us make a similar transformation as we did in the regular case from special syntax diagrams to finite automata. We write the algorithm in a formal way (see Algorithm 3).

Algorithm 3.
Input: a finite set of rail-road diagrams.
1. Let the middle point of the start arrow of the main diagram be chosen to place the initial state.
2. Let the middle point of the finishing arrow of the main diagram be chosen to place the final state.
3. Let every junction of the main diagram be a state of the automaton.
4. Let every midpoint of an arrow connecting two terminals directly without having any junctions between them, be a state of the automaton.
5. Apply steps 1–4 to the other elements of the set of railroad diagrams.
6. Let the label of a transition (an arrow from a state to a state) be the terminal that can be found between the two connected states if any, if there is not any terminal between two states, then let the empty word ε the label of that transition.
7. Substitute the diagrams obtained instead of the nonterminals appear (in the main diagram) iteratively. In a substitution by putting a subdiagram, the arrow that was going to the substituted nonterminal, is replaced by an arrow that is, at the same time, the starting arrow of the subdiagram. And the finishing arrow of the subdiagram is joined to the arrow which was starting from the substituted nonterminal.

We should note that Algorithm 3 is an infinite procedure, and therefore depending on the used terminology, it may not be counted as an algorithm if the finiteness of the execution is required. On the other hand, apart from this, it fulfills all the usual requirements of the algorithms. In one usual terminology all Turing machines are counted as algorithms and their computations as executions of these algorithms even if some of those computations are infinitely long (this concept of algorithm is connected to the recursively enumerable class of languages). In another terminology, only those Turing machines are counted as algorithms which halts on any input (this concept of algorithm is connected to the class of recursive languages). The former concept of the algorithm is more general than the latter one and we used Algorithm 3 according to this former category. However, using the more restricted terminology, Algorithm 3 can be called a procedure, but not an algorithm.

The automaton (theoretically) obtained by Algorithm 3 is a fractal automaton for the given context-free language. Since the recursion can be arbitrarily deep in these diagrams, this process results an infinite – but somehow regularly obtained, self-similar – system. If the nonterminal of a railroad diagram does not appear in the main diagram by the iterative use of step 7, then that diagram does not play any role in the concept defined by the main diagram.

Observe that the resulting automaton is very similar to finite automata but has an infinite number of states. The transformation from a set of railroad diagrams may be done, first by the construction of a finite automaton (allowing nonterminals) for each diagram, and then these automata are used to substitute instead of the nonterminals.

To have a formal definition and description of the fractal automata, we first introduce an addressing scheme to handle the infinite number of states.

Let Q denote the set of states of a fractal automaton, we use the alphabet Λ to give a unique address (label) for each state.

Definition 1 (Labeling). *The label alphabet Λ contains two disjoint finite sets $\Lambda = \Lambda_a \cup \Lambda_n$, where Λ_n refers for the names of the states (can be imagined as identifying the location, the state itself inside a railroad diagram based automaton obtained by steps 1–6 of Algorithm 3) and Λ_a refers for the symbols that are used to address the nonterminals appearing in the railroad diagrams, i.e., this part of the address of the state refers to show where the current railroad diagram is embedded in the recursion. In every railroad diagram describing our language we identify each occurrence of a nonterminal by a unique element of the set Λ_a. Every state $q \in Q$ can be identified by its label $u \cdot p$ from the set $\Lambda_a^* \Lambda_n$ ($u \in \Lambda_a^*, p \in \Lambda_n$). The states for which their address $u = \varepsilon$ are the states that are located in the original main railroad diagram. Each state r of a railroad diagram based automaton ($r \in \Lambda_n$) that corresponds to the railroad diagram α being substituted to a nonterminal A of a rail road diagram β will get address $u \cdot J \cdot r$, where $u \in \Lambda_a^*$ is used to address the states that are located in railroad diagram β and $J \in \Lambda_a$ is the label of the substituted nonterminal A in α.*

As the states with $u = \varepsilon$ are located in the original main railroad diagram, in the case of a regular language, having only one railroad diagram, these addresses are not used, consequently the result is a finite automaton. When a railroad diagram is directly put into the main railroad diagram (by substituting a nonterminal of the original main railroad diagram), then every of its states is addressed by the address symbol of that nonterminal of the main railroad diagram.

To describe the transition function and the set of states more formally, let Λ_A be the set of states inside the railroad diagram describing/defining nonterminal A, such that $\Lambda_A \cap \Lambda_B = \emptyset$ if $A \neq B$ (where A and B are arbitrary nonterminals of the railroad diagrams). Let s and f be the initial and the accepting state inside the main railroad diagram. Then Λ_n is the set of states inside all railroad diagrams, i.e., $\Lambda_n = \bigcup_{A \in N} \Lambda_A$ where N is the set of nonterminals that used to describe the language by railroad diagrams. We can restrict the definition to states that can be reached from the initial state s, and thus we can define the set of states in an iterative way, as follows:

Definition 2 (Set of states). *Let*

- *$Q_0 = \Lambda_A \cup \{J \mid J \in \Lambda_a$ is an index of a nonterminal in the automaton obtained from the main diagram$\}$, where A is the nonterminal referring for the main railroad diagram, thus Q_0 already includes s and f.*
- *Starting from the set Q_i the set Q_{i+1} is obtained: $Q_{i+1} = (Q_i \cap \Lambda_a^* \Lambda_n) \cup \{uJp \mid u \in \Lambda_a^i, J \in \Lambda_a, p \in \Lambda_A, uJ \in Q_i$ and J is an identifier of the nonterminal $A\} \cup \{uJK \mid u \in \Lambda_a^i, J \in \Lambda_a, uJ \in Q_i, K \in \Lambda_a$ such that J is an identifier of the nonterminal A and K is an identifier of a nonterminal in the railroad based automaton of nonterminal $A\}$, where Λ_a^i refers for the words of Λ_a^* with length i. Thus Q_{i+1} allows us to go one step deeper in the recursion chain than Q_i allows, and it is done by substituting the automata obtained from the railroad diagrams instead of each current nonterminal, respectively.*

With this infinite process, in the limit one may obtain the infinite set of states $Q = \lim_{i \to \infty} Q_i$.

From the process given above it is clear that Q_i contains states and nonterminals on level i of the recursion. On the other hand, $Q_i \cap \Lambda_a^* \Lambda_n \subset Q_{i+1} \cap \Lambda_a^* \Lambda_n$, the set of states is always expanded and the new states has longer and longer labels. Thus, the limit exists.

Now we are ready to define formally the fractal automata.

Definition 3 (Fractal automaton). *The tuple $R = (Q, \Sigma, \Lambda, \delta, s, f)$ with the (infinite) set of states Q, the (input) alphabet Σ, the label alphabet Λ, the transition function $\delta : Q \times (\Sigma \cup \{\varepsilon\}) \to 2^Q$ (only to finite subsets of Q), the initial state $s \in Q$ and the accepting/final state $f \in Q$, is a fractal automaton (fra) where the transition function δ is defined as follows.*

- *$up \in \delta(ur, b)$ with $u \in \Lambda_a^*$, $p, r \in \Lambda_A(\subset \Lambda_n)$, $b \in \Sigma \cup \{\varepsilon\}$ if the transition $p \in \delta(r, b)$ was in the "finite automaton" obtained from the railroad diagram describing/defining nonterminal A. (Assuming $up, ur \in Q$.)*
- *$uJp \in \delta(ur, b)$ with $u \in \Lambda_a^*$, $J \in \Lambda_a$, $r \in \Lambda_A$, $p \in \Lambda_B$, $b \in \Sigma \cup \{\varepsilon\}$ if in the automata obtained from the railroad diagram of A there is a transition from state r with b to the nonterminal B addressed by J and p is the initial state of the automaton representing the railroad diagram of nonterminal B. (Assuming $uJp, ur \in Q$.)*
- *$up \in \delta(uJr, b)$ with $u \in \Lambda_a^*$, $J \in \Lambda_a$, $r \in \Lambda_B$, $p \in \Lambda_A$), $b \in \Sigma \cup \{\varepsilon\}$ if r is the final state of the automaton obtained from the railroad diagram of the nonterminal B and in the automaton obtained from the railroad diagram of A there is a transition from the nonterminal B addressed by J to the state p with b. (Assuming $up, uJr \in Q$.)*

Actually $Q \subset \Lambda_a^* \Lambda_n$ (it is restricted to contain only valid states that can be reached from s by the transition function for some input words).

We note also that for every word $w \in \Sigma^*$ there is a value $i \geq 0$ such that its acceptance can be decided using the finite set Q_i instead of the infinite set Q. Even if the set of states is infinite, as we have seen, there is a convenient way to address (name) the states of a fractal automaton.

The fractal automaton works in a similar way as a finite automaton (the only difference is that the former has an infinite number of states), thus the computations, the accepting computations/walks and the accepted language are defined analogously.

An example for a fractal automaton is shown in Fig. 5. This automaton accepts the context-free language of the correct bracketed expressions using two binary operators $+, -$ and binary (nonnegative) integers. The self-similar feature of the automaton can easily be observed.

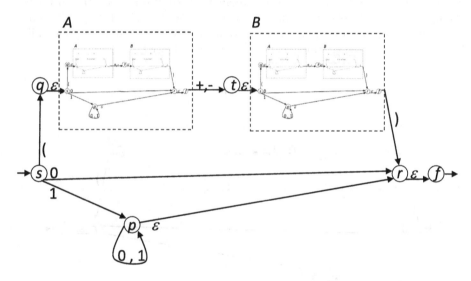

Fig. 5. Fractal automaton accepting a non-regular context-free language (in the figure we have used the recursion up to Q_2).

By our construction method it is obvious that for every context-free language there is a fractal automaton that accepts it. When more than one railroad diagrams are used to describe the language, the recursions (the parts that we can zoom in as in fractals) can be varied. The minimal number of different parts that must be embedded into each other to describe a language could be a new interesting complexity measure of context-free languages.

5   Properties of the Fractal Automata

We have seen that context-free languages can be accepted by fractal automata. Therefore, fractal automata seem to be useful tools to present some properties of context-free languages, e.g., pumping lemmas: during the acceptance of long enough words, the accepting walk allows to go more deeply in the fra (using a more deeper recursion indicating the acceptance of similar-structure longer words). Because the lack of space we do not give a formal proof of a pumping lemma by fra in this paper. Instead, we show that fractal automata cannot accept more languages than the class of context-free languages.

The representation of an fra can be done by the finite set of finite-looking automata obtained from the set of railroad diagrams, linking them together (by the nonterminals) according to the recursions. (In this way the fractal automaton can be represented in a finite way, i.e., when one does a computation with a fractal automaton, she or he can use the finite representation with the theoretically infinite set of state labels. We show this finite representation for our example, in Fig. 6). The chain of the recursion may be traced by the help of a pushdown stack (as it is done in computers as well in recursive function calls). It is the idea of the next construction (shown in Algorithm 4).

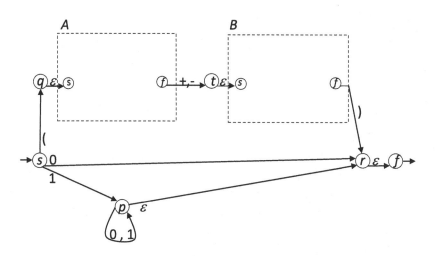

Fig. 6. Finite representation of a fractal automaton.

Algorithm 4.

Input: a fractal automaton $R = (Q, \Sigma, \Lambda, \delta, s, f)$.

1. Let us construct a pda $P = (Q', \Sigma, \Gamma, \delta', s, B, \{f\})$ that accepts the same language as R:

2. Let $Q' = \Lambda_n$ and $\Gamma = \Lambda_a$ (w.l.o.g. we assume that $B \notin \Lambda_a$).

3. Further let δ' be defined as follows:

- let $(p, C) \in \delta'(r, b, C)$ if $up \in \delta(ur, b)$ with some $u \in \Lambda_a^*$, $p, r \in Q'(= \Lambda_n)$, $b \in \Sigma \cup \{\varepsilon\}$ for every $C \in \Gamma \cup \{B\}$;

- let $(p, CJ) \in \delta'(r, b, C)$ if $uJp \in \delta(ur, b)$ with some $u \in \Lambda_a^*$, $J \in \Gamma(= \Lambda_a)$, $r, p \in Q'$, $b \in \Sigma \cup \{\varepsilon\}$ for every $C \in \Gamma \cup \{B\}$;

- let $(p, \varepsilon) \in \delta'(r, b, J)$ if $up \in \delta(uJr, b)$ with $u \in \Lambda_a^*$, $J \in \Gamma$, $p, r \in Q'$, $b \in \Sigma \cup \{\varepsilon\}$.

In this way P will simulate R storing the (possibly infinite) address part of a state of R in its stack and the name part of the state in its own state. The acceptance can go by empty stack and final state.

By the previous construction one could see that every context-free language can be accepted by a pda using only three types of restricted transitions:

- push operation: a new element is pushed to the stack and the next state is independent of the earlier stack contents;
- pop operation: the top element is popped out from the stack and the next state depends on that symbol as well;
- no change: in this transition the stack is not used, the next state does not depend on the stack contents, and it has not been changed during this transition.

Thus, there is an equivalent pda for every other pda (in terms of accepting the same language) by using only these three types of transitions. Actually, these operations are the basic operations when computer programs uses the stack at recursive calls. When a new call happens we push to the stack the place where the actual function should be continued after the return and we start to execute the new function, (somewhat similar as we enter to the new part of the automaton based on another railroad diagram in an accepting walk). When a function terminates, i.e., in our case, the final state of an automaton obtained from a railroad diagram is reached, then if the stack is nonempty, we return back to continue the process at the caller level.

Figure 7 shows a graphical representation of the pda obtained from our fractal automaton (the stack operations are written with various colors at the transitions, e.g., push is written by blue color). The shown no change transitions (written by red color) refer to transitions where the stack does not play any role, and they are corresponding to 'normal' transitions of the automaton based on a railroad diagram (these transitions neither start a recursion, nor finish it in the corresponding fra and railroad diagram).

Pushdown automata are frequently used tools to represent context-free languages. During the computation the stack contains important information. By the connection between fra and pda there is another view of the pushdown stack:

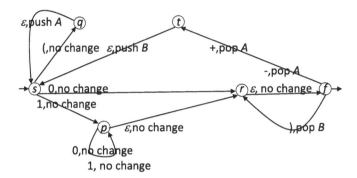

Fig. 7. Pushdown automaton that accepts the same language as the fra that shown in Fig. 5. (Color figure online)

with the infinite state fra, the stack content of the pda is used somehow to address the states in the computation (accepting walk). In fra it is very straightforward to see that if the computation/walk goes more deeply in the recursion, then it must come back (in a longer way).

6   Conclusions

Based on visual representations of regular and context-free languages and the description of context-free languages by (sets of) railroad diagrams, the fractal automata are investigated as an infinite state model that can be defined by a finite description. This new representation of context-free languages, by representing recursions with fractals, can be used to understand better this family of languages. We have also given a link between pushdown automata and the pushdown stack used in various programming languages (in an automatic way) at recursive calls of functions (or other types of subprograms) by the help of our new concept. This explanation can also be very helpful for students to understand these concepts better.

The new concept opens also a series of questions for future research. How the well known subfamilies of context-free languages, e.g., linear languages, one-counter languages, deterministic context-free languages can be represented and characterized by this new automata model? How the new complexity measure can be determined for context-free languages: can we compute how many finite state looking automata we need to link together to describe the given context-free language?

Acknowledgements. Comments of the reviewers are gratefully acknowledged.

References

1. Backus, J.W.: The syntax and semantics of the proposed international algebraic language of the Zurich ACM-GAMM Conference. In: Proceedings of the International Conference on Information Processing, pp. 125–132. UNESCO (1959)
2. Chomsky, N.: Three models for the description of language. IRE Trans. Inf. Theory IT **2**(3), 113–124 (1956)
3. Fisher, A.E., Grodzinsky, F.S.: The Anatomy of Programming Languages. Prentice-Hall, Hoboken (1993)
4. Harrison, M.A.: Introduction to Formal Language Theory. Addison-Wesley (1978)
5. Hopcroft, J.E., Ullman, J.D.: Introduction to Automata Theory, Languages and Computation. Addison-Wesley Publishing Company, Reading (1979)
6. Linz, P.: An Introduction to Formal Languages and Automata, 4th edn. Jones and Bartlett Publishers (2006)
7. Nagy, B.: A normal form for regular expressions. In: Eighth International Conference on Developments in Language Theory, DLT 2004, Auckland, New Zealand, Supplemental Material, (CDMTCS-252 report), p. 10 (2004)
8. Nagy, B.: Programnyelvek elemeinek szintaktikus leírása normál formában (Syntactic description of the elements of the programming languages in a normal form. In: e-Proceedings of IF 2005: Conference Information Higher Education, Debrecen, p. 6 (CD-ROM Proceedings) (2005). (in Hungarian)
9. Nagy, B.: Graphical representations of context-free languages. In: Dwyer, T., Purchase, H., Delaney, A. (eds.) Diagrams 2014. LNCS (LNAI), vol. 8578, pp. 48–50. Springer, Heidelberg (2014). https://doi.org/10.1007/978-3-662-44043-8_7
10. Nagy, B.: Fractal automata, talk in SWORDS 2014: Szeged Workshop on Discrete Structures, Szeged, Hungary (2014)
11. Révész, Gy.E.: Introduction to Formal Languages. McGraw-Hill, New York (1983)
12. Rozenberg, G., Salomaa, A. (eds.): Handbook of Formal Languages, 3rd edn. Springer, Heidelberg (1997). https://doi.org/10.1007/978-3-642-59136-5
13. Savage, J.E.: Models of Computation: Exploring the Power of Computing. Addison-Wesley, Amsterdam (1998)
14. Tucker, A., Noonan, R.: Programming Languages: Principles and Paradigms. Mc Graw Hill, Boston (2002)
15. Wirth, N.: The Programming Language Pascal, July 1973

Closure Properties of Subregular Languages Under Operations

Viktor Olejár[1,2]([✉]) [iD] and Alexander Szabari[2]

[1] Mathematical Institute, Slovak Academy of Sciences, Košice, Slovakia
olejar@saske.sk
[2] Department of Computer Science, P. J. Šafárik University, Košice, Slovakia
alexander.szabari@upjs.sk

Abstract. A class of languages is closed under a given operation if the resulting language belongs to this class whenever the operands belong to it. We examine the closure properties of various subclasses of regular languages under basic operations of intersection, union, concatenation and power, positive closure and star, reversal, and complementation. We consider the following classes: symmetric definite languages and their variants (left ideal, finitely generated left ideal, and combinational), two-sided comets and their variants comets and stars, and the classes of singleton, finite, ordered, star-free, and power-separating languages. We also give an overview about subclasses of convex languages (classes of ideal, free, and closed languages), union-free languages, and group languages. For all pairs of a class and an operation, we provide an answer whether this class is closed under this operation or not.

1 Introduction

The class of regular languages is the simplest class in the standard version of the Chomsky hierarchy. Despite this, it has still attracted the attention of many researchers who examine its related decidability and descriptional complexity problems. Every regular language can be expressed as an iterated composition of unions, concatenations, and Kleene stars applied to singleton sets of symbols from a given alphabet. If we permit only unions and concatenations, we get the class of finite languages. With unions, concatenations, and complements, we get star-free languages [9,13], and with concatenations and stars we get union-free languages [8,21]. Using various other restrictions, we are able to obtain plenty of subclasses of regular languages with most of them having been studied in the past for their interesting properties.

One of the first examined subregular classes were the definite languages. These languages and their variants were first investigated by Brzozowski [4], Perles et al. [23], and Paz and Peleg [22]. The class of star-free languages was exhaustively studied in [24] by Schützenberger and in [20] by Meyer. Subsequently, group languages, which were called permutation regular sets at the

---

Research supported by VEGA grants 2/0132/19 and 1/0177/21.

time, were studied by Thierrin in [28]. Shyr and Thierrin investigated ordered and power-separating languages in [25] and [26], respectively. Since the introduction of these classes decades ago, intensive research has been conducted in regards to them with many fruitful outcomes.

Operational state complexity is a hot topic in theoretical computer science. It is often beneficial to focus on the case, where the operands of a considered operation belong to some specific subclass. Due to this belonging to a subclass, in certain cases the resulting state complexity may significantly decrease compared to the general regular case. Some examples for this from more recent publications include results in the classes of prefix- and suffix-free languages by Han et al. [10,11]. Brzozowski et al. examined the classes of factor- and subword-free languages [3], ideal languages [6], and closed languages [7]. Efforts to jointly investigate prefix-, suffix-, factor-, and subword-convex languages and their subclasses were made by Hospodár et al. [15,17]. Not only the complexity of various operations on regular languages, but also ranges of state complexities were examined, for example in [12,16]. In papers about operational state complexity on subclasses, sometimes the closure and non-closure properties of the considered class under operations are provided.

A class of languages is closed under a given operation if the resulting language belongs to this class whenever the operands belong to it. In this paper, we look at the classes of combinational, finitely generated left ideal (alternatively called noninitial definite), left ideal (alternatively called ultimate definite), symmetric definite, star, comet, two-sided comet, singleton, finite, ordered, star-free, and power-separating languages, and provide closure and non-closure properties for intersection, union, concatenation, power, positive closure, Kleene star, reversal, and complementation. Some of these properties are already known from the literature. For the others, we provide arguments for the closure property or a counterexample, called a witness, for non-closure. At the end of the paper, we provide an overview of the closure and non-closure properties, together with mostly known results for the subclasses of convex languages (right ideal, prefix- and suffix-closed, -free, and -convex), union-free languages, and group languages.

2   Preliminaries

We assume that the reader is familiar with some standard notions and notation in automata theory. For additional details and explanations, we refer the reader to [14,27].

Let Σ be a non-empty *alphabet* of symbols. Then Σ^* denotes the set of all strings over Σ, including the empty string ε. A *language* over Σ is any subset of Σ^*. We often refer to a language over a single symbol alphabet as unary, and to a language over a two-symbol alphabet as binary. The length of a string w is denoted by $|w|$, and the number of occurrences of a symbol a in w is denoted by $|w|_a$. The *reversal of a string* w over Σ denoted w^R is defined as $w^R = \varepsilon$ if $w = \varepsilon$, and $w^R = a_n a_{n-1} \cdots a_2 a_1$ if $w = a_1 a_2 \cdots a_{n-1} a_n$ with $a_i \in \Sigma$. The *reversal of a language* L is the language $L^R = \{w^R \mid w \in L\}$. The *complement* of a language L over Σ is the language $L^c = \Sigma^* \setminus L$. The *intersection* of languages K and L is the language $K \cap L = \{w \mid w \in K \text{ and } w \in L\}$, while the *union* of K and L is $K \cup L = \{w \mid w \in K \text{ or } w \in L\}$. The *concatenation* of languages K and L is the language $KL = \{uv \mid u \in K \text{ and } v \in L\}$. For a given positive integer k, the *k-th power* of a language L is the language $L^k = LL^{k-1}$ with $L^0 = \{\varepsilon\}$. The *positive closure* of a given language L is $L^+ = \bigcup_{k \geq 1} L^k$, while the *star* of L is defined as $L^* = \bigcup_{k \geq 0} L^k$ and it is equal to $\{\varepsilon\} \cup L^+$. Given two strings $u, v \in \Sigma^*$ and a positive integer k we define the *shuffle* of two strings $u \sqcup\!\!\sqcup v$ as

$$u \sqcup\!\!\sqcup v = \{u_1 v_1 \cdots u_k v_k \mid u_1, \ldots, u_k, v_1, \ldots, v_k \in \Sigma^*$$
$$\text{and } u = u_1 \cdots u_k$$
$$\text{and } v = v_1 \cdots v_k\}.$$

The *shuffle of languages* K and L over some alphabet Σ is the language

$$K \sqcup\!\!\sqcup L = \bigcup_{u \in K} \bigcup_{v \in L} u \sqcup\!\!\sqcup v.$$

We use the notation of *regular expressions* over Σ in a standard way with $\emptyset$ (empty set), ε, and each $\sigma \in \Sigma$ being regular expressions; furthermore if r and s are regular expressions, then rs (concatenation), $r + s$ (union), and r^* (star) are also regular expressions. For a regular expression r, the expression r^k denotes the k-th power of the language of r, and the expressions $r^{\leq k}$ and $r^{\geq k}$ are shorthands for $r^0 + r^1 + \cdots + r^k$ and $r^k + r^{k+1} + \cdots$, respectively.

A *nondeterministic finite automaton with multiple initial states* (MNFA) is a quintuple $M = (Q, \Sigma, \cdot, I, F)$ where Q is a finite non-empty set of *states*, Σ is a finite non-empty set of input symbols (*i.e., input alphabet*), $I \subseteq Q$ is the set of *initial states*, $F \subseteq Q$ is the set of *final (accepting) states*, and $\cdot : Q \times \Sigma \to 2^Q$ is the *transition function* which can be naturally extended to the domain $2^Q \times \Sigma^*$. The language accepted by the MNFA M is

$$L(M) = \{w \in \Sigma^* \mid I \cdot w \cap F \neq \emptyset\}.$$

We call an MNFA a *(complete) deterministic finite automaton* (DFA) if $|I| = 1$ and $|q \cdot \sigma| = 1$ for each $q \in Q$ and each $\sigma \in \Sigma$; in such a case, $\cdot$ is a mapping from $Q \times \Sigma$ to Q.

A given language L is called *regular* if and only if there exists an MNFA M for which $L = L(M)$. Two MNFAs A and B are *equivalent* if they accept the same language. For a given MNFA $M = (Q, \Sigma, \cdot, I, F)$, we can construct the MNFA $M^R = (Q, \Sigma, \cdot^R, F, I)$ with $q \cdot^R \sigma = \{p \mid q \in p \cdot \sigma\}$ for each state q and symbol σ. The MNFA M^R recognizes the reverse of the language $L(M)$. Every MNFA $M = (Q, \Sigma, \cdot, I, F)$ can be converted into an equivalent complete DFA

$$\mathcal{D}(M) = (2^Q, \Sigma, \cdot, I, \{S \in 2^Q \mid S \cap F \neq \emptyset\})$$

by the *subset construction* [14] where $\cdot$ is the extension of the transition function of M to the domain $2^Q \times \Sigma$. Such DFA $\mathcal{D}(M)$ is called the *subset automaton*.

Next, we present the language classes that are the main focus in this paper. Most of these were recently jointly investigated in [2] in regards to the NFA to DFA conversion problem. A language L is

- *combinational* (class abbreviation CB): if $L = \Sigma^* H$ for some $H \subseteq \Sigma$;
- *finitely generated left ideal* (FGLID): if $L = \Sigma^* H$ for some finite language H (in [2] called noninitial definite);
- *left ideal* (LID): if $L = \Sigma^* L$ (in [2] called ultimate definite);
- *symmetric definite* (SYDEF): if $L = G\Sigma^* H$ for some regular languages G, H;
- *star* (STAR): if $L = G^*$ for a regular language G [5] (equivalently, $L = L^*$);
- *comet* (COM): if $L = G^* H$ for some regular languages G, H with $G \notin \{\emptyset, \{\varepsilon\}\}$;
- *two-sided comet* (2COM): if $L = EG^* H$ for regular E, G, H with $G \notin \{\emptyset, \{\varepsilon\}\}$;
- *singleton* (SINGL): if it consists of one string;
- *finite* (FIN): if it consists of finitely many strings;
- *ordered* (ORD): if it is accepted by a (possibly non-minimal) DFA with ordered states such that $p \preceq q$ implies $p \cdot \sigma \preceq q \cdot \sigma$ for each symbol σ (the relation $\preceq$ on the states of the DFA is a total order) [25];
- *star-free* (STFR): if L is constructable from finite languages by concatenation, union, and complementation only (equivalently, if L has an aperiodic DFA) [24];
- *power-separating* (PSEP): if for every x in Σ^* there exists an integer m such that $x^{\geq m} \subseteq L$ or $x^{\geq m} \subseteq L^c$ [26];

The following language classes are mentioned in a summarizing table in the Conclusions section to provide a more complete overview of other studied subregular language classes. A language L over Σ is a *right ideal* (RID) if $L = L\Sigma^*$, it is a *two-sided ideal* (TSID) if $L = \Sigma^* L\Sigma^*$, and it is an *all-sided ideal* (ASID) if $L = L \sqcup\!\sqcup \Sigma^*$. If L is a left (right, two-sided, all-sided) ideal, then it is equal to $\Sigma^* G$ ($G\Sigma^*$, $\Sigma^* G\Sigma^*$, $G \sqcup\!\sqcup \Sigma^*$) for some language G which is called a *generator* of L. The smallest such language with respect to set inclusions is called the *minimal generator* of L. The minimal generator of a left ideal L is the language $G = L \setminus \Sigma^+ L$, cf. [6, p. 45]. The minimal generators of right, two-sided, and all-sided languages are obtained similarly. If the minimal generator of L is infinite, then L has no finite generator.

For a given string w, a string x is called a *factor* (resp. *prefix*, *suffix*) of w if there exist strings u and v such that $w = uxv$ (resp. $w = xv$, $w = ux$). This factor (prefix, suffix) is called *proper* if $uv \neq \varepsilon$ ($v \neq \varepsilon$, $u \neq \varepsilon$). Given some string v we call u a *subword* of v if there exist strings $u_1 \ldots u_k$ and $v_1 \ldots v_k$ for a positive integer k such that $u = u_1 \cdots u_k$ and $v = u_1 v_1 \cdots u_k v_k$. A language L is *prefix-closed* (PRCL) if for every string of L, each its prefix is in L, and it is *prefix-free* (PRFR) if for every string of L, none of its proper prefixes are in L. Suffix- (SUCL), factor- (FACL), subword-closed (SWCL), and suffix- (SUFR), factor- (FAFR), and subword-free (SWFR) languages are defined analogously. A language L is $\prec$-*convex* with respect to a partial order $\prec$ if for every strings u, v in L and each x with $u \prec x \prec v$, we have $x \in L$. Each prefix-free, prefix-closed, or right ideal language is prefix-convex (PRCV), and similar inclusions hold also for suffix- (factor-, subword-) free, -closed, and left (two-sided, all-sided) ideal languages in regards to suffix-convex (SUCV) (factor-convex (FACV), subword-convex (SWCV)) languages. A language L is called a *group* language (GRP) if it is accepted by a DFA whose transition function forms a permutation on its set of states, and it is called *union-free* (UNFR) if L is constructible from finite languages by concatenation and star only.

The following lemmas encapsulate some properties of the considered language classes that are utilized in the upcoming proofs. The results presented here are known. In Lemma 1, for the reader's convenience, we provide a proof for inclusions, but not for their strictness since it is not used and it follows from the different properties for different classes.

Lemma 1 (Inclusions of classes, cf. [25,26], and [2, Fig. 2]). *We have*

(a) CB $\subsetneq$ FGLID $\subsetneq$ LID $\subsetneq$ SYDEF,
(b) STAR $\subsetneq$ COM $\subsetneq$ 2COM, *where the first inclusion does not apply for* $\{\varepsilon\}$,
(c) SINGL $\subsetneq$ FIN $\subsetneq$ ORD $\subsetneq$ STFR $\subsetneq$ PSEP.

Proof. (a) Every combinational language L is equal to $\Sigma^* H$ for some $H \subseteq \Sigma$. Since H is finite, L is a finitely generated left ideal. Next, finitely generated left ideals are left ideals by definition, and left ideals are symmetric definite languages $G\Sigma^* H$ with $G = \{\varepsilon\}$.

(b) If L is a star different from $\{\varepsilon\}$, then it is the comet $G^* H$ with $G = L$ and $H = \{\varepsilon\}$. Next, if L is a comet, then it is equal to $EG^* H$ with $E = \{\varepsilon\}$.

(c) Every singleton language consists of one string, so it is finite. In a DFA for a finite language, only states from which no string is accepted can form a cycle of transitions, so the other states can be ordered right compatible relatively to the concatenation of strings, hence every finite language is ordered, cf. [25, Proposition 11(3)]. Next, in a DFA for an ordered language, for each state q there exists an integer k such that $q \cdot \sigma^k = q \cdot \sigma^{k+1}$ for each symbol σ. It follows that every ordered language is star-free, cf. [25, Proposition 12]. Finally, for every star-free language L there exists an integer k such that for each $x, y, z \in \Sigma^*$, we have $xy^k z \in L$ if and only if $xy^{k+1} z \in L$. Let $m = k + 1$. Then for every string v we have $v^{\geq m} \subseteq L$ or $v^{\geq m} \subseteq L^c$. Hence every star-free language is power-separating, cf. [26, Proposition 3]. $\square$

Lemma 2 (cf. [22, Theorem 9.2]). *Let* $A = (Q, \Sigma, \cdot, s, F)$ *be a minimal DFA. Then A is symmetric definite if and only if there exists a state $\overline{s} \in Q$ with the following properties:*

- *for each $w \in L(A) \cap \Sigma^{\leq |Q|-2}$, there exists a prefix u such that $s \cdot u = \overline{s}$;*
- *the DFA $(Q, \Sigma, \cdot, \overline{s}, F)$ accepts a left ideal language.* $\square$

The first condition of the previous lemma can be read as follows: If A is reading a string w with $|w| \leq |Q| - 2$ which is in $L(A)$, then A goes through the specified state $\overline{s}$. The state $\overline{s}$ is called *decomposition state*. For the following lemma, a proof idea is provided to illustrate the connection between the considered congruence classes and DFAs.

Lemma 3 (cf. [25, Proposition 9]). *Let L be a language over Σ. Then the following are equivalent:*

(1) L is an ordered language;

(2) L is the union of some classes of a right congruence of finite index over Σ^* and the set of the classes of this right congruence is a totally ordered set with an order which is right compatible relatively to the concatenation of strings.

Proof Idea. Assume (1) and let $M = (Q, \Sigma, \cdot, s, F)$ be a DFA with $L = L(M)$. Let the relation R on Σ^* be defined as

$$u R v \text{ if and only if } s \cdot u = s \cdot v.$$

Such R is a right congruence relation (with respect to string concatenation to the right), the number of its congruence classes is finite, and L is the union of some of them. Denote the total order on Q as $\preceq$ and the congruence classes of R as $C = \{[w] \mid w \in \Sigma^*\}$. Let the total order $\leq$ on C be defined as

$$[u] \leq [v] \text{ if and only if } s \cdot u \preceq s \cdot v.$$

Statement (2) holds since $(C, \leq)$ is a totally ordered set which is right compatible relatively to the concatenation of strings.

Conversely, assume (2) and denote the totally orderable set of right congruence classes as $C = \{[w] \mid w \in \Sigma^*\}$. Define the DFA $M = \{C, \Sigma, \cdot, s, F\}$, where $s = [\varepsilon]$, $F = \{[w] \mid w \in L\}$, and $\cdot$ simulates right string concatenation in a standard way. The states of M are orderable by assumption and $L = L(M)$, thus statement (1) holds.   □

3   Results

In this section, we discuss closure and non-closure properties of the main languages of interest introduced in the preliminaries. We focus on the binary operations of intersection, union, concatenation, and unary operations of power, positive closure, star, reversal, and complementation.

For closure properties, we show that the resulting language has the property of being in the same class as the operands which are K and L for binary operations and L for unary operations. To show non-closure properties, we find witness languages belonging to the class such that the result of the operation is not in the respective class. The provided witnesses are numbered throughout the paper.

It is known that the class of left ideals is closed under intersection, union [22, Lemma 3.4], and concatenation [22, Lemma 3.6], and finitely generated left ideals are closed under positive closure [4, p. 559]. In the following two lemmas, we consider the classes of combinational, finitely generated left ideal, left ideal, and symmetric definite languages. First, we present closures under the considered operations and subsequently non-closures.

Lemma 4. *Let K and L be languages and k a given positive integer.*

(a) If K and L are finitely generated left ideal (combinational), then $K \cap L$, $K \cup L$, and L^+ are finitely generated left ideal (combinational) as well.

(b) If L is left ideal, then L^k and L^+ are left ideal as well.

(c) If K and L are symmetric definite, then KL, L^k, L^+, and L^R are symmetric definite as well.

Proof. First we show that $L = L^+$ in all classes, and as a result, all classes are closed under positive closure. If a language L is in one of the considered classes, then it is symmetric definite, so we have $L = G\Sigma^*H$ for some regular languages G and H. Next, for every $i \geq 1$ we have $L^i = G(\Sigma^*HG)^{i-1}\Sigma^*H$. Hence $L^i \subseteq G\Sigma^*H = L$, so $L^+ \subseteq L$. Taking into account that $L \subseteq L^+$, we get $L^+ = L$. Now we continue with the remaining operations.

(a) First, let K and L be in FGLID, so $K = \Sigma^*G$ and $L = \Sigma^*H$ for some finite languages G and H. Let

$$m = \max\{|w| \mid w \in G \cup H\} \text{ and } n = \min\{|w| \mid w \in G \cup H\}.$$

We aim to show that there exists a finite language I such that $\Sigma^*G \cap \Sigma^*H = \Sigma^*I$.
Set

$$G' = \{\Sigma^{\leq m-|w|}w \mid w \in G\} \text{ and } H' = \{\Sigma^{\leq m-|w|}w \mid w \in H\}$$

and let

$$I = \bigcup_{i=n}^{m} (G' \cap H' \cap \Sigma^i).$$

First we show that $\Sigma^*G \cap \Sigma^*H \subseteq \Sigma^*I$. Let $w \in \Sigma^*G \cap \Sigma^*H$. Then there exists a suffix u of w in G and a suffix v of w in H. Without loss of generality, let u be a suffix of v. Then $v \in G' \cap H' \cap \Sigma^{|v|}$, and since $n \leq |v| \leq m$, we have $v \in I$. Hence $w \in \Sigma^*I$. Next we show that $\Sigma^*I \subseteq \Sigma^*G \cap \Sigma^*H$. Let $w \in \Sigma^*I$. Then there exists a suffix v of w with $v \in I$, so $v \in G' \cap H' \cap \Sigma^{|v|}$. Since $v \in G'$, there exists a suffix of v in G, and since $v \in H'$, there exists a suffix of v in H as well. It follows that $w \in \Sigma^*G$ and $w \in \Sigma^*H$. Thus $\Sigma^*G \cap \Sigma^*H = \Sigma^*I$.

Similarly, we can show that for the following finite language

$$U = \bigcup_{i=n}^{m} ((G' \cup H') \cap \Sigma^i)$$

we have $\Sigma^*G \cup \Sigma^*H = \Sigma^*U$. First, let us prove the inclusion $\Sigma^*G \cup \Sigma^*H \subseteq \Sigma^*U$. Let $w \in \Sigma^*G \cup \Sigma^*H$ and $w = xv$ such that $x \in \Sigma^*$ and $v \in G \cup H$. Thus, from the definitions of G' and H', we have $v \in G' \cup H'$, subsequently resulting in $v \in (G' \cup H') \cap \Sigma^{|v|}$. It follows that $v \in U$, and $xv = w \in \Sigma^*U$. To show the inclusion $\Sigma^*U \subseteq \Sigma^*G \cup \Sigma^*H$, let $w \in \Sigma^*U$ and $w = xv$ such that $x \in \Sigma^*$ and $v \in U$. From the definition of U, we have $v \in (G' \cup H') \cap \Sigma^{|v|}$. Therefore we have $v \in G' \cap \Sigma^{|v|}$ or $v \in H' \cap \Sigma^{|v|}$, and so $v \in G'$ or $v \in H'$. It follows that $v = x'v'$ where $v' \in G$ or $v' \in H$. Hence $w = xv = xx'v'$ where $xx' \in \Sigma^*$ and $v' \in G \cup H$. Thus $w \in \Sigma^*G \cup \Sigma^*H$, and $\Sigma^*G \cup \Sigma^*H = \Sigma^*U$.

Hence $K \cap L$ and $K \cup L$ are finitely generated left ideals. Moreover, if languages $K = \Sigma^*G$ and $L = \Sigma^*H$ are combinational, then each string in $G \cup H$ is of length one, so both $K \cap L$ and $K \cup L$ are combinational as well.

(b) Since left ideals are closed under concatenation [22, Lemma 3.6], they are closed under power.

(c) Let $K = G_1\Sigma^*H_1$ and $L = G_2\Sigma^*H_2$ for some languages G_1, H_1, G_2, H_2. Then $KL = G_1\Sigma^*(H_1G_2\Sigma^*H_2)$, which is a symmetric definite language. Next, since symmetric definite languages are closed under concatenation, they are closed under power as well. For reversal, we have $L^R = (G\Sigma^*H)^R = H^R\Sigma^*G^R$, hence L^R is symmetric definite.   □

Lemma 5. *The following statements hold:*

(a) *The binary language $L_1 = (a+b)^*a$ is combinational, but $L_1L_1 = L_1^2$ is not a finitely generated left ideal, and L_1^*, L_1^R, and L_1^c are not left ideals.*

(b) *The binary languages $K_1 = a(a+b)^*$ and $L_1 = (a+b)^*a$ are symmetric definite, but their intersection is not symmetric definite.*

(c) *The binary languages $K_2 = a(a+b)^*a$, $L_2 = b(a+b)^*b$, and unary language $L_3 = a^*aa$ are symmetric definite, but $K_2 \cup L_2$, L_3^*, and L_3^c are not symmetric definite.*

Proof. (a) We have $L_1^2 = (a+b)^*ab^*a$, which is a left ideal and its minimal generator is

$$(a+b)^*ab^*a \setminus (a+b)(a+b)^*ab^*a = ab^*a.$$

Hence it is not generated by any finite language. Next, we have $\varepsilon \in L_1^*$ but $b \notin L_1^*$, $a \in L_1^R$ but $ba \notin L_1^R$, and $\varepsilon \in L_1^c$ but $a \notin L_1^c$. It follows that L_1^*, L_1^R and L_1^c are not left ideals.

(b) We have $K_1 \cap L_1 = a + a(a+b)^*a$. Assume for a contradiction that $K_1 \cap L_1$ is symmetric definite. Then it is equal to $G\Sigma^*H$ for some regular languages G, H. Since $a \in K_1 \cap L_1$, we must have either $\varepsilon \in G$ and $a \in H$, or $a \in G$ and $\varepsilon \in H$, so either $G\Sigma^* = \Sigma^*$ or $\Sigma^*H = \Sigma^*$. But it would mean that $K_1 \cap L_1$ is either a left or a right ideal, which is a contradiction since $a \in K_1 \cap L_1$ but $\{ba, ab\} \cap K_1 \cap L_1 = \emptyset$. Hence $K_1 \cap L_1$ is not symmetric definite.

(c) Assume that $K_2 \cup L_2$ is a symmetric definite language. Then, by Lemma 2, it is accepted by a DFA with a decomposition state $\bar{s}$. Next, the state $\bar{s}$ is neither initial nor final since $K_2 \cup L_2$ is neither a left nor a right ideal. It follows that when processing the string aa, the DFA is in the state $\bar{s}$ after reading a, and when processing the string bb, the DFA is in the same state $\bar{s}$ after reading b. But this would mean that ab is accepted by this DFA, which is a contradiction with the fact that $ab \notin K_2 \cup L_2$. Hence $K_2 \cup L_2$ is not symmetric definite. Notice that if a symmetric definite language contains the empty string, then it is equal to Σ^*. It follows that L_3^* is not symmetric definite since $\varepsilon \in L_3^*$ but $a \notin L_3^*$. Next, $L_3^c = \{\varepsilon, a\}$ is not symmetric definite since it is a finite non-empty language.   □

In the following two lemmas, we consider the classes of star, comet, and two-sided comet languages.

Lemma 6. *Let K and L be languages and k a given positive integer.*

(a) *If K and L are stars, then $K \cap L$, L^k, L^+, L^*, and L^R are stars.*
(b) *If K and L are comets, then KL, L^k, and L^+ are comets, and L^* is a comet if $L \neq \emptyset$.*
(c) *If K and L are two-sided comets, then KL, L^k, L^+, and L^R are two-sided comets, and L^* is a two-sided comet if $L \neq \emptyset$.*

Proof. (a) Let K and L be stars. We aim to show that $K \cap L = (K \cap L)^*$. The inclusion $K \cap L \subseteq (K \cap L)^*$ follows from definition of the star operation. To show the converse, assume that a string w is in $(K \cap L)^*$. Hence it can be factorized to $v_1 v_2 \cdots v_k$ with $v_i \in K \cap L$ for each $i = 1, 2, \ldots, k$. Thus for each i we have $v_i \in K$ and $v_i \in L$. Since $K = K^*$ and $L = L^*$, it then follows that $v_1 v_2 \cdots v_k = w$ is in both K and L, so $w \in K \cap L$. Hence resulting in $K \cap L = (K \cap L)^*$. Next, we have $L^k = L^+ = L^* = L$ for star languages. Finally, for a star language L we have $L^R = (L^*)^R = (L^R)^*$, thus the reverse of L is a star language as well.

(b) We have $K = G_1^* H_1$ and $L = G_2^* H_2$ for some regular languages G_1, H_1, G_2, H_2 such that G_1 and G_2 are non-empty. Next, we have $KL = G_1^*(H_1 G_2^* H_2)$, which is a comet. Hence comets are closed under concatenation, and consequently under power. We have $\emptyset^+ = \emptyset$ and for a non-empty comet L, we have $L^+ = L^* L$ where $L \notin \{\emptyset, \{\varepsilon\}\}$. Thus L^+ is a comet in both cases. Finally, $L^* = L^*\{\varepsilon\}$, so it is a comet unless $L = \emptyset$.

(c) Let $L = EG^* H$ for some languages E, G, H with $G \notin \{\emptyset, \{\varepsilon\}\}$. Then similar arguments as for comets hold for concatenation, power, positive closure, and star. Next, we have $L^R = H^R (G^R)^* E^R$, so L^R is a two-sided comet.   □

Lemma 7. *The following statements hold:*

(a) *The binary languages $K_4 = (ab^*a + b)^*$ and $L_4 = (ba^*b + a)^*$ are star languages, while $K_4 \cup L_4$, $K_4 L_4$, and L_4^c are not star languages.*
(b) *The binary languages $K_5 = a^* ba$ and $L_5 = b^* a$ are comets, while $K_5 \cap L_5$ and $K_5 \cup L_5$ are not even two-sided comets, and L_5^R is not a comet.*
(c) *The unary language $L_6 = a^* a$ is a comet, but L_6^c is not even a two-sided comet.*

Proof. (a) By definition, the languages K_4 and L_4 are star languages. Next, we have $\{a, b\} \subseteq K_4 \cup L_4$ but $ab \notin K_4 \cup L_4$, $\{a, b\} \subseteq K_4 L_4$ but $ab \notin K_4 L_4$, and $b \in L_4^c$ but $bb \notin L_4^c$. It follows that $K_4 \cup L_4$, $K_4 L_4$, and L_4^c are not star languages.

(b) We have $K_5 \cap L_5 = \{ba\}$, which is a non-empty finite language, hence it is not a two-sided comet. For every string w in $K_5 \cup L_5 = a^* ba + b^* a$, we have $|w|_a = 1$ or $|w|_b = 1$. Assume that $a^* ba + b^* a = EG^* H$ for some regular languages E, G, H with $G \notin \{\emptyset, \{\varepsilon\}\}$. Let w be a string in $EG^* H$. Then $w = ux^i v$

for some non-negative integer i. We cannot have both a and b as factors of x since then we would have $|w|_a \geq i$ and $|w|_b \geq i$. Thus $x \in a^* + b^*$. Let $x \in a^*$. Then a string of the form a^*ba is in EG^*H only if $ba \in H$. But this is a contradiction with $a \in a^*ba + b^*a$. So let $x \in b^*$. Then, if $a^iba \in K_5 \cup L_5$ for some $i \geq 2$, also $a^ib^ia \in K_5 \cup L_5$, but such a string is not in $a^*ba + b^*a$. It follows that $a^*ba + b^*a$ is not a two-sided comet. Finally, assume that $L_5^R = ab^*$ is a comet. Then $ab^* = G^*H$ with $G \notin \{\emptyset, \{\varepsilon\}\}$. It follows that a string starting with a is in G. But then strings with more than two occurrences of a are in G^*H, which is a contradiction with $G^*H = ab^*$. Thus ab^* is not a comet.

(c) The language $L_6^c = a^* \setminus a^*a = \{\varepsilon\}$ is non-empty and finite, so it is not a two-sided comet. □

We give an observation about the classes of singletons and finite languages.

Proposition 8. *Let K and L be languages and k a given positive integer.*

(a) If K and L are singletons, then KL, L^k, and L^R are singletons.
(b) If K and L are finite, then $K \cap L$, $K \cup L$, KL, L^k, and L^R are finite.
(c) Let $K_7 = \{\varepsilon\}$ and $L_7 = \{a\}$. Then K_7 and L_7 are singletons, $K_7 \cap L_7$ and $K_7 \cup L_7$ are not singletons, and L_7^+, L_7^*, and L_7^c are not even finite.

Proof. (a) Let $K = \{u\}$ and $L = \{v\}$. Then we have $KL = \{uv\}$, $L^k = \{v^k\}$, and $L^R = \{v^R\}$, which are singleton languages.

(b) The sets $K \cap L$, $K \cup L$, KL, and L^R are finite sets by definition of operations. Next, we have $L^k = LL^{k-1}$, thus the closure property for power follows from the closure property for concatenation.

(c) We have $K_7 \cap L_7 = \emptyset$ and $K_7 \cup L_7 = \{\varepsilon, a\}$, thus both sets $K_7 \cap L_7$ and $K_7 \cup L_7$ have size different from one. Next, we have $L_7^+ = a^+$, $L_7^* = a^*$, and $L_7^c = \varepsilon + a^{\geq 2}$, which are infinite languages. □

In the final two lemmas, we consider the classes of ordered, star-free, and power-separating languages. These language classes have been studied in [20,25], and [26, Proposition 5], where the closure and non-closure properties for Boolean operations and concatenation were shown. Specifically, all these classes are closed under complementation, but only star-free and power-separating languages are closed under intersection and union, and only star-free languages are closed under concatenation. For the non-closures, notice that $b^*a(a + b)^*$ and $a^*b(a + b)^*$ are ordered, but their intersection is not, $\{b^*ab^*\}$ and $\{a^*ba^*\}$ are ordered, but their concatenation is not, and $(abab)^*a$ and $bab(abab)^*$ are power-separating, but their concatenation is not. The closure properties for operations of power, plus, star and reversal are shown next.

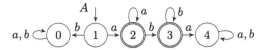

Fig. 1. A DFA for the ordered language L_8 whose second power is not ordered.

Lemma 9. *Let L be a language and k a given positive integer.*

(a) If L is power-separating, then L^R is power-separating as well.
(b) If L is star-free, then L^k and L^R are star-free as well.

Proof. (a) Notice that $(L^c)^R = (L^R)^c$ and $(w^k)^R = (w^R)^k$ for every $k \geq 0$ and $w \in \Sigma^*$. Let $x \in \Sigma^*$. Since L is power-separating, for the string x^R there exists an integer m such that $(x^R)^{\geq m} \subseteq L$ or $(x^R)^{\geq m} \subseteq L^c$. Thus $x^{\geq m} \subseteq L^R$ or $x^{\geq m} \subseteq (L^R)^c$, so L^R is power-separating.

(b) The class of star-free languages is constructible from elementary symbols by union, complementation, and concatenation. Hence the power of a star-free language, which is an iterated concatenation, is star-free. Since all these operations commute with reversal, the reverse of a star-free language is star-free as well.   □

Lemma 10. *The following statements hold:*

(a) The binary language $L_8 = aa^*b^*$ is ordered, but its second power is not ordered.
(b) The binary language $L_9 = b + a(baba)^*$ is power-separating, but its second power is not power-separating.
(c) The unary language $L_{10} = \{aa\}$ is ordered, but L_{10}^+ and L_{10}^* are not even power-separating.
(d) The binary language $L_{11} = b^*aa^*ba^*$ is ordered, but its reverse is not ordered.

Proof. (a) The language L_8 is ordered since it is accepted by the ordered DFA A shown in Fig. 1. Assume that $L_8^2 = aa^*b^*aa^*b^*$ is ordered. Therefore it is accepted by an ordered DFA as described in Lemma 3 where states corresponds to the classes of a right congruence with an order right compatible relatively to the concatenation of strings. The class $[\varepsilon]$ is different from both $[a]$ and $[b]$ since no string starting with b is in L_8^2, and there exists a string w with $aw \in L_8^2$ and $w \notin L_8^2$. The classes $[a]$ and $[aa]$ are different since their corresponding states have different finality. Next, we have $[aaa] = [aa]$ but $[aaba] \neq [aab]$, $[aabb] = [aab]$ but $[aabab] \neq [aaba]$, and $[aabaa] = [aaba]$ but for every string w in $[aababa]$ we have $w(a + b)^* \cap L_8^2 = \emptyset$. It follows that $[\varepsilon]$, $[a]$, $[aa]$, $[aab]$, $[aaba]$, and $[aabab]$ are different classes, while $[b]$ and $[aababa]$ correspond to some states from which no string is accepted. Next, the class $[ab]$ is different from all previously mentioned classes since it corresponds to a non-final state from which a is accepted and aba is rejected. Assume that $[\varepsilon] < [a]$. Then $[a] < [aa]$ and $[aa] = [aaa]$. Next, we cannot have $[\varepsilon] < [b] < [a]$ since then we would have $[aa] < [baa] < [aaa]$. We also cannot have $[\varepsilon] < [a] < [b]$ since it would mean that $[b] < [ab] < [bb]$, but we have $[b] = [bb]$ and only strings starting with a are in L_8^2. So we have $[b] < [\varepsilon] < [a]$. By similar arguments, we have $[\varepsilon] < [a] < [aa] < [aab] < [aaba] < [aabab]$. Now we want to place the class $[ab]$ in the order. If $[ab] < [aa]$, then $[aba] < [aaa]$, which is a contradiction with $[aba] = [aaba]$. Next, if $[aa] < [ab] < [aab]$, then $[aab] < [abb]$, which is a contradiction with $[abb] = [ab]$. Finally, if $[a] < [aab] < [ab]$, then $[ab] < [aabb]$, which is a contradiction since $[aabb] = [aab]$ (See Fig. 2 for illustration).

(b) Every string in L_9 is of odd length and symbols a and b alternate. But every power of a string of even length is also of even length, and every power of a string of odd length ℓ has the same symbol on the first and the $(\ell + 1)$-th position. Hence for every $w \in \{a, b\}^*$ and $k \geq 2$, we have $w^k \in L_9^c$, so L_9 is power-separating. Now let $k \geq 0$. Then we have $(ba)^{2k+1} = b \cdot a(baba)^k \in L_9^c$, and $(ba)^{2k} \notin L_9^c$ since every string in L_9^c is of length 2 mod 4.

(c) Since $L_{10} = \{aa\}$ is finite, it is ordered. We have $L_{10}^+ = \bigcup_{i=1}^{\infty} \{a^{2i}\}$. Consequently, it follows that for the string a, there does not exist an integer m such that $a^{\geq m} \subseteq L_{10}^+$ or $a^{\geq m} \subseteq (L_{10}^+)^c$. The same holds for $L_{10}^* = \bigcup_{i=0}^{\infty} \{a^{2i}\}$.

(d) The language L_{11} is ordered since it is accepted by the ordered DFA C shown in Fig. 3, left. Striving for contradiction, assume that also $L_{11}^R = a^*ba^*ab^*$ is ordered. Therefore it is accepted by an ordered DFA as described in Lemma 3 where states corresponds to the classes of a right congruence with an order right compatible relatively to the concatenation of strings. The classes $[\varepsilon]$ and $[a]$ coincide since for each string aw in L_{11}^R, we have $w \in L_{11}^R$. The class $[b]$ is different from $[\varepsilon]$ since each string in L_{11}^R has a factor ba, but if $bw \in L_{11}^R$, we may have $w \notin L_{11}^R$. The class $[ba]$ is different from both $[\varepsilon]$ and $[b]$ since it includes strings in L_{11}^R, unlike $[\varepsilon]$ and $[a]$. The class $[bab]$ is different from previous three classes since it includes strings in L_{11}^R, but for every string w in $[bab]$, we have $wa \notin L_{11}^R$, while for every string v in $[ba]$, we have $va \in [ba]$. It follows that the class $[baba]$ corresponds to a state from which no string is accepted. Without loss of generality, let $[\varepsilon] < [b]$. Then $[a] < [ba]$ since the order is right compatible to concatenation, so $[\varepsilon] < [ba]$. It follows that $[b] < [bab]$. Next, we have $[bb] < [babb]$ and $[babb] = [bab]$. But by the definition of L_{11}^R, the class $[bb]$ corresponds to a state from which no string is accepted. This is a contradiction with the fact that $[\varepsilon] < [b]$ and $[ba] < [baba]$. Thus L_{11}^R is not an ordered language. □

Notice that an alternative proof is provided for non-closure of power-separating languages under concatenation.

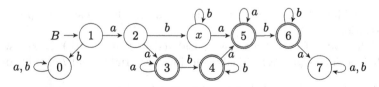

Fig. 2. A DFA for the second power of the language $(aa^*b^*)^2$. The problematic state that arises for the total order is denoted with x.

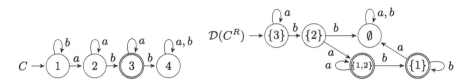

Fig. 3. Left: A DFA C for the ordered language L_{11} whose reverse is not ordered. Right: The DFA $\mathcal{D}(C^R)$ for the language L_{11}^R.

4   Conclusions

We conclude with a summary of the obtained properties in an upcoming table with a description of lemmas and cited known results used to obtain them. For better context we also provide an overview of closure properties of some other subclasses of regular languages, shown in its bottom part.

The already mentioned class of left ideals is a subclass of suffix-convex languages. For other classes of ideal languages, it is known that they are closed under intersection, union, and concatenation, but not under star and complementation [29]. In [1], some closure and non-closure properties for classes of closed, free, and convex languages are provided as well. For the sake of completeness of our overview, in the following proposition we provide all the other closure and non-closure properties for right, two-sided, and all-sided ideals, as well as for prefix-, suffix-, factor-, and subword-closed, -free, and -convex languages. We include them separately from the main results due to the fact that the closure of these considered classes is mostly a direct consequence of the corresponding language class definitions and non-closure can be shown in a straightforward manner.

Proposition 11. *The following statements hold:*

(a) The classes of ideal, closed, and free languages are closed under power.
(b) The classes of ideal languages are closed under positive closure.
(c) The classes of free languages are not closed under union, positive closure, and complementation.
(d) The classes of convex languages are not closed under positive closure.
(e) The right ideal, prefix- and suffix-closed, prefix- and suffix-free, and prefix- and suffix-convex classes are not closed under reversal, while classes of the two-sided and all-sided ideal, factor- and subword-closed, factor- and subword-free, and factor- and subword-convex classes are closed under reversal.

Proof. (a) The closure property follows from the closure property under concatenation.

(b) The class of left ideals was considered in Lemma 4(b). Next, two-sided and all-sided ideals are right ideals, and for every right ideal L, we have

$$L \subseteq L^+ = LL^* \subseteq L\Sigma^* = L,$$

thus we have $L^+ = L$. Hence L^+ is in the same class as L.

(c) The languages $K_7 = \{\varepsilon\}$ and $L_7 = \{a\}$ from Lemma 8(c) are subword-free since every singleton language is subword-free. Next, $\{\varepsilon, a\} \subseteq K_7 \cup L_7$ while ε is a prefix and suffix of a, $\{a, aa\} \subseteq L_7^+$ while a is a prefix and suffix of aa, and $\{\varepsilon, aa\} \subseteq L_7^c$ while ε is a prefix and suffix of aa. It follows that $K_7 \cup L_7$, L_7^+, and L_7^c are neither prefix-free nor suffix-free.

(d) The language $L_{10} = \{aa\}$ from Lemma a(c) is subword-convex since it is a singleton. But $\{aa, aaaa\} \subseteq L_{10}^+$ while $aaa \notin L_{10}^+$. Hence L_{10}^+ is neither prefix-convex nor suffix-convex.

(e) The closure property follows from the definitions of classes. For the non-closure property, consider the right ideal language $L_{12} = a(a + b)^*$, prefix-closed language $L_{13} = \{\varepsilon, a, ab\}$, and prefix-free language $L_{14} = \{a, baa\}$. Then we have $\{a, aba\} \subseteq L_{12}^R$ but $ab \notin L_{12}^R$, next $\{\varepsilon, ba\} \subseteq L_{13}^R$ but $b \notin L_{13}^R$, and finally $\{a, aab\} \subseteq L_{14}^R$ but $aa \notin L_{14}^R$. Hence the languages L_{12}^R, L_{13}^R, and L_{14}^R are not even prefix-convex. The non-closure property for classes of suffix-closed and suffix-free languages can be shown using L_{13}^R and L_{14}^R as witnesses. □

All results of this paper together with already known properties are summarized in the following theorem.

Theorem 12. *For each cell in Table 1, the class corresponding to the row is closed under the operation corresponding to the column if the cell displays ✓, and it is not closed if the cell displays ×.*

Proof. The closure and non-closure properties of left ideal languages are shown in [22] for intersection and union [22, Lemma 3.4], concatenation [22, Lemma 3.6], star [22, Lemma 3.7], and complementation [22, Lemma 3.10]. The other closure and non-closure properties of combinational, finitely generated and general left ideal, and symmetric definite languages are shown in Lemmas 4 and a, respectively. The closure and non-closure properties of star, comet, and two-sided comet languages are shown in Lemmas 6 and a, respectively. The closure and non-closure properties of singletons and finite languages are provided by Proposition 8. The results for Boolean operations and concatenation on star-free, ordered, and power-separating languages are taken from [20], [25], and [26], respectively. The other closure and non-closure properties of ordered, star-free, and power-separating languages are shown in Lemma 9 and a, respectively.

In the second part of the table, we provide properties of the subclasses of convex languages, and the classes of union-free and group languages. The closure and non-closure properties of ideal, closed, and convex languages under Boolean operations, concatenation, and star are taken from [29]. In [1], the properties of convex classes under power [1, Remark 5], free classes under star [1, Remark 6], concatenation [1, Corollary 8], and intersection [1, Proposition 10], and closed classes under positive closure [1, Proposition 11] are shown. The other closure and non-closure properties for classes of ideal, closed, free, and convex languages, are provided by Proposition 11. The closure and non-closure properties for union-free languages is shown in [21], with the closure under reversal for this class previously shown in [19, Theorem 1]. Finally, the closure and non-closure properties for group languages are shown in [18, Theorem 8]. □

Table 1. Closure and non-closure properties for each considered class.

	$K \cap L$	$K \cup L$	KL	L^k	L^+	L^*	L^R	L^c
CB	✓	✓	×	×	✓	×	×	×
FGLID	✓	✓	×	×	✓[4]	×	×	×
LID	✓[22]	✓[22]	✓[22]	✓	✓	×[22]	×	×[22]
SYDEF	×	×	✓	✓	✓	×	✓	×
STAR	✓	×	×	✓	✓	✓	✓	×
COM	×	×	✓	✓	✓	✓^{a}	×	×
2COM	×	×	✓	✓	✓	✓	✓	×
SINGL	×	×	✓	✓	×	×	✓	×
FIN	✓	✓	✓	✓	×	×	✓	×
ORD	×[25]	×[25]	×[25]	×	×	×	×	✓[25]
STFR	✓[20]	✓[20]	✓[20]	✓	×	×	✓	✓[20]
PSEP	✓[26]	✓[26]	×[26]	×	×	×	✓	✓[26]
RID	✓[29]	✓[29]	✓[29]	✓	✓	×[29]	×	×[29]
TSID	✓[29]	✓[29]	✓[29]	✓	✓	×[29]	✓	×[29]
ASID	✓[29]	✓[29]	✓[29]	✓	✓	×[29]	✓	×[29]
PRCL	✓[29]	✓[29]	✓[29]	✓	✓[1]	✓[29]	×	×[29]
SUCL	✓[29]	✓[29]	✓[29]	✓	✓[1]	✓[29]	×	×[29]
FACL	✓[29]	✓[29]	✓[29]	✓	✓[1]	✓[29]	✓	×[29]
SWCL	✓[29]	✓[29]	✓[29]	✓	✓[1]	✓[29]	✓	×[29]
PRFR	✓[1]	×	✓[1]	✓	×	×[1]	×	×
SUFR	✓[1]	×	✓[1]	✓	×	×[1]	×	×
FAFR	✓[1]	×	✓[1]	✓	×	×[1]	✓	×
SWFR	✓[1]	×	✓[1]	✓	×	×[1]	✓	×
PRCV	✓[29]	×[29]	×[29]	×[1]	×	×[29]	×	×[29]
SUCV	✓[29]	×[29]	×[29]	×[1]	×	×[29]	×	×[29]
FACV	✓[29]	×[29]	×[29]	×[1]	×	×[29]	✓	×[29]
SWCV	✓[29]	×[29]	×[29]	×[1]	×	×[29]	✓	×[29]
UNFR	×[21]	×[21]	✓[21]	✓[21]	✓[21]	✓[21]	✓[19]	×[21]
GRP	✓[18]	✓[18]	×[18]	×[18]	×[18]	×[18]	✓[18]	✓[18]

^{a} Closure for comets and two-sided comets under star applies for all L except $L = \emptyset$.

Acknowledgment. We would like to thank Martin Kutrib and Jeffrey Shallit for providing us some relevant literature.

References

1. Ang, T., Brzozowski, J.A.: Languages convex with respect to binary relations, and their closure properties. Acta Cybern. 19(2), 445–464 (2009). https://cyber.bibl.u-szeged.hu/index.php/actcybern/article/view/3776
2. Bordihn, H., Holzer, M., Kutrib, M.: Determination of finite automata accepting subregular languages. Theor. Comput. Sci. **410**(35), 3209–3222 (2009). https://doi.org/10.1016/j.tcs.2009.05.019
3. Brzozowski, J., Jirásková, G., Li, B., Smith, J.: Quotient complexity of bifix-, factor-, and subword-free regular languages. Acta Cybern. **21**(4), 507–527 (2014). https://doi.org/10.14232/actacyb.21.4.2014.1
4. Brzozowski, J.A.: Canonical regular expressions and minimal state graphs for definite events. In: Proceedings of Symposium on Mathematical Theory of Automata. MRI Symposia Series, vol. 12, pp. 529–561. Polytechnic Press, New York (1962)
5. Brzozowski, J.A.: Roots of star events. J. ACM **14**(3), 466–477 (1967). https://doi.org/10.1145/321406.321409
6. Brzozowski, J.A., Jirásková, G., Li, B.: Quotient complexity of ideal languages. Theor. Comput. Sci. **470**, 36–52 (2013). https://doi.org/10.1016/j.tcs.2012.10.055
7. Brzozowski, J., Jirásková, G., Zou, C.: Quotient complexity of closed languages. Theory Comput. Syst. **54**(2), 277–292 (2013). https://doi.org/10.1007/s00224-013-9515-7
8. Crvenković, S., Dolinka, I., Ésik, Z.: On equations for union-free regular languages. Inf. Comput. **164**(1), 152–172 (2001). https://doi.org/10.1006/inco.2000.2889
9. Davies, S., Hospodár, M.: Square, power, positive closure, and complementation on star-free languages. In: Hospodár, M., Jirásková, G., Konstantinidis, S. (eds.) DCFS 2019. LNCS, vol. 11612, pp. 98–110. Springer, Cham (2019). https://doi.org/10.1007/978-3-030-23247-4_7
10. Han, Y., Salomaa, K.: State complexity of basic operations on suffix-free regular languages. Theor. Comput. Sci. **410**(27–29), 2537–2548 (2009). https://doi.org/10.1016/j.tcs.2008.12.054
11. Han, Y., Salomaa, K., Wood, D.: Operational state complexity of prefix-free regular languages. In: Ésik, Z., Fülöp, Z. (eds.) Automata, Formal Languages, and Related Topics - Dedicated to Ferenc Gécseg on the Occasion of his 70th Birthday, pp. 99–115. Institute of Informatics, University of Szeged, Hungary (2009)
12. Holzer, M., Hospodár, M.: The range of state complexities of languages resulting from the cut operation. In: Martín-Vide, C., Okhotin, A., Shapira, D. (eds.) LATA 2019. LNCS, vol. 11417, pp. 190–202. Springer, Cham (2019). https://doi.org/10.1007/978-3-030-13435-8_14
13. Holzer, M., Kutrib, M., Meckel, K.: Nondeterministic state complexity of star-free languages. Theor. Comput. Sci. **450**, 68–80 (2012). https://doi.org/10.1016/j.tcs.2012.04.028
14. Hopcroft, J.E., Ullman, J.D.: Introduction to Automata Theory, Languages and Computation. Addison-Wesley, Boston (1979)
15. Hospodár, M.: Power, positive closure, and quotients on convex languages. Theor. Comput. Sci. **870**, 53–74 (2021). https://doi.org/10.1016/j.tcs.2021.02.002
16. Hospodár, M., Holzer, M.: The ranges of accepting state complexities of languages resulting from some operations. Int. J. Found. Comput. Sci. **31**(8), 1159–1177 (2020). https://doi.org/10.1142/S0129054120420083
17. Hospodár, M., Jirásková, G., Mlynárčik, P.: Nondeterministic complexity in subclasses of convex languages. Theor. Comput. Sci. **787**, 89–110 (2019). https://doi.org/10.1016/j.tcs.2018.12.027

18. Hospodár, M., Mlynárčik, P.: Operations on permutation automata. In: Jonoska, N., Savchuk, D. (eds.) DLT 2020. LNCS, vol. 12086, pp. 122–136. Springer, Cham (2020). https://doi.org/10.1007/978-3-030-48516-0_10
19. Jirásková, G., Masopust, T.: Complexity in union-free regular languages. Int. J. Found. Comput. Sci. **22**(07), 1639–1653 (2011). https://doi.org/10.1142/S0129054111008933
20. Meyer, A.R.: A note on star-free events. J. ACM **16**(2), 220–225 (1969). https://doi.org/10.1145/321510.321513
21. Nagy, B.: Union-freeness, deterministic union-freeness and union-complexity. In: Hospodár, M., Jirásková, G., Konstantinidis, S. (eds.) DCFS 2019. LNCS, vol. 11612, pp. 46–56. Springer, Cham (2019). https://doi.org/10.1007/978-3-030-23247-4_3
22. Paz, A., Peleg, B.: Ultimate-definite and symmetric-definite events and automata. J. ACM **12**(3), 399–410 (1965). https://doi.org/10.1145/321281.321292
23. Perles, M., Rabin, M.O., Shamir, E.: The theory of definite automata. IEEE Trans. Electron. Comput. **EC-12**(3), 233–243 (1963). https://doi.org/10.1109/PGEC.1963.263534
24. Schützenberger, M.P.: On finite monoids having only trivial subgroups. Inf. Control **8**(2), 190–194 (1965). https://doi.org/10.1016/S0019-9958(65)90108-7
25. Shyr, H., Thierrin, G.: Ordered automata and associated languages. Tamkang J. Math. **5**, 9–20 (1974)
26. Shyr, H., Thierrin, G.: Power-separating regular languages. Math. Syst. Theory **8**(1), 90–95 (1974). https://doi.org/10.1007/BF01761710
27. Sipser, M.: Introduction to the Theory of Computation. Cengage Learning, Boston (2012)
28. Thierrin, G.: Permutation automata. Math. Syst. Theory **2**, 83–90 (1968). https://doi.org/10.1007/BF01691347
29. Thierrin, G.: Convex languages. In: Nivat, M. (ed.) ICALP 1972, pp. 481–492. North-Holland, Amsterdam (1972)

P Systems with Evolutional Communication and Separation Rules

David Orellana-Martín[1,2(✉)] , Luis Valencia-Cabrera[1,2] ,
and Mario J. Pérez-Jiménez[1,2]

[1] Research Group on Natural Computing, Department of Computer Science
and Artificial Intelligence, Universidad de Sevilla,
Avda. Reina Mercedes s/n, 41012 Sevilla, Spain
{dorellana,lvalencia,marper}@us.es
[2] SCORE Laboratory, I3US, Universidad de Sevilla, Avda. Reina Mercedes s/n,
41012 Sevilla, Spain

Abstract. In the framework of membrane computing, several interesting results concerning frontiers of efficiency between the complexity classes **P** and **NP** have been found by using different ingredients. One of the main characteristics of cell-like membrane systems is their rooted tree-like structure, where a natural parent-children membrane relationship exists, and objects can travel through the membranes. Separation rules are used as a method to obtain an exponential workspace in terms of membranes in polynomial time. Inspired by cell *meiosis*, objects from the original membrane are distributed between the two new membranes. In this work, P systems with evolutional symport/antiport rules and separation rules are used to give a solution to SAT, a well known **NP**-complete problem. One of the advantages of this solution is the use of the environment as a passive agent.

Keywords: Membrane computing · Computational complexity theory · P vs. NP problem · Evolutional communication · Symport/antiport

1   Introduction

Membrane Computing is a model of computation within the field of *Natural Computing*. The devices of such a model of computation, called membrane systems or P systems, are inspired by the structure of living cells, using the concept of compartments as the organelles situated within eukaryotic cells [18]. A wide spectrum of different membrane systems can be constructed by changing the "ingredients" used for each of them: the structure and connection between the regions of the systems [2,5,17], the types of objects used [4,9,24], the nature and behavior of the rules [1,6,8], among others [3,7,16].

From all of them, cell-like membrane systems were the first ones introduced and one of the most studied types of P systems. Cell-like P systems are structured with a tree-like graph, where the *skin* membrane abstracts the cytoplasmic

J. Durand-Lose and G. Vaszil (Eds.): MCU 2022, LNCS 13419, pp. 143–157, 2022.
https://doi.org/10.1007/978-3-031-13502-6_10

membrane of a living cell, and its contents represent the chemical compounds that reside within the cell. In this structure, the concept of *parent* membrane and *children* membranes are naturally defined. The only region allowed to communicate with the environment of the cell is the one enclosed by the skin membrane.

Integral membrane proteins are involved in the process of transporting molecules from one region to other region [13]. Compounds that travel along in the same direction are moved with the help of a *symporter*, while compounds that move in different directions (that is, they "interchange" positions) are moved with the help of a *antiporter*. This is the inspiration for classical symport/antiport rules. In fact, if we think about the process of transport, the elements involved in this process (both the elements moving and the integral membrane proteins) can change their nature, giving these objects the ability to "evolve". Evolutional symport/antiport rules were first introduced in tissue P systems [23], while trying to demonstrate their ability to solve presumably hard problems. Later, in [15] separation rules [14] were used as a method to create an exponential workspace in terms of cells in polynomial time. An improvement of the results of the previous papers was presented in [11]. In [12], evolutional communication rules were introduced in the framework of cell-like P systems besides the use of division rules as a method to create an exponential workspace in terms of membranes. In this paper, we change division rules by separation rules as it was made with the tissue-like counterparts. In the tissue-like framework, the results changed depending on the fission type of rule, and it seems straightforward to study it in the cell-like framework to see if it holds.

Originally, the environment played a passive role in cell-like membrane systems [18], given that it could only receive objects from the P systems. In the framework of tissue P systems [10], a new way to transport objects were introduced, where the environment, apart from receiving objects, it could also have the ability to send objects to the cells of the system. In order to give it a special role, a special alphabet (referred to as the environment alphabet, and usually denoted as $\mathcal{E}$) is defined and all the objects in it are supposed to appear an arbitrary number of times (it can be though as an infinite number of appearances) at the beginning of the computation in the environment (it is an inspiration from the real tissues and their communication with the environment, that has chemical components coming from other places). In [21], authors simulated the environment through an initial stage where a sufficient number of objects, necessary for an efficient solution to a presumably hard problem, could be created in polynomial time at the beginning of the computation just by using a duplication process. In this way, authors proved that in some types of P systems, the environment can be recreated by means of an initial creation of all the necessary objects for the computation.

The paper is organized as follows: In Sect. 2, some concepts are introduced in order to be used later in the paper. Section 3 is devoted to introduce P systems with evolutional communication and separation rules defining directly their recognizing versions. In the following section, a solution to the **NP**-complete problem SAT is given, besides an overview of the computation. Finally, some remarks and future research lines are depicted in the last section.

2   Preliminaries

In this section, we provide some concepts used through the whole paper.

2.1   Alphabets and Sets

An *alphabet* Γ is a (finite) non-empty set. The elements of an alphabet are named *symbols*. A *word* over Γ is a *finite ordered succession* of elements from Γ; that is, it is an application from a natural number n onto the set Γ. The number n is denominated the *length* of a string. The *empty string* is the string with length 0, and it is denoted by λ.

Given two sets A and B, the *relative complement* $A \setminus B$ of B in A is defined as follows: $A \setminus B = \{x \in A \mid x \notin B\}$. For each set A, we note by $|A|$ the *cardinal* (number of elements) of the set A.

A *multiset* M can be described explicitly as follows:

$$\{(a_1, M(a_1)), \ldots, (a_n, M(a_n))\}$$

and we will use the notation $M = a_1^{M(a_1)} \ldots a_n^{M(a_n)}$. The cardinal of a finite multiset over $\Gamma = \{a_1, \ldots, a_n\}$ is defined as follows: $|M| = M(a_1) + \ldots + M(a_n)$. We denote by $M_f(\Gamma)$ the set of all the finite multisets over Γ, and $M_f^+(\Gamma) = M_f(\Gamma) \setminus \emptyset$. For a more specific concepts in this area, we refer the reader to [22].

2.2   Propositional Boolean Logic

The language of propositional logic consists on: (a) an enumerable set, PV, of propositional variables; (b) some logic connectives ($\neg$, negation and $\vee$, disjunction); and (c) some auxiliary symbols "("and")".

The set $PForm$ of *propositional formula* is the smallest set Γ that contains PV and verifies the following conditions: (a) if $P \in \Gamma$, then $\neg P \in \Gamma$; and (b) if $P, Q \in \Gamma$, then $(P \vee Q) \in \Gamma$. From $\neg$ and $\vee$ the logic connectives $\wedge$, $\rightarrow$ and $\leftrightarrow$ are defined according to the usual truth tables. We denote the formulas $\neg P$, $P \vee Q$ and $P \wedge Q$ by $\overline{P}$, $P + Q$ and $P \cdot Q$.

A *literal* is a propositional variable or the negation of a propositional variable. A *clause* is the disjunction of a finite number of literals. A propositional formula is in *conjunctive normal form* (CNF) if it is a conjunction of a finite number of clauses. Besides, we can suppose that, without loss of generality, every propositional formula in CNF is in *simplified form*; that is, in each clause of such a formula, there cannot exist neither a literal and its negation, nor two repeated literals.

A *truth assignment* is an application from PV onto $\{0, 1\}$. Every truth assignment is extended in a natural way to an application from $PForm$ onto $\{0, 1\}$

(through the corresponding *truth tables*). A *relevant* truth assignment for a formula φ is an application from the set of variables of such a formula onto the set $\{0, 1\}$. Therefore, if a propositional formula φ has n variables, then the total number of possible relevant truth assignments of φ is 2^n.

We say that a propositional formula, φ, is *satisfiable* if and only if there exists, at least, a truth assignment, σ, such that $\sigma(\varphi) = 1$. The SAT problem is a decision problem $\text{SAT} = (I_{\text{SAT}}, \theta_{\text{SAT}})$ such that the elements from I_{SAT} are simplified propositional formulas in CNF and $\theta_{\text{SAT}}(\varphi) = 1$ if and only if the formula φ is satisfiable.

2.3   Cantor Pairing Function

The *Cantor pairing function* encodes pairs of natural numbers through individual natural numbers and it is defined as follows: for each $m, n \in \mathbb{N}$,

$$\langle m, n \rangle = \frac{(m + n)(m + n + 1)}{2} + n$$

The Cantor pairing function is a recursive primitive bijective function from $\mathbb{N} \times \mathbb{N}$ onto $\mathbb{N}$. Therefore, for each natural number $t \in \mathbb{N}$ there exist two (unique) natural numbers $m, m \in \mathbb{N}$ such that $t = \langle m, n \rangle$.

3   Recognizer Cell-Like Membrane Systems with Evolutional Symport/Antiport and Separation Rules

Let h be a label of a membrane. Then $p(h)$ is the label of the parent membrane of the membrane labelled by h. A recognizer P system with evolutional communication and separation rules of degree $q \geq 1$ is a tuple

$$\Pi = (\Gamma, \Gamma_0, \Gamma_1, \Sigma, \mathcal{E}, H, H_0, H_1, \mu, \mathcal{M}_1, \ldots, \mathcal{M}_q, \mathcal{R}, i_{in}, i_{out})$$

where:

1. Γ is a finite alphabet, with $\Sigma, \mathcal{E} \subseteq \Gamma$, $\Sigma \cap \mathcal{E} = \emptyset$, and Γ contains two special objects **yes** and **no**.
2. $\{\Gamma_0, \Gamma_1\}$ is a partition of Γ; that is, $\Gamma_0 \cap \Gamma_1 = \emptyset$ and $\Gamma_0 \cup \Gamma_1 = \Gamma$.
3. H is the set of labels, and $\{H_0, H_1\}$ is a partition of H.
4. μ is a rooted tree whose nodes are bijectively labelled with elements from H. We say that the label of the root is i_{skin}, and the "label" of the environment is env or 0.
5. $\mathcal{R}$, is a finite set of rules over Γ of the following forms:
   (a) Evolutional send-in (symport) rules: $[u [\ ]_j]_i \rightarrow [[u']_j]_i$, with $0 \leq i, j \leq q, i \neq j, i = p(j), u \in M_f^+(\Gamma), u' \in M_f(\Gamma)$.
   (b) Evolutional send-out (symport) rules: $[[u]_j]_i \rightarrow [u' [\ ]_j]_i$, with $0 \leq i, j \leq q, i \neq j, i = p(j), u \in M_f^+(\Gamma), u' \in M_f(\Gamma)$.

(c) Evolutional antiport rules: $[u\,[v]_j]_i \to [v'\,[u']_j]_i$, with $0 \le i,j \le q, i \ne j, i = p(j), u,v \in M_f^+(\Gamma), u',v' \in M_f(\Gamma)$.

(d) Separation rules: $[a]_i \to [\Gamma_0]_i[\Gamma_1]_i$, with $1 \le i \le q, i \notin \{i_{out}, i_{skin}\}, a \in \Gamma$ (being i_{skin} the label of the skin membrane).

6. $i_{in} \in \{1, \ldots, q\}$ and $i_{out} = env$.

A recognizer P system with evolutional symport/antiport and separation rules of degree $q \ge 1$ $\Pi = (\Gamma, \Gamma_0, \Gamma_1, \Sigma, \mathcal{E}, H, H_0, H_1, \mu\mathcal{M}_1, \ldots, \mathcal{M}_q, \mathcal{R}, i_{in}, i_{out})$ with input $m \subseteq M_f(\Sigma)$ can be seen as a set of q membranes labelled by $1, \ldots, q$ organized in a rooted-tree graph defined by μ, where the parent-children membrane relationship is described in a natural way, and where the environment is the parent region of the skin (outermost) membrane, such that: (a) $\mathcal{M}_1, \ldots, \mathcal{M}_q$ represent the initial multisets of objects situated at the beginning in the q membranes of the system; (b) $\mathcal{E}$ is the set of objects situated initially in the environment, each of them with an arbitrary number of copies; (c) $\mathcal{R}$ is a finite set of rules over Γ that rule the dynamics of the system; and (d) i_{in} and i_{out} represent distinguished *regions* (or *zones*), that represent the zone where the encoded instance is placed initially in the case of i_{in}, and where the encoded solution will be placed in the last step of the computation. We use the terms *zone* or *region* i $(0 \le i \le q)$ to refer to the membrane i, in the case $1 \le i \le q$, or to the environment, in the case $i = 0$. The environment can play an active role in this framework, in the sense that it can both receive objects from and send objects to the P system. There are two definitions of length defined in the case of evolutional symport/antiport rules. The length of a rule $r \equiv [u\,[v]_j]_i \to [v'\,[u']_j]_i$ can be defined as a natural number $length(r) = |u| + |v| + |u'| + |v'|$. Another way to define it is as a pair $length(r) = (|u| + |v|, |u'| + |v'|)$.

A *configuration* of a P system Π in an instant t is described by the structure of membranes in that instant, the multisets of objects from Γ in each membrane of the structure and the multiset of objects over $\Gamma \backslash \mathcal{E}$ situated in the environment. The initial configuration of Π is $(\mu, \mathcal{M}_1, \ldots, \mathcal{M}_{i_{in}} + w, \ldots, \mathcal{M}_q, \emptyset)$, where w is the encoded instance of the problem. If the environment plays a passive role, then $\mathcal{E}$ is usually omitted from the definition of the P system.

An *evolutional send-in* rule $[u\,[\;\;]_j]_i \to [\,[u']_j]_i$ is applicable to a configuration $\mathcal{C}_t$ at an instant t if in such a configuration, there exists a membrane labelled by i that contains the multiset of objects u and it has a child membrane labelled by j. The application of such a rule to that membrane i produces the following effects: objects from u are consumed from that membrane and, in the same step, objects from u' are created in the child membrane labelled by j.

An *evolutional send-out* rule $[\,[u]_j]_i \to [u'\,[\;\;]_j]_i$ is applicable to a configuration $\mathcal{C}_t$ at an instant t if in such a configuration, there exists a membrane labelled by i that has a child membrane labelled by j that contains the multiset of objects u. The application of such a rule to that membrane i produces the following effects: objects from u are consumed from the membrane labelled by j and, in the same step, objects from u' are created in the membrane labelled by i.

An *evolutional antiport* rule $[u[v]_j]_i \rightarrow [v'[u']_j]_i$ is applicable to a configuration $\mathcal{C}_t$ at an instant t if in such a configuration, there exists a membrane labelled by i that contains the multiset of objects u and it has a child membrane labelled by j that contains the multiset of objects v. The application of such a rule to that membrane i produces the following effects: objects from u and v are consumed from their respective membranes and, in the same step, objects from u' are created in the membrane labelled by j and objects from v' are created in the membrane labelled by i.

A *separation* rule $[a]_i \rightarrow [\Gamma_0]_i[\Gamma_1]_i$ is applicable to a configuration $\mathcal{C}_t$ at an instant t if in such a configuration, there exists a membrane labelled by i that contains the object a. The application of such a rule to that membrane i produces the following effects: object a is consumed, the membrane i disappears and in the same steps, two new membranes with label i are created, with the contents of the original membrane distributed between the two of them according to the partition $\{\Gamma_0, \Gamma_1\}$. If the separated membrane is a non-elementary membrane, then the internal membranes are distributed into the two new membranes in such a way that membranes from H_0 will be present in one membrane and membranes from H_1 will be present in the other new membrane. If no separation rules for non-elementary membranes are used, then H_0 and H_1 are omitted in the definition of the P system.

We say that a configuration $\mathcal{C}_t$ of a recognizer P system with evolutional symport/antiport and separation rules Π produces a configuration $\mathcal{C}_{t+1}$ in one *transition step*, we denote it by $\mathcal{C}_t \Rightarrow_\Pi \mathcal{C}_{t+1}$ and we say that $\mathcal{C}_{t+1}$ is a following configuration of $\mathcal{C}_t$ if we can pass from $\mathcal{C}_t$ to $\mathcal{C}_{t+1}$ by applying the rules from $\mathcal{R}$ according to the following principles:

- An arbitrary object of a membrane can fire, at most, one rule (selected, in such a case, in a non-deterministic way); that is, if a specific object is used to apply a rule, then the object cannot be used to apply another rule (even if it is the same rule).
- To each membrane, there can only be applied each evolutional communication rules or separation rules. In the case of applying evolutional communication rules to the membrane i in the configuration $\mathcal{C}_t$, these will be applied in a non-deterministic, parallel and maximal way; that is, all the communication rules from $\mathcal{R}_i$ that can be applied in a single step will be applied. In the case of applying a separation rule to the membrane i in the configuration $\mathcal{C}_t$, it will be selected in a non-deterministic way. In this sense, when a separation rule is applied to a membrane i, then it is blocked and cannot communicate with other membranes.

The new membranes resulting from the separation will be able to interact with other membranes only from the following transition step, only if they are not separated again. Besides, these membranes will have the same labels as the original one and will provide new edges to the tree-like graph.

The computation of a P system Π is defined as a sequence of configurations $\mathcal{C} = (\mathcal{C}_0, \mathcal{C}_1, \ldots, \mathcal{C}_n)$, where $\mathcal{C}_0$ is the initial configuration of Π and $\mathcal{C}_t \Rightarrow_\Pi \mathcal{C}_{t+1}, 1 \leq t \leq n-1$, and we say that it takes n steps.

As a recognizer P system, some conditions need to be fulfilled:

- All the computations of a P system Π with input, denoted by $\Pi + w$, halt and send an object **yes** or an object **no** (but not both) to the environment, and only in the last step of the computation. We say that it is an *accepting* (respectively, *rejecting*) computation if an object **yes** (resp., **no**) is sent to the environment.
- The system must be *confluent*, in the sense that all the possible computations of $\Pi + w$ are either accepting computations or rejecting computations.

We say that a family of recognizer P systems with evolutional communication and separation rules solve a decision problem $X = (I_X, \theta_X)$ if the following holds:

1. We can define (cod, s) a pair of polynomially computable functions over I_X such that (a) $s(u)$ is a natural number (obtained by a reasonable encoding scheme); (b) for each $k \in \mathbb{N}$, the set $s^{-1}(k)$ is finite; and (c) for each $u \in I_X$, $cod(u)$ is an input multiset of the P system $\Pi(s(u))$.

Definition 1. *Let $X = (I_X, \theta_X)$ a decision problem, $\mathbf{\Pi} = \{\Pi(n) \mid n \in \mathbb{N}\}$ a family of recognizer P systems and (cod, s) a polynomial encoding of the problem X in the family $\mathbf{\Pi}$.*

- *We say that the family $\mathbf{\Pi}$ is* sound *with respect to (X, cod, s) if for each instance $u \in I_X$ such that it exists, at least, one accepting computation of the system $\Pi(s(u)) + cod(u)$, it holds that $\theta_X(u) = 1$.*
- *We say that the family $\mathbf{\Pi}$ is* complete *with respect to (X, cod, s) if for each instance $u \in I_X$ such that $\theta_X(u) = 1$, it holds that all the computations of $\Pi(s(u)) + cod(u)$ are accepting computations.*

The set of problems solvable by uniform families of P systems from a class $\mathcal{R}$ is denoted by $\mathbf{PMC}_\mathcal{R}$. The class of recognizer P systems with evolutional communication and separation rules of length at most k (respectively, (k_1, k_2)) is denoted by $\mathcal{CSEC}(k)$ (resp., $\mathcal{CSEC}(k_1, k_2)$).

All of these concepts among many others in the framework of Membrane Computing can be found in a more comprehensive way in [19, 20].

4 A Solution to SAT in $\mathcal{CSEC}(2, 2)$

Let $\varphi = C_1 \wedge \ldots \wedge C_p$ be a Boolean formula with n variables and p clauses, such that $C_j = l_{j,1} \vee \ldots \vee l_{j,r_j}$ is the j-th clause and $l_{j,k}$ is a literal that can be either a variable x_i or its negation $\neg x_i$. We define the encoding of such a formula as follows: $cod(\varphi) = \{x_{i,j,0} \mid x_i \in C_j\} \cup \{\overline{x}_{i,j,0} \mid \neg x_i \in C_j\}$. We define $s(\varphi) = \langle n, p \rangle$, where $\langle a, b \rangle$ is the Cantor pairing function of a and b. Then, for each $n, p \in \mathbb{N}$, we consider the recognizer P system

$$\Pi(\langle n, p \rangle) = (\Gamma, \Gamma_0, \Gamma_1, \Sigma, H, \mu, \mathcal{M}_1, \ldots, \mathcal{M}_q, \mathcal{R}, i_{in}, i_{out})$$

from $\mathcal{CSEC}(2, 2)$ defined as follows:

1. Working alphabet Γ:
   $\{\text{yes}, \text{no}, y_1, y_2, n_1, n_2, \#\} \cup$
   $\{a_{i,j} \mid 1 \le i \le n, 0 \le j \le i\} \cup$
   $\{a'_{i,j} \mid 2 \le i \le n, 0 \le j \le i-1\} \cup$
   $\{a^L_{i,j}, a^R_{i,j} \mid 2 \le i \le n, 1 \le j \le i-1\} \cup$
   $\{\alpha_j, \alpha'_j, \alpha^L_j, \alpha^R_j \mid 1 \le j \le p+1\} \cup$
   $\{t_i, f_i, t'_i, t''_i f''_i, t^L_i, t^R_i, f^L_i, f^R_i \mid 1 \le i \le n\} \cup$
   $\{\beta_{l,k}, \beta'_{l,k}, \beta^L_{l,k}, \beta^R_{l,k} \mid 0 \le k \le n, 1 \le l \le n\} \cup$
   $\{x_{i,j,k}, \overline{x}_{i,j,k}, x^*_{i,j,k} \mid 1 \le i \le n, 1 \le j \le p, 1 \le k \le n+j-1\} \cup$
   $\{x'_{i,j,k}, \overline{x}'_{i,j,k}, x^{*\prime}_{i,j,k}, x''_{i,j,k}, \overline{x}''_{i,j,k}, x^{*\prime\prime}_{i,j,k}, x'''_{i,j,k}, \overline{x}'''_{i,j,k}, x^{*\prime\prime\prime}_{i,j,k}, \mid$
   $0 \le i \le n, 1 \le j \le p, 1 \le k \le n\} \cup$
   $\{c_{j,k} \mid 1 \le j \le p, j \le k \le p\} \cup \{\delta_i \mid 0 \le i \le 4n+p+2\} \cup$
   $\{\delta'_i \mid 0 \le i \le 4n+p\} \cup \{\gamma_k \mid 0 \le k \le n+1\}$.
2. $\Gamma_1 = \Gamma \setminus \Gamma_0$, $\Gamma_0 = \{a^L_{i,j} \mid 2 \le i \le n, 1 \le j \le i-1\} \cup$
   $\{\alpha^L_j \mid 1 \le j \le p+1\} \cup \{t^L_i, f^L_i \mid 1 \le i \le n\} \cup$
   $\{\beta^L_{l,k} \mid 0 \le k \le n, k+1 \le l \le n\}$
3. Input alphabet Σ: $\{x_{i,j,0}, \overline{x}_{i,j,0}, x^*_{i,k,0} \mid 1 \le i \le n, 1 \le j \le p\}$.
4. $H = \{1, 2, 3\}$
5. $\mu = [[\ \ ]_2 [\ \ ]_3]_1$.
6. $\mathcal{M}_1 = \{\delta_0, \delta'_0, \gamma_0^{2n^2+6np+4n+2p+6}\}$,
   $\mathcal{M}_2 = \{a_{i,0} \mid 1 \le i \le n\} \cup \{\alpha_j \mid 1 \le j \le p+1\}$,
   $\mathcal{M}_3 = \{\gamma_0^{2n^2+6np+4n+2p+6}\} \cup \{\beta_{l,0}^{n+p+1} \mid 1 \le l \le n\}$.
7. The set $\mathcal{R}$ consists of the following rules:

   0.1 Rules to generate the objects γ to simulate the environment

   $$\left. \begin{array}{l} [[\gamma_k]_3]_1 \to [\gamma_{k+1}^2 [\ \ ]_3]_1 \\ [\gamma_k [\ \ ]_3]_1 \to [[\gamma_{k+1}^2]_3]_1 \end{array} \right\} \text{for } 1 \le k \le n$$
   $$[[\gamma_{n+1}]_3]_1 \to [\gamma [\ \ ]_3]_1$$
   $$[\gamma_{n+1} [\ \ ]_3]_1 \to [[\gamma]_3]_1$$

   1.1 Rules for steps $(4k+1)$.

   $$[\gamma [a_{i,i-1}]_2]_1 \to [[a'_{i,i-1} t'_i]_2]_1 \text{, for } 1 \le i \le n$$
   $$\left. \begin{array}{l} [\gamma [t_i]_2]_1 \to [[t''_i]_2]_1 \\ [\gamma [f_i]_2]_1 \to [[f''_i]_2]_1 \end{array} \right\} \text{for } 1 \le i \le n$$
   $$[\gamma [a_{i,j}]_2]_1 \to [[a'_{i,j}]_2]_1 \text{, for } 2 \le i \le n, 0 \le j \le i-2$$
   $$[\gamma [\alpha_j]_2]_1 \to [[\alpha'_j]_2]_1 \text{, for } 1 \le j \le p+1$$
   $$[\gamma [\beta_{l,k}]_3]_1 \to [[\beta'_{l,k}]_3]_1 \} \text{ for } \begin{array}{l} 0 \le k \le n, \\ k+1 \le l \le n \end{array}$$
   $$\left. \begin{array}{l} [x_{i,j,k} [\gamma]_3]_1 \to [x'_{i,j,k} [\ \ ]_3]_1 \\ [\overline{x}_{i,j,k} [\gamma]_3]_1 \to [\overline{x}'_{i,j,k} [\ \ ]_3]_1 \\ [x^*_{i,j,k} [\gamma]_3]_1 \to [x^{*\prime}_{i,j,k} [\ \ ]_3]_1 \end{array} \right\} \text{ for } \begin{array}{l} 1 \le i \le n, \\ 1 \le j \le p, \\ 0 \le k \le n-1 \end{array}$$

1.2 Rules for steps $(4k + 2)$.

$$\left.\begin{array}{l} [\gamma [a'_{i,i-1}]_2]_1 \to [[a_{i,i}f^R_i]_2]_1 \\ [\gamma [t'_i]_2]_1 \to [[t^L_i]_2]_1 \end{array}\right\} \text{ for } 1 \le i \le n$$

$$\left.\begin{array}{l} [\gamma [t''_i]_2]_1 \to [[t^L_i t^R_i]_2]_1 \\ [\gamma [f''_i]_2]_1 \to [[f^L_i f^R_i]_2]_1 \end{array}\right\} \text{ for } 1 \le i \le n$$

$$[\gamma [a'_{i,j}]_2]_1 \to [[a^L_{i,j+1}a^R_{i,j+1}]_2]_1, \text{ for } \begin{array}{l} 2 \le i \le n, \\ 0 \le j \le i-1 \end{array}$$

$$[\gamma [\alpha'_j]_2]_1 \to [[\alpha^L_j \alpha^R_j]_2]_1, \text{ for } 1 \le j \le p+1$$

$$[\gamma [\beta'_{l,k}]_3]_1 \to [[\beta^L_{l,k+1}\beta^R_{l,k+1}]_3]_1, \text{ for } \begin{array}{l} 0 \le k \le n, \\ k+1 \le l \le n \end{array}$$

$$\left.\begin{array}{l} [x'_{i,j,k}[\gamma]_3]_1 \to [x''^2_{i,j,k+1}[\ ]_3]_1 \\ [\overline{x}'_{i,j,k}[\gamma]_3]_1 \to [\overline{x}''^2_{i,j,k+1}[\ ]_3]_1 \\ [x^{*'}_{i,j,k}[\gamma]_3]_1 \to [x^{*''2}_{i,j,k+1}[\ ]_3]_1 \end{array}\right\} \begin{array}{l} 1 \le i \le n, \\ 1 \le j \le p, \\ 0 \le k \le n-1 \end{array}$$

1.3 Rules for steps $(4k + 3)$.

$$[a_{i,i}]_2 \to [\Gamma_0]_2[\Gamma_1]_2, \text{ for } 1 \le i \le n$$

$$\left.\begin{array}{l} [[\beta^O_{k,k}]_3]_1 \to [\beta^O_{k,k}[\ ]_3]_1 \\ [[\beta^O_{l,k}]_3]_1 \to [\beta_{l,k}[\ ]_3]_1 \end{array}\right\} \begin{array}{l} O \in \{L, R\}, \\ \text{for } 1 \le k \le n, \\ k+1 \le l \le n \end{array}$$

$$\left.\begin{array}{l} [x''_{i,j,k}[\gamma]_3]_1 \to [x'''_{i,j,k}[\ ]_3]_1 \\ [\overline{x}''_{i,j,k}[\gamma]_3]_1 \to [\overline{x}'''_{i,j,k}[\ ]_3]_1 \\ [x^{*''}_{i,j,k}[\gamma]_3]_1 \to [x^{*'''}_{i,j,k}[\ ]_3]_1 \end{array}\right\} \begin{array}{l} 1 \le i \le n, \\ \text{for } 1 \le j \le p, \\ 1 \le k \le n \end{array}$$

1.4 Rules for steps $(4k)$.

$$\left.\begin{array}{l} [\beta^O_{k,k}[a^O_{i,j}]_2]_1 \to [[a_{i,j}]_2]_1 \\ [\beta^O_{k,k}[r^O_i]_2]_1 \to [[r_i]_2]_1 \end{array}\right\} \begin{array}{l} O \in \{L, R\}, \\ r \in \{t, f\}, \\ \text{for } 1 \le i \le n, \\ 1 \le j \le n, \\ 1 \le k \le n \end{array}$$

$$[\beta^O_{k,k}[\alpha^O_j]_2]_1 \to [[\alpha_j]_2]_1, \begin{array}{l} O \in \{L, R\}, \\ \text{for } 1 \le j \le p+1, \\ 0 \le k \le n \end{array}$$

$$\left.\begin{array}{l} [x'''_{i,j,k}[\gamma]_3]_1 \to [x_{i,j,k}[\ ]_3]_1 \\ [\overline{x}'''_{i,j,k}[\gamma]_3]_1 \to [\overline{x}_{i,j,k}[\ ]_3]_1 \\ [x^{*'''}_{i,j,k}[\gamma]_3]_1 \to [x^*_{i,j,k}[\ ]_3]_1 \end{array}\right\} \begin{array}{l} 1 \le i \le n, \\ \text{for } 1 \le j \le p, \\ 0 \le k \le n \end{array}$$

$$[\beta_{l,k}[\ ]_3]_1 \to [[\beta_{l,k}]_3]_1, \text{ for } 0 \le k \le n, k+1 \le l \le n$$

2.1 Rules to check satisfied clauses.

$$\left.\begin{array}{l} [\,x_{i,j,n+j-1}\,[\,t_i\,]_2\,]_1 \to [\,[\,c_{j,j}t_i\,]_2\,]_1 \\ [\,\overline{x}_{i,j,n+j-1}\,[\,t_i\,]_2\,]_1 \to [\,[\,t_i\,]_2\,]_1 \\ [\,x^*_{i,j,n+j-1}\,[\,t_i\,]_2\,]_1 \to [\,[\,t_i\,]_2\,]_1 \\ [\,x_{i,j,n+j-1}\,[\,f_i\,]_2\,]_1 \to [\,[\,f_i\,]_2\,]_1 \\ [\,\overline{x}_{i,j,n+j-1}\,[\,f_i\,]_2\,]_1 \to [\,[\,c_{j,j}f_i\,]_2\,]_1 \\ [\,x^*_{i,j,n+j-1}\,[\,f_i\,]_2\,]_1 \to [\,[\,f_i\,]_2\,]_1 \end{array}\right\} \text{ for } 1 \le i \le n, 1 \le j \le p$$

$$\left.\begin{array}{l} [\,x_{i,j,n+k}\,[\,\gamma\,]_3\,]_1 \to [\,x_{i,j,n+k+1}\,[\quad]_3\,]_1 \\ [\,\overline{x}_{i,j,n+k}\,[\,\gamma\,]_3\,]_1 \to [\,\overline{x}_{i,j,n+k+1}\,[\quad]_3\,]_1 \\ [\,x^*_{i,j,n+k}\,[\,\gamma\,]_3\,]_1 \to [\,x^*_{i,j,n+k+1}\,[\quad]_3\,]_1 \end{array}\right\} \begin{array}{l} 1 \le i \le n, \\ \text{for } 1 \le j \le p, \\ 0 \le k \le j-2 \end{array}$$

$$[\,\gamma\,[\,c_{j,k}\,]_2\,]_1 \to [\,[\,c_{j,k+1}\,]_2\,]_1 \,, \text{ for } 1 \le j \le p, j \le k \le p-1$$

3.1 Rules to check if all clauses are satisfied by a given truth assignment.

$$[\,\delta'_{4n+p}\,[\,\alpha_{p+1}\,]_2\,]_1 \to [\,[\,\alpha'_{p+1}\,]_2\,]_1$$
$$[\,[\,\alpha_j\,c_{j,p}\,]_2\,]_1 \to [\,\#\,[\quad]_2\,]_1 \,, \text{ for } 1 \le j \le p$$

4.1 General counters.

$$[\,\delta_i\,[\,\gamma\,]_3\,]_1 \to [\,\delta_{i+1}\,[\quad]_3\,]_1 \,, \text{ for } 0 \le i \le 4n+p+1$$
$$[\,\delta'_{4i+1}\,[\,\gamma\,]_3\,]_1 \to [\,\delta'^2_{4i+2}\,[\quad]_3\,]_1 \,, \text{ for } 0 \le i \le n-1$$
$$[\,\delta'_{4i+k}\,[\,\gamma\,]_3\,]_1 \to [\,\delta'_{4i+k+1}\,[\quad]_3\,]_1 \,, \text{ for } 0 \le i \le n-1, k \in \{0,2,3\}$$
$$[\,\delta'_{4n+i}\,[\,\gamma\,]_3\,]_1 \to [\,\delta'_{4n+i+1}\,[\quad]_3\,]_1 \,, \text{ for } 0 \le i \le p-1$$

4.2 Rules to return a negative answer.

$$[\,[\,\alpha_j\alpha'_{p+1}\,]_2\,]_0 \to [\,n_1\,[\quad]_2\,]_0 \,, \text{ for } 1 \le j \le p$$
$$[\,n_1\,[\quad]_2\,]_1 \to [\,[\,n_1\,]_2\,]_1$$
$$[\,\delta_{4n+p+2}\,[\,n_1\,]_2\,]_1 \to [\,n_2\,[\quad]_2\,]_1$$
$$[\,[\,n_2\,]_1\,]_0 \to [\,\mathbf{no}\,[\quad]_1\,]_0$$

4.3 Rules to return a positive answer.

$$[\,\delta_{4n+p+2}\,[\,\alpha'_{p+1}\,]_2\,]_1 \to [\,[\,y_1\,]_2\,]_1$$
$$[\,[\,y_1\,]_2\,]_1 \to [\,y_2\,[\quad]_2\,]_1$$
$$[\,[\,y_2\,]_1\,]_0 \to [\,\mathbf{yes}\,[\quad]_1\,]_0$$

8. The input membrane is the membrane labelled by 1 ($i_{in} = 1$) and the output region is the environment ($i_{out} = env$).

4.1 Overview of the Computations

We denote by $cod_k(\varphi)$ the set of elements from $cod(\varphi)$ with the third subscript equal to k.

Here, we give an informal description of how the system works. The proposed solution follows a brute-force algorithm in the framework of recognizer P systems with evolutional symport/antiport and separation rules, and consists on the following stages:

- *Pregeneration stage*: In order to simulate the environment, we want to generate enough objects γ to use them as "assistants" to fire other rules of the system. This will lead to the creation of an exponential number of objects γ in a linear number of steps by using the rules from 0.1 in both the membranes 1 and 3. In particular, this stage takes $n + 1$ steps. In fact, these objects are necessary for the next computational steps, since all of them use the object γ (or some other object created by some rule that needs γ to be applied), thus no other rules can be fired until objects γ are finally created.
- *Generation stage*: Using separation rules each 4 steps, we produce 2^n membranes labelled by 2 that will contain all the possible truth assignments with rules from 1.1, 1.2, 1.3 and 1.4. With these rules, at the same time, we generate 2^n copies of $cod_n(\varphi)$. This stage takes $4n$ steps of computation. In the first step, rules from 1.1 are applied, and objects start to be prepared for when the membrane is separated. In the second step, all the objects o^L and o^R, where $o\{a, \alpha_j, t_i, f_i, \beta_{l,k}\}$ are created since they will be sent to different membranes in the next computational step. In the third step, the separation will be executed and it will be followed by some rules used to return to the first configuration so a new loop can be executed. Apart from this, rules for generating an exponential number of copies of $cod(\varphi)$ are executed in membrane 1 using objects γ from the membrane 3.
- *First checking stage*: With rules from 2.1, we can check which clauses from the formula φ are satisfied with each of the possible truth assignments. This stage takes exactly p steps. In this stage, objects from $cod(\varphi)$ interact with objects t_i and f_i in order to generate objects $c_{j,j}$, that represent that the clause C_j is satisfied by the truth value corresponding to the membrane where it is created.
- *Second checking stage*: With rules from 3.1, we remove the objects α_j such that are removed from a membrane if and only if the corresponding truth assignment associated to such a membrane makes true the clause C_j. This stage takes exactly 1 computation step. In this stage, two different behaviors can be observed. On the one hand, Objects α_j react with objects $c_{j,p}$ and, at the same time, objects δ_{4n+p} react with objects α_{p+1}.
- *Output stage*: With rules from 4.2 and 4.3, we return an afirmative answer (i.e. an object **yes**) or a negative answer (i.e. an object **no**) to the environment depending on the satisfiability of the formula φ. This stage takes exactly 4 computation steps, independently of the satisfiability of the formula φ. In this stage, if there exists an object α_j in a specific membrane, it means that the corresponding truth assignment in that membrane does not satisfy the clause C_j, and then the object n_1 is created in the membrane 1 If there exists a membrane where no objects α_j appear, it means that the truth assignment corresponding to that membrane makes true the Boolean formula φ. In that case, the object δ_{4n+p+2} reacts with the object α'_{p+1} in that membrane creating an object y_1. This object will be transported finally to the environment as an object **yes**. If the object y_1 is not generated, it means that the formula φ is not satisfiable, therefore the object δ_{4n+p+2} does not react with the object y_1, and it will be able to react with the object n_1 when it is in a membrane

labelled by 2. From that moment, this object will be transported finally to the environment as an object no.

Since objects γ are necessary for the execution of the following stages, the rest of the objects are considered "dormant" during the first stage, and that is why the final index of δ_i is $4n + p + 2$.

Theorem 1. SAT $\in$ **PMC**$_{\mathcal{CSEC}(2,2)}$

Proof. The family of recognizer P systems constructed previously verifies the following:

- Every system from $\mathbf{\Pi} = \{\Pi(n) \mid n \in \mathbb{N}\}$ is a recognizer P system from $\mathcal{CSEC}(2,2)$.
- The family $\mathbf{\Pi}$ is polynomially uniform by Turing machines given that, for each $n, p \in \mathbb{N}$, the rules from $\Pi(\langle n, p \rangle)$ are recursively defined by $n, p \in \mathbb{N}$, and the amount of resources needed for constructing an element of the family is of polynomial order with respect to n and p:
  - Alphabet size: $\Theta(max\{p^2, n^2 p\})$
  - Initial number of membranes: $2 \in \Theta(1)$
  - Initial number of objects in membranes: $\Theta(max\{n^2, np\})$
  - Number of rules: $\Theta(max\{n^3, n^2 p\})$
  - Maximum number of objects involved in a rule: $4 \in \Theta(1)$

The pair (cod, s) of polynomial-time computable functionsdefined fill the following: for each formula φ of the SAT problem, $s(\varphi)$ is a natural number, $cod(\varphi)$ is an input multiset of the system $\Pi(s(\varphi))$ and for each $k \in \mathbb{N}$, $s^{-1}(k)$ is a finite set.

The family $\mathbf{\Pi}$ is polynomially bounded in time: in fact, for each formula φ of the SAT problem, the recognizer P system $\Pi(s(\varphi)) + cod(\varphi)$ takes exactly $5n + p + 6$ steps to return a positive or a negative answer, being n the number of variables and p the number of clauses of φ.

The family $\mathbf{\Pi}$ is sound with respect to (SAT, cod, s): in fact, if the computations of $\Pi(s(\varphi)) + cod(\varphi)$ are *accepting* computations, then φ is satisfiable.

The family $\mathbf{\Pi}$ is complete with respect to (SAT, cod, s): in fact, for each formula φ that is satisfiable, then all the computations of $\Pi(s(\varphi)) + cod(\varphi)$ are *accepting* computations.

Corollary 1. $\mathbf{NP} \cup \mathbf{co} - \mathbf{NP} \subseteq \mathbf{PMC}_{\mathcal{CSEC}(2,2)}$

Proof. It is enough to see that SAT is a **NP**-complete problem, SAT $\in$ **PMC**$_{\mathcal{CSEC}(2,2)}$ and the complexity class **PMC**$_{\mathcal{CSEC}(2,2)}$ is closed under polynomial-time reducibility and under complementary.

In fact, as it is explained in the design, in the pregeneration stage we create objects γ that, instead of the environment in an arbitrary number of copies, they are available in the membrane 1 with enough copies for the whole computation. Therefore, as the environment plays a passive role, the following holds:

Corollary 2. $NP \cup co - NP \subseteq PMC_{\widehat{CSEC}(2,2)}$

Using the first definition of length of the rules, we see that the maximum number of objects involved in a rule is 4. Therefore:

Corollary 3. $NP \cup co - NP \subseteq PMC_{\widehat{CSEC}(4)}$

5   Conclusions and Future Work

In this work, we have introduced recognizer P systems with evolutional symport/antiport and separation rules, and we have provided an efficient solution to the problem SAT, a well-known **NP**-complete problem. In previous works, similar results were obtained, while changing the cell-like framework by the tissue-like framework, but in the previous case the environment was used in an active way; that is, it could send objects back to the system. In this case, the environment of the system only receives an object yes or an object no in the last step of the computation as the answer.

The maximum number of objects used in evolutional communication rules of this solution is 4, thus a good research line is to prove if this number can be decreased. In this sense, using the second definition of length, the maximum length of a rule is $(2, 2)$. This would be a good point of view while trying to reduce the number of maximum objects involved in evolutional communication rules. While using division rules, the maximum length of the rules with the first definition (respectively, second definition) was 3 (resp., $(2, 1)$). We want to analyze if it is possible to obtain a similar result while using separation rules. As stated above, we do not make use of the environment as an active agent, it would be interesting to see if the active role can be also omitted in their tissue-like counterparts. In fact, if it holds, the underlying structure (i.e. directed graph vs rooted tree structure) does not matter while measuring the ability of these systems to solve presumably hard problems. It seems that separation rules have, in this case, at least, the same computational power than division rules in terms of the problems that they can deal in an efficient way.

Another interesting research line is to find frontiers of efficiency; that is, what is the maximum length of evolutional communication rules allowed while maintaining the systems being non-efficient; that is, with the ability to only solve efficiently problems from the class **P**.

Acknowledgements. This work was supported by the following research project: FEDER/Junta de Andalucía - Paidi 2020/ _Proyecto (P20_00486). D. Orellana-Martín acknowledges Contratación de Personal Investigador Doctor. (Convocatoria 2019) 43 Contratos Capital Humano Línea 2. Paidi 2020, supported by the European Social Fund and Junta de Andalucía.

References

1. Alhazov, A., Ivanov, S., Rogozhin, Y.: Polymorphic P systems. In: Gheorghe, M., Hinze, T., Păun, G., Rozenberg, G., Salomaa, A. (eds.) CMC 2010. LNCS, vol.

6501, pp. 81–94. Springer, Heidelberg (2010). https://doi.org/10.1007/978-3-642-18123-8_9

2. Cabarle, F.G.C., Zeng, X., Murphy, N., Song, T., Rodríguez-Patón, A., Liu, X.: Neural-like P systems with plasmids. Inf. Comput. **281**, 104766 (2021). https://doi.org/10.1016/j.ic.2021.104766, https://www.sciencedirect.com/science/article/pii/S089054012100081X

3. Cienciala, L., Ciencialová, L., Sosík, P.: P colonies with agent division. Inf. Sci. **589**, 162–169 (2022). https://doi.org/10.1016/j.ins.2021.12.094

4. Csuhaj-Varjú, E., Vaszil, G.: P systems with string objects and with communication by request. In: Eleftherakis, G., Kefalas, P., Păun, G., Rozenberg, G., Salomaa, A. (eds.) WMC 2007. LNCS, vol. 4860, pp. 228–239. Springer, Heidelberg (2007). https://doi.org/10.1007/978-3-540-77312-2_14

5. Freund, R., Păun, G.H., Pérez-Jiménez, M.J.: Tissue P systems with channel states. Theor. Comput. Sci. **330**(1), 101–116 (2005). https://doi.org/10.1016/j.tcs.2004.09.013, https://www.sciencedirect.com/science/article/pii/S0304397504006085, insightful Theory insightful Theory

6. Freund, R., Sosík, P.: On the power of catalytic P systems with one catalyst. In: Rozenberg, G., Salomaa, A., Sempere, J.M., Zandron, C. (eds.) CMC 2015. LNCS, vol. 9504, pp. 137–152. Springer, Cham (2015). https://doi.org/10.1007/978-3-319-28475-0_10

7. Gheorghe, M., Ipate, F.: A kernel P systems survey. In: Alhazov, A., Cojocaru, S., Gheorghe, M., Rogozhin, Y., Rozenberg, G., Salomaa, A. (eds.) CMC 2013. LNCS, vol. 8340, pp. 1–9. Springer, Heidelberg (2014). https://doi.org/10.1007/978-3-642-54239-8_1

8. Hamshawi, Y., Bîlbîe, F.D., Păun, A., Malka, A., Piran, R.: P systems with protein rules. J. Franklin Inst. **359**(8), 3779–3807 (2022). https://doi.org/10.1016/j.jfranklin.2022.02.017, https://www.sciencedirect.com/science/article/pii/S0016003222001247

9. Krishna, S.N., Rama, R., Krithivasan, K.: P systems with picture objects. Acta Cybern. **15**(1), 53–74 (2001)

10. Martín-Vide, C., Păun, G., Pazos, J., Rodríguez-Patón, A.: Tissue P systems. Theor. Comput. Sci. **296**(2), 295–326 (2003). https://doi.org/10.1016/S0304-3975(02)00659-X, https://www.sciencedirect.com/science/article/pii/S030439750200659X. Machines, Computations and Universality

11. Orellana-Martín, D., Valencia-Cabrera, L., Song, B., Pan, L., Pérez-Jiménez, M.J.: Tuning frontiers of efficiency in tissue P systems with evolutional communication rules. Complex, **2021**, 7120840:1–7120840:14 (2021). https://doi.org/10.1155/2021/7120840

12. Orellana-Martín, D., Valencia-Cabrera, L., Pérez-Jiménez, M.J.: P systems with evolutional communication and division rules. Axioms, **10**(4), 327 (2021). https://doi.org/10.3390/axioms10040327, https://www.mdpi.com/2075-1680/10/4/327

13. Padan, E., Landau, M.: Sodium-proton (Na^+/H^+) antiporters: properties and roles in health and disease. In: Sigel, A., Sigel, H., Sigel, R.K.O. (eds.) The Alkali Metal Ions: Their Role for Life. MILS, vol. 16, pp. 391–458. Springer, Cham (2016). https://doi.org/10.1007/978-3-319-21756-7_12

14. Pan, L., Ishdorj, T.: P systems with active membranes and separation rules. J. Univers. Comput. Sci. **10**(5), 630–649 (2004). https://doi.org/10.3217/jucs-010-05-0630

15. Pan, L., Song, B., Valencia-Cabrera, L., Pérez-Jiménez, M.J.: The computational complexity of tissue P systems with evolutional symport/antiport rules. Complex, **2018**, 3745210:1–3745210:21 (2018). https://doi.org/10.1155/2018/3745210

16. Pavel, A., Arsene, O., Buiu, C.: Enzymatic numerical P systems - a new class of membrane computing systems. In: 2010 IEEE Fifth International Conference on Bio-Inspired Computing: Theories and Applications (BIC-TA), pp. 1331–1336 (2010). https://doi.org/10.1109/BICTA.2010.5645071
17. Păun, Gh.: P systems with active membranes: attacking NP complete problems. J. Automata Lang. Comb. **6**, 75–90 (1999)
18. Păun, G.H.: Computing with membranes. J. Comput. Syst. Sci. **61**(1), 108–143 (2000). https://doi.org/10.1006/jcss.1999.1693, https://www.sciencedirect.com/science/article/pii/S0022000099916938
19. Păun, Gh.: Membrane Computing: An Introduction. Springer-Verlag, Berlin, Heidelberg (2002). https://doi.org/10.1007/978-3-642-56196-2
20. Păun, Gh., Rozenberg, G., Salomaa, A.: The Oxford Handbook of Membrane Computing. Oxford University Press Inc, USA (2010)
21. Pérez-Jiménez, M.J., Riscos-Núñez, A., Rius-Font, M., Romero-Campero, F.J.: A polynomial alternative to unbounded environment for tissue p systems with cell division. Int. J. Comput. Math. **90**(4), 760–775 (2013). https://doi.org/10.1080/00207160.2012.748898
22. Thomas, W.: Languages, automata, and logic. In: Rozenberg, G., Salomaa, A. (eds.) Handbook of Formal Languages, pp. 389–455. Springer, Heidelberg (1997). https://doi.org/10.1007/978-3-642-59126-6_7
23. Song, B., Zhang, C., Pan, L.: Tissue-like P systems with evolutional symport/antiport rules. Inf. Sci. **378**, 177–193 (2017)
24. Sweety, F., Sasikala, K., Kalyani, T., Thomas, D.G.: Partial array-rewriting P systems and basic puzzle partial array grammars. In: AIP Conference Proceedings, vol. 2277, no. 1, p. 030003 (2020). https://doi.org/10.1063/5.0027078, https://aip.scitation.org/doi/abs/10.1063/5.0027078

Computational Universality
and Efficiency in Morphogenetic Systems

Petr Sosík[(✉)] [iD] and Jan Drastík

Institute of Computer Science, Faculty of Philosophy and Science,
Silesian University in Opava, Opava, Czech Republic
`petr.sosik@fpf.slu.cz`

Abstract. The topic of computational universality and efficiency of various types of abstract machines is still subject of intensive research. Besides many crucial open theoretical problems, there are also numerous potential applications, e.g., in construction of small physical computing machines (nano-automata), harnessing algorithmic processes in biology or biochemistry, efficient solving of computationally hard problems and many more. The study of computability and complexity of new abstract models can help to understand the borderline between non-universality and universality, or between tractable and intractable problems.

Here we study computational universality (in Turing sense) and computational complexity in the framework of morphogenetic (M) systems—computational models combining properties of membrane systems and algorithmic self-assembly of pre-defined atomic polytopes. Even very simple morphogenetic systems can exhibit complex self-organizing behaviour and phenomena such as controlled growth, self-reproduction, homeostasis and self-healing. We present two small universal M systems, one of which is additionally self-healing. Then we show how the borderline **P** versus **NP** can be characterized by some properties of morphogenetic systems.

Keywords: Morphogenetic system · Membrane computing ·
Self-assembly · Universal computation · **P** versus **NP**

1 Introduction

In recent decades we have witnessed a strong and still growing interconnection of computer science with disciplines like biology, chemistry and even physics. The relation is often bi-directional, in the sense that not only these disciplines use computer science tools to process and organize data they depend on (as, typically, various *-omics in biology). But also computer science is inspired and driven by biological, chemical and physical phenomena, resulting in new algorithms and both theoretical and physical computational models. Naturally, the computability and complexity aspects of these new models are under investigation.

© The Author(s), under exclusive license to Springer Nature Switzerland AG 2022
J. Durand-Lose and G. Vaszil (Eds.): MCU 2022, LNCS 13419, pp. 158–171, 2022.
https://doi.org/10.1007/978-3-031-13502-6_11

This paper studies properties of abstract computational model of so-called morphogenetic (M) systems introduced in [17,18] inspired by morphogenetic phenomena such as controlled and programmed growth of individuals and colonies, their dynamics possibly oscillating or leading to a homoeostasis, as well as more complex phenomena as self-reproduction and self-healing. The relation between morphogenesis, mathematics and computational models was established already in the 1950s by Alan Turing [19] and John von Neumann [6]. Morphogenetic systems studied here are based on mathematical abstraction of chemical reactions and mechanical forces which define self-control and self-organization in natural morphogenesis. Chemical reactions and molecules are formalized by the use of principles of *membrane computing* [9], a multiset-based computing model. The crucial concept of membrane computing is an abstract membrane dividing the space into separate compartments. The compartments host abstract molecules and chemical reactions developing independently and interchanging information between compartments. M systems are inspired by a specific variant of membrane systems with proteins on membranes [7,8]. Proteins serve both as catalysts of reactions and as protein channels between compartments. Importantly, membrane systems treat an abstract shapeless cell as a given atomic assembly unit, while M systems assume no implicit membranes. Instead, compartments can be self-assembled from simpler geometrical primitives.

The self-assembly in M systems is defined by principles inspired by the *abstract Tile Assembly Model* (aTAM) [4,21]. We generalized the original aTAM which uses square 2D tiles forming patterns in 2D. M systems use building elements in form of 1D rods or 2D convex polygons (dD polytopes in general) that can assemble into 2D or 3D structures due to explicitly predefined angles and glue relations. Their explicit geometrical shapes and sizes represents a spatial arrangement determining resulting self-assembled spatial forms. Some non-trivial examples of M systems inspired by cell formation and division were presented in the survey paper [14].

Besides theoretical studies of computational aspects of morphogenesis, we also intended to carry out experiments with artificial morphogenesis based on M systems. For this purpose, a freely available visual 3D simulator of M systems *Cytos* has been released and described in [12]. Further details and download links can be found at the M systems web page at http://sosik.zam.slu.cz/msystem/.

This paper deals with computability and complexity aspects of M systems and presents several new results. It was already shown in [17,18] that M systems are both computationally universal in the Turing sense, and also capable of efficient solving of **NP**-complete problems by trading space for time. Here we focus on the problem of minimal Turing-universal M systems, and on the problem of characterization of the P versus NP borderline. The paper is organized as follows. M systems are described in Sect. 2. The Sect. 3 contains results related to minimal Turing-universal M systems. Section 4 then provides a characterization of the relation **P** versus **NP** within the framework of M systems. Theorems are presented without proofs, which will be available in an extended version of this paper [13]. Section 5 contains concluding remarks and discussion.

2   Morphogenetic Systems

Morphogenetic systems self-assemble cellular-like (but, in principle, arbitrary) forms in a 2D or 3D (generally, dD) Euclidean space $\mathbb{R}^d$. They have three types of elementary objects at their disposal: *protions*, *tiles* and *floating objects*. All objects have their specified position (and, in case of tiles, also orientation) in space at every moment.

Floating objects play the role of abstract molecules participating in mutual reaction or passing through protion channels (which are placed on tiles). They do not have any pre-defined shape but they have a certain nonzero volume. They float freely within the environment with a Brownian motion.

Tiles (also called fixed objects) have their pre-defined nonzero size and shape, in the form of bounded convex polytopes. They can have *glues* on their edges and vertices (or, generally, on any places) which allow them to self-assemble into interconnected structures. The connecting edges or points are called (*connectors*) and their connection is controlled by a pre-defined *glue relation*. Unlike the aTAM, tiles do not exist in arbitrary numbers but they can be created, destroyed and disconnected only by reactions with floating objects.

Protions are point objects placed on tiles playing roles of both protion channels letting floating objects pass through, as well as catalysts allowing selected reactions of floating objects. The term *protion* was chosen to avoid possible confusion between biological proteins and these abstract objects.

2.1   Polytopic Tiling

The formalism defining shapes, connection, angles and further parameters of tiles is called the *polytopic tiling*. It efficiently controls the process of self-assembly of tiles in an M systems It can be viewed as a generalization of aTAM [4,21], which is itself related to Wang tiling [10]. In M systems we generalize the aTAM to d dimensions and the tiles can adopt shapes of bounded convex polytopes [22]. Note that a 1D polytope is shaped as a rod.

A polytope is the convex hull of an ordered list of its extreme points in ordinary 2D or 3D (generally, dD) space, called *vertices*. Position of each vertex is given by an d-tuple of real numbers. Two-dimensional tiles have faces of dimension 1, called *facets*, separating them from the exterior. Formally, a *d-dimensional tile* is defined as

$$t = (\Delta, \{c_1, \ldots, c_k\}, g_s), \text{ for } k \geq 0, \text{ where}$$

Δ is a bounded convex d-dimensional polytope,
$c_1, \ldots, c_k$ are its connectors,
$g_s \in G$ is the *surface glue*, where G is a finite set of *glues*.

Connectors define possible attachments of the tile to other tiles. They are sites on the surface of a tile specified by their shape, glue and connecting angles: $c = (\Delta_c, g, (\varphi_1, \varphi_2))$, where

$\Delta_c \subset \Delta$ is a bounded convex k-polytope where $0 \le k < d$,
$g \in G$ is a glue,
$\varphi_1, \varphi_2 \in (-\pi, \pi)$ are connecting angles (φ_2 being void when only one angle is applicable).

A connector may be shaped as a point, a segment or a polygon. Two connectors on neighboring tiles can connect together if they have identical shapes and their glues match in the glue relation defined below. To specify precisely connecting angles of 1D or 2D tiles embedded in $\mathbb{R}^3$, we define the tiles as yaw-pitch-roll angles (DIN 9300), as used in aviation, with the "aircraft" being placed on the new tile that is being connected to an existing one, with its tail pointing to the connector. The order of rotations of a tile in 3D space is given by the pair of angles (φ_1, φ_2) defined in the following table, where d is the dimension of the tile and k is the dimension of the connector.

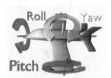

d	k	φ_1	φ_2
1	0	roll	yaw
2	0	yaw	pitch
2	1	pitch	–

Aircraft principal axes.
Wikimedia Commons.

An unspecified angle of a connector can be chosen randomly.

Definition 1. *A polytopic tile system in $\mathbb{R}^3$ is a tuple $T = (Q, G, \gamma, d_g, S)$, where*

Q is the set of tiles of dimensions ≤ 3;
G is the set of glues;
$\gamma \subseteq G \times G$ is the glue relation;
$d_g \in \mathbb{R}_0^+$ is the gluing radius (assumed to be small compared to tile sizes);
S is a finite multiset of seed tiles from Q randomly distributed in space.

2.2   M System

A polytopic tile system defined in the previous subsection specifies the geometrical structure of growth in an M system. However, the creation, destruction and eventual disconnection of tiles is controlled by more elementary *floating objects* available in environment of the M system. These reactions are subject to rules inspired by those used in P systems with proteins on membranes. Formally, for a finite alphabet O we denote by O^* the free monoid generated by O by the operation of concatenation, with identity element λ. As usual, $O^+ = O^* \setminus \{\lambda\}$. A multiset S over alphabet O can be represented by a string $x \in O^*$ such that $|x|_a = |S|_a$. For a string or multiset S and $a \in O$, $|S|_a$ denotes the multiplicity of occurrences of a in S.

Definition 2. *A morphogenetic system (*M system*) in* $\mathbb{R}^3$ *is a tuple*

$$\mathcal{M} = (F, P, T, \mu, R, \sigma),$$

where

$F = (O, m, \rho, \epsilon)$ *is a catalog of floating objects, where*
  O *is a set of floating objects;*
  $m : O \longrightarrow \mathbb{R}^+$ *is the* mean mobility *of each floating object;*
  $\rho : O \longrightarrow \mathbb{R}_0^+$ *specifies the* radius *(size) of the floating objects in* O*;*
  $\epsilon : O \longrightarrow \mathbb{R}_0^+$ *likewise gives the (initial)* concentration *of each floating object in the environment;*
P *is a set of protions;*
$T = (Q, G, \gamma, d_g, S)$ *is a polytopic tile system in* $\mathbb{R}^3$*, with* O*,* P*,* Q*,* G *all pairwise disjoint;*
μ *is the mapping assigning to each tile* $t \in Q$ *a multiset of protions placed on* t *together with their positions:* $\mu(t) \subset P \times \Delta$ *where* Δ *is the underlying polytope of* t*;*
R *is a finite set of reaction rules;*
$\sigma : \gamma \longrightarrow O^*$ *is the mapping assigning to each glue pair* $(g_1, g_2) \in \gamma$ *a multiset of floating objects which are released to the environment when a connection with glues* (g_1, g_2) *is established.*

Reaction rules in the set R have the form $u \to v$, where u and v are strings/multisets which may contain floating objects, protions, glues and/or tiles as specified below. A rule $u \to v$, is applicable when each floating object $o \in u$ is located within the radius $m(o)$ from the reaction site (which may be a protion, a connector or a whole tile), and eventual further rule-specific conditions are also met.

Metabolic Rules
Let $u, v \in O^+$ be nonempty multisets of floating objects and $p \in P$ be a protion. If the symbol $[$ is specified in the rule, then the protion must be placed on a 2D-tile with distinguished *in* (denoted by $[p]$) and *out* (denoted by $p[$) sides. This applies only to $(d-1)$D tiles in dD Euclidean space. Metabolic rules are of several subtypes:

Type	Rule	Effect
Simple	$u \to v$	Objects in multiset u react to produce v
Catalytic	$pu \to pv$	Objects in u react in presence of p to produce v
	$u[p \to v[p$	Similar as above but both u, v must be on the side "out" of a tile on which p is placed (applicable only to $(d-1)$D tiles in dD space)
	$[pu \to [pv$	Similar as above but both u, v must be on the side "in" of a tile on which p is placed;
Symport	$u[p \to [pu$	u Passes through protion channel p
	$[pu \to u[p$	To the other side of the tile
Antiport	$u[pv \to v[pu$	Interchange of u and v through protion channel p

During application of the rule, objects at the left-hand side react, are consumed (except protions) and produce objects at the right-hand side, eventually passing through a 2D tile indicated in the rule.

Creation Rules $u \to t$,
create a tile t while consuming the floating objects in u, where $u \in O^+$ and $t \in Q$. Furthermore, t must be able to connect to an existing fixed object at some of its connectors.

Destruction Rules $ut \to v$,
destroy a tile t, while consuming the floating objects in u and producing floating objects in v, where $u, v \in O^+$ and $t \in Q$.

Division Rules $g \xrightarrow{u} h \to g, h$,
cause the two connectors to disconnect and the multiset u to be consumed, where $g—h$ is a pair of glues on connectors of two connected tiles, and $u \in O^+$.

2.3 Computation of the M System

An M system evolves in *discrete time steps* by applying rules in its set R in maximally parallel manner (such that no more rules can be applied at each step), and thereby passing between configurations. A rule is applied (completely) in a single time step, that is, rules cannot span multiple time steps before all their products are realized. A *configuration* of an M system is given by

- the set of all tiles in the environment and their relative positions at a certain time;
- an interconnection graph of connectors on these tiles;
- positions for all floating objects modulo their mobility.

The computation starts in the *initial configuration* containing seed tiles in S (either randomly positioned or in specific locations) and floating objects randomly distributed due to their initial concentration. $\epsilon(a)$ for each $a \in O$. At each step, each floating object can be subject to at most one rule, each connector can be subject to at most one creation or division rule, and each tile can be subject to at most one destruction rule. After application of rules at each step, all floating objects change their position in accordance with the Brownian motion principle [3] with mean mobility $m(o)$ for each object $o \in O$.

Naturally, positions of any two objects (either tiles or floating objects) cannot overlap. Newly created tiles can push already existing tile structures and also floating objects to make the necessary room for themselves. Although we consider shapes of tiles and volumes of floating objects, we abstract from some other physical parameters as weights, forces, pressure etc.

The computation can eventually stop when there are no more applicable rules, or it can continue forever when the system reaches a homoeostatic equilibrium, transiting cyclically within a certain set of configurations.

2.4 Example

We provide a very simple example of an M system producing a set of self-replicating boxes in 3D. Originally we called it *Boxy Hallows* due to the inspiration by a scene from the Harry Potter movie. The M system is formally described as follows: $\mathcal{M} = (F, \emptyset, T, \emptyset, R, \emptyset)$, where

$F = (\{a\}, m(a) = 5, \rho(a) = 0.05, \epsilon(a) = 10)$, i.e., there is a single floating object a with a nonzero concentration in the environment;

$T = (\{d\}, \{g1\}, \{(g1, g1)\}, 0.1, \{d\})$ is a tiling with a single square 2D tile d, having four identical connectors occupying its four edges, with connecting glue g_1 and angle $\varphi_1 = 90°$ as specified in Sect. 2.1;

R contains the two reaction rules:

Rule	Effect
$a \rightarrow d$	Creates new tile d while consuming one floating object a
$g1 \overset{a}{-} g1 \rightarrow g1, g1$	Divides two tiles connected with glues $g1$ while consuming one object a

Fig. 1. Visualization of development of the M system "Boxy Hallows".

The described M system operates as follows. The seed tile d serving as a box base attaches four other tiles to its four connectors at all four edges in the first step. These connectors allow to connect four new tiles under the angle of 90°. New tiles are produced from abundant floating objects a due to the creation rule. By the same principle, a box completes with another tile in the second step. Meanwhile, original connections of the tiles attached in the first step to the seed tile are released by the division rule. In the third step, new tiles are immediately connected to all free connectors, both on the seed tile and the four tiles from the second step. As a result, the seed tile is connected to new four tiles (similarly as in step 2), pushing the original (now incomplete) box aside. The original box is simultaneously completed by another tile replacing the seed one. All these new tiles are created by the same creation rule. In the next step the new box completes and the process continues in an analogous way, generating an exponentially growing group of mutually pushing boxes as in Fig. 1. The image was produced by the simulation package *Cytos*.

3   Small Universal M Systems

Let us start this section with a review of a known result about simulation of Turing machines (TMs) by morphogenetic systems which will be needed later. An *M system generating strings* is such that produces a unique sequence of interconnected closed cells, where each cell contains at most one floating object from a specific tape alphabet. The sequence of these floating objects in a specific configuration forms the string which is a result of computation of the M system. Such an M system can generate a set of strings thanks to its possible nondeterminism (induced by the underlying Turing machine). Please consult [16] for more details of the construction.

Proposition 1 ([16]). *Every (nondeterministic) Turing machine starting with an empty tape can be simulated in linear time by an M system that produces exactly the same set of strings. Furthermore, the M system only requires metabolic and creation rules.*

The proof is based on a direct simulation of a TM by an M system unfolding in 2D, which builds a tape-like structure (tape cells interlaced with auxiliary cells) populated with objects representing states and alphabet symbols of the Turing machine, see Fig. 2. Note that, if the same construction is used to simulate a *deterministic* Turing machine, the computation of the M systems has a unique result. However, the effect of the random Brownian motion of floating object may result, with a very small probability, to a small delay in simulation (e.g., a one step delay can occur with the probability of $p << 1$ and, in general, a delay by n steps occurs with the probability of p^n. Hence the probability the delay decreases exponentially with its growing length.

Let us now focus on the construction of small universal M systems. By that we mean a *unique* M system which can (with a proper input/output encoding) simulate any register or Turing machine, and thus generate or accept any recursively enumerable set of integers. To formalize the term "small", recall that small Turing machines are usually characterized by the number of states, tape symbols

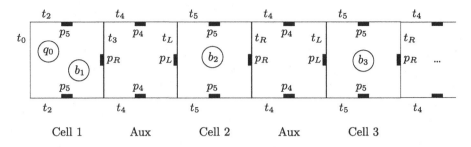

Fig. 2. A snapshot of an M system simulating a Turing machine. Odd-numbered squares (left to right, starting from 1) represent tape cells while even-numbered squares are auxiliary cells controlling movements of floating objects. Objects $b_1 b_2 b_3 \dots$ represent tape symbols, while q_0 is the object representing TM's state.

and rules. Let us assume the following values as the key ones characterizing size/ descriptional complexity of an M system:

- the number of tiles in the set Q;
- the number of floating objects in the set O;
- the number of protions in the set P;
- the number of rules.

To construct a small universal M system, we employ an approach based on the paper [1] dealing with simulations of strongly universal register machines by parallel multiset rewriting systems. Let $\Phi_0, \Phi_1, \Phi_2, \dots$ be a fixed admissible enumeration of the set of unary partial recursive functions. Then, a register machine U computing a binary function Φ_U^2 is said to be *strongly universal* if there exists a recursive function g such that $\Phi_x(y) = \Phi_U^2(g(x), y)$ holds for all $x, y \in \mathbb{N}$ [1].

In the same sense as in [1], we call an M system *universal* if it can simulate a strongly universal register machine, representing contents of its registers by numbers of designated floating objects. Now the following result can be established:

Theorem 1. *There exists a universal M system in 2D with three tiles, 26 floating objects, one protion and 26 rules.*

3.1 Self-healing Universal M System

In this section we aim at a construction of a universal M system which is simultaneously self-healing. Self-healing, i.e., the capability of recovery from certain damages, is a characteristic property of M systems. The phenomenon of self-healing, self-repair and self-stabilization was studied in many different contexts within the general framework of distributed systems. For an interested reader, the study [2] on self-stabilizing algorithms can be a source of inspiration.

An experimental study of M system forming self-reproducing cell-like structures which is also self-healing, i.e., resistant to various types of injuries (in the form of destruction of randomly chosen tiles), has been provided in [15,17]. The-oretical framework of self-healing in an M systems is based on its *computation graph*, i.e., a directed graph M whose nodes are *all* configurations which can be reached from the initial configuration by any computation of the M system. Arcs of the graph are computational steps of the M systems described above.

We further define the *configuration space* M^c of the M system, obtained from M by adding all the configurations (and transitions among them) which are unreachable by normal computation of the M system, but from which one can reach some node of M. In other words, M^c is obtained as an inverse transitive closure of M in the larger graph consisting of all possible configurations and transitions.

Another crucial concept is the *homeostatic (h) component* of M^c. Informally, it is each minimum subgraph of M^c from which there is no transition to other nodes of M^c. In particular, each cycle in M^c and its transitive closure belongs to some h-component. For the formal definition please consult [15].

Definition 3 ([17]). *Given a morphogenetic system M, an* injury *is a change from configuration x to y such that there is no directed arc from x to y in the configuration space M^c. The* degree *of the injury is the undirected* distance *between x and y in M^c.*

An injury (x, y) is sustainable *if both x and y belong to the same h-component.*

An M system is self-healing *(of degree m, respectively) if and only if the probability that a random injury (of degree at most m, respectively) to any home-ostatic node is sustainable is at least 0.5.*

Therefore, an injury is any change of configuration of M which cannot be the result of a single step of the system. An injury is sustainable if it does not take the M system out of its current h-component, i.e., it remains in the same set of homeostatic states as before the injury.

Here we introduce a small universal self-healing M system which is based on the construction of a self-healing M system simulating a Turing machine in [15]. Geometrically, the construction is very similar to that in Proposition 1 which is presented at Fig. 2. A detailed examination of this construction, together with the gallery of small universal Turing machines presented by Yurii Rogozhin in [11] which can be simulated by that M systems, yields the following result.

Theorem 2. *There exists an M system in 2D with 8 tiles, 28 floating objects, 4 protions and 100 rules, that simulates a universal Turing machine M on any given input in linear time, and it is self-healing of degree 1, provided that injuries at each step only affect tiles and objects belonging to a single tape cell.*

4   P Versus NP in Morphogenetic Systems

We start with recalling the capability of M systems to solve the NP-complete problem 3-SAT in a randomized polynomial time [17]. As M systems are inher-ently nondeterministic, their computation depending among others on a random

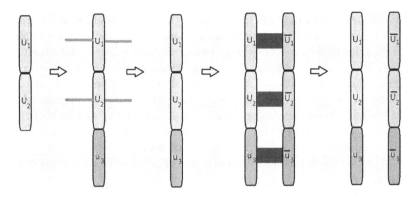

Fig. 3. A chain of tiles representing an assignment to variables x_1, x_2 is extended and duplicated to cover also the variable x_3. Capital U_i represents an arbitrary assignment $(0/1)$ to x_i, for $i = 1, 2$, while $\overline{U_i}$ represents its negation. Small u_3 represents $x_3 \leftarrow 1$, while $\overline{u_3}$ represents $x_3 \leftarrow 0$.

movement of floating objects, it is mostly impossible to construct a fully deterministic M system which would conclude its computation in a pre-defined number of steps. Therefore, the concept of Monte Carlo M systems has been defined in [17]: either at least $1/2$ of its computations are accepting, or all computations are rejecting. Then, a semi-uniform family of M systems solving a decision problem was constructed: for each instance of the problem, a specific Monte Carlo M system is constructed (by a Turing machine in polynomial time), solving that particular instance. The following result was established:

Proposition 2 ([17]). *The* **NP***-complete problem 3-SAT can be solved in randomized polynomial time by a semi-uniform family of Monte Carlo M systems using only context-free rules.*

Figure 3 illustrates the generation of all possible assignments to logical variables $x_1, \ldots, x_n$ of the formula, by stepwise prolonging and duplicating chains of rods in 2D, each representing one partial assignment. Note that the need for a physical representation of sequence of variables $x_1, \ldots, x_n$ allowing for its duplication necessarily led us to the form of a double strand of information-bearing elements, very much alike DNA double-stranded molecule.

4.1 M Systems with Mass

An important guideline in design of M systems was to find a compromise between physical-chemical realism, computational realism and biological realism. Yet, Proposition 2 shows their capability of solving NP-complete problems in randomized polynomial time. This, of course, contradicts the so-called *invariance thesis* understood as an extension of the Church-Turing thesis: 'Reasonable' machines can simulate each other within a polynomially bounded overhead in time and a constant-factor overhead in space [20]. To make M systems more physically realistic, we define the variant called *M system with mass*, where the chained pushing of objects at each step is limited by a certain fixed distance d_{push}. The following result can be then demonstrated.

Theorem 3. *Any M system with mass can be simulated by a Turing machine in polynomial time.*

Corollary 1. *M systems with mass can solve in polynomial time exactly the class of problems* **P**.

Proof. By inspection of details of the proof of Proposition 1 which is given in [16], one can easily deduce that the M system constructed there to simulate any Turing machine in a linear time is with mass, as it does not use any pushing of tiles (or floating objects). Hence, problems in **P** can be solved by M systems in polynomial time, on one hand. On the other hand, Theorem 3 implies that M systems with mass can only solve in polynomial time the problems in P.   □

5   Conclusions

We have studied computational aspects of morphogenetic systems: their computational universality (in the Turing sense) and computational efficiency according to the measures of the computational complexity theory. In the section devoted to computability, two universal M systems are constructed, in the sense of a universal computer: that each of them can, with proper input encoding, simulated any Turing machine encoded as a part of the input. The second presented universal M system is also self-healing of degree 1. The section devoted to complexity then presents a characterization of the relation **P** versus **NP** with the help of morphogenetic systems.

Among open problems, we would like to mention whether it is possible to construct a universal M system which would be self-healing of degree greater than 1. Some studies of self-repairing Turing machines such as, e.g., [5] may be helpful in this sense. It is also possible (or rather probable) that still smaller universal M systems can be constructed.

The precise characterization of the class of problems solvable by morphogenetic systems in polynomial time also remains open. Previous study [17] demonstrated only their capability of solving NP-complete problems in randomized polynomial time. Upper bound of this class of problems, however, is not known yet.

Acknowledgments. This work was supported by the Silesian University in Opava under the Student Funding Scheme, project SGS/8/2022.

References

1. Alhazov, A., Verlan, S.: Minimization strategies for maximally parallel multiset rewriting systems. Theor. Comput. Sci. **412**(17), 1581–1591 (2011)
2. Altisen, K., Devismes, S., Dubois, S., Petit, F.: Introduction to distributed self-stabilizing algorithms. Synth. Lect. Distrib. Comput. Theory **8**(1), 1–165 (2019)
3. Einstein, A.: Über die von der molekularkinetischen theorie der wärme geforderte bewegung von in ruhenden flüssigkeiten suspendierten teilchen. Ann. Phys. **322**(8), 549–560 (1905)
4. Krasnogor, N., Gustafson, S., Pelta, D., Verdegay, J.: Systems Self-Assembly: Multidisciplinary Snapshots. Studies in Multidisciplinarity. Elsevier Science (2011)
5. Mange, D., Madon, D., Stauffer, A., Tempesti, G.: Von Neumann revisited: a Turing machine with self-repair and self-reproduction properties. Robot. Auton. Syst. **22**(1), 35–58 (1997)
6. von Neumann, J.: Probabilistic logics and the synthesis of reliable organisms from unreliable components. Ann. Math. Stud. **34**, 43–98 (1956)
7. Păun, A., Popa, B.: P systems with proteins on membranes. Fund. Inform. **72**(4), 467–483 (2006)
8. Păun, A., Popa, B.: P systems with proteins on membranes and membrane division. In: Ibarra, O.H., Dang, Z. (eds.) DLT 2006. LNCS, vol. 4036, pp. 292–303. Springer, Heidelberg (2006). https://doi.org/10.1007/11779148_27
9. Păun, G., Rozenberg, G., Salomaa, A. (eds.): The Oxford Handbook of Membrane Computing. Oxford University Press, Oxford (2010)
10. Qang, H.: Proving theorems by pattern recognition - II. Bell Syst. Tech. J. **40**(1), 1–41 (1961)
11. Rogozhin, Y.: Small universal Turing machines. Theor. Comput. Sci. **168**(2), 215–240 (1996)
12. Smolka, V., Drastík, J., Bradík, J., Garzon, M., Sosík, P.: Morphogenetic systems: models and experiments. Biosystems **198**, Article no. 104270 (2020). https://doi.org/10.1016/j.biosystems.2020.104270
13. Sosík, P.: Morphogenetic computing: computability and complexity results. Nat. Comput. (2022, submitted)
14. Sosík, P., Drastík, J., Smolka, V., Garzon, M.: From P systems to morphogenetic systems: an overview and open problems. J. Membrane Comput. **2**(4), 380–391 (2020). https://doi.org/10.1007/s41965-020-00057-9
15. Sosík, P., Garzon, M., Drastík, J.: Turing-universal self-healing computations in morphogenetic systems. Nat. Comput. **20**, 739–750 (2021)
16. Sosík, P., Garzon, M., Smolka, V., Drastík, J.: Morphogenetic systems for resource bounded computation and modeling. Inf. Sci. **547**, 814–827 (2021)
17. Sosík, P., Smolka, V., Drastík, J., Bradík, J., Garzon, M.: On the robust power of morphogenetic systems for time bounded computation. In: Gheorghe, M., Rozenberg, G., Salomaa, A., Zandron, C. (eds.) CMC 2017. LNCS, vol. 10725, pp. 270–292. Springer, Cham (2018). https://doi.org/10.1007/978-3-319-73359-3_18
18. Sosík, P., Smolka, V., Drastík, J., Moore, T., Garzon, M.: Morphogenetic and homeostatic self-assembled systems. In: Patitz, M.J., Stannett, M. (eds.) UCNC 2017. LNCS, vol. 10240, pp. 144–159. Springer, Cham (2017). https://doi.org/10.1007/978-3-319-58187-3_11
19. Turing, A.: The chemical basis of morphogenesis. Philos. Trans. R. Soc. Lond. B **237**, 7–72 (1950)

20. van Emde Boas, P.: Machine models and simulations. In: van Leeuwen, J. (ed.) Handbook of Theoretical Computer Science, vol. A: Algorithms and Complexity, pp. 1–66. Elsevier, Amsterdam (1990)
21. Winfree, E.: Self-healing tile sets. In: Chen, J., Jonoska, N., Rozenberg, G. (eds.) Nanotechnology: Science and Computation. Natural Computing Series, pp. 55–66. Springer, Cham (2006). https://doi.org/10.1007/3-540-30296-4_4
22. Ziegler, G.: Lectures on Polytopes. Graduate Texts in Mathematics, Springer, New York (1995)

Adaptive Experiments for State Identification in Finite State Machines with Timeouts

Aleksandr Tvardovskii[1]([✉])[iD] and Nina Yevtushenko[2][iD]

[1] National Research Tomsk State University, Tomsk 634050, Russia
`tvardal@mail.ru`
[2] Ivannikov Institute for System Programming of the RAS, Moscow 109004, Russia

Abstract. Homing and synchronizing sequences are used for the current state identification in finite state machines (FSMs). Adaptive homing and synchronizing sequences for which the next input depends on the outputs to the previous ones, exist more often and usually are shorter than the preset. Thus, a lot of attention is paid to the existence check, derivation complexity and length of shortest adaptive state identification sequences. In this paper, we adapt the notions of adaptive homing and synchronizing sequences for FSMs with timeouts which are widely used for solving verification and testing problems of components of telecommunication systems. Based on the corresponding FSM abstraction, the procedures for deriving adaptive homing and synchronizing sequences are proposed for FSMs with timeouts when such sequences exist.

Keywords: Finite state machines · Timeouts · Homing sequence · Synchronizing sequence

1 Introduction

The state identification problem for Finite State Machines (FSM) has a long history; it has been studied since the middle of the 20th century [1–4]. Homing and synchronizing sequences (HS and SS) are used for determining a current state of a system, i.e., the system state after applying a corresponding HS or SS [3,5–8]. Such knowledge allows to set a system of interest into a known state or to determine such a state by observing external system responses. The latter is used to minimize testing efforts in both active and passive testing (monitoring) [9,10]. In active testing, each test sequence must be preceded by a reset to the known initial state. When testing is performed via monitoring, it is useful to know a current state of the system based on observed communication as such knowledge can reduce the check of necessary test purposes/invariants. Thus, the state identification can be efficiently used for testing optimization.

Nowadays time aspects become very important for discrete and hybrid systems, and, respectively, classical FSMs have been extended with clock variables

[11–15]. Components of a telecommunication system often have timers and time-outs, for example, for implementing a disconnection when there is no answer from the other side during an appropriate time period. In order to identify states of such non-classical FSM components, so-called Timed FSMs (TFSMs) are utilized. In this work we consider FSMs with timeouts, i.e., FSMs extended by a single clock variable and special timeout transitions. Given a state, the timeout determines how long a system can stay at a given state waiting for an input. If an input is not applied before the timeout expires, then the TFSM can spontaneously move to another prescribed state.

Sufficient and necessary conditions for the existence of preset [5,6,8,9] and adaptive [16–18] HS and SS are established for various kinds of classical FSMs and corresponding derivation algorithms are proposed. A preset state identification sequence is known before an experiment (before the start of testing procedures, for example) and is not modified during the experiment. In the paper [19], the authors define the SS notion for a timed automaton, investigate various kinds of such automata for the SS existence and evaluate the complexity of this check. Since the authors consider automata where the set of actions is not divided into inputs and outputs, only preset SS are considered. When inputs and outputs are involved adaptive state identification sequences can be also studied. The next input of an adaptive state identification sequence depends on its responses to the previous inputs, which sometimes makes it more difficult to conduct the experiment, but in some cases allows cutting the sequence length from the exponential up to plolynomial, for example, for FSMs [2,7,20]. It is also known that the probability that an adaptive state identification sequence exists for a nondeterministic FSM is higher than for the existence of a corresponding preset sequence. In this work we investigate the existence check and derivation of adaptive state identification sequences for possibly non-deterministic FSMs with timeouts.

The main contributions of the paper are as follows. We introduce the notion of a timed test case for an FSM with timeouts that represents an adaptive HS or an adaptive SS. Such a test case is a partial acyclic TFSM where at each intermediate state either a timeout or an input with all outputs is defined. Therefore, applying an HS or an SS means that we wait for appropriate time units and then apply an input. Depending on the produced output, the next step is chosen. By definition, an adaptive SS can be defined only for machines with inputs and outputs. Necessary and sufficient conditions are established for the existence check of adaptive HS and SS for FSMs with timeouts and procedures for deriving corresponding timed test cases are proposed when such sequences exist. The check conditions and derivation procedures are based on the FSM abstraction of a given FSM with timeouts [14]. The number of states of such FSM abstraction does not exceed the number of states of the given TFSM multiplied by the maximum finite timeout at a state. If the FSM abstraction is represented by special arrays [21] both procedures have the polynomial complexity with respect to the product of the number of states and outputs. For complete non-initialized possibly non-deterministic FSMs with timeouts, the length of both shortest HS and SS is at most cubic with respect to the number of states of the FSM abstraction when such sequences exist. In both cases, the complexity coincides with that for classical FSMs.

The rest of the paper has the following structure. Section 2 contains necessary definitions and notations for classical FSMs and FSMs with timeouts. In Sect. 3, the notion of an adaptive homing sequence for FSMs with timeouts is introduced. A procedure for deriving a homing test case for a TFSM based on the FSM abstraction is presented in Sect. 4. In Sect. 5, we discuss how a synchronizing test case for an FSM with timeouts can be derived based on an adaptive homing sequence. Section 6 concludes the paper.

2   Preliminaries

In this section, we briefly remind the notions of classical Finite State Machines and Finite State Machines with timeouts.

2.1   Finite State Machines

A Finite State Machine (FSM) is a 4-tuple $P = (P, I, O, h_P)$ where P is a finite non-empty set of states, I and O are finite non-empty input and output alphabets, and $h_P \subseteq P \times I \times O \times P$ is the transition (behavior) relation. By definition, a non-initialized FSM can start at any state of the set P. A transition (p, i, o, p') describes the situation when an input i is applied to P at the current state p and P moves to state p' producing the output (response) o. In this work, if the converse is not explicitly stated, we consider complete observable, possibly non-deterministic FSMs, i.e., given an FSM P, for every input i and state p, there exists at least one transition $(p, i, o, p') \in h_P$. If there exist several such transitions then for each two transitions (p, i, o, p_1) and (p, i, o, p_2) of h_P, it holds that $p_1 = p_2$.

The FSM has an input/output transition $p \xrightarrow{io} p'$ if $(p, i, o, p') \in h_P$. A trace of the FSM P at state p is a sequence of input/output transitions starting at the state p. Given a trace $tr = p \xrightarrow{i_1 o_1} p_1 \xrightarrow{i_2 o_2} \ldots \xrightarrow{i_n o_n} p_n$ at state p of FSM P, $\alpha = i_1, i_2, \ldots, i_n$ is the input sequence, $\gamma = o_1, o_2, \ldots, o_n$ is the corresponding output sequence and $\alpha/\gamma = i_1/o_1, i_2/o_2, \ldots, i_n/o_n$ is the IO-projection of the trace or simply an input/output sequence. State p_n is the tr-successor of state p in FSM P. In this case, an input sequence α is said to induce a trace with IO-projection α/γ at state p. Moreover, in a non-deterministic FSM, input sequence α can induce several traces with different IO-projections.

2.2   Timed Finite State Machines

An FSM with timeouts is a 5-tuple $S = (S, I, O, \lambda_S, \Delta_S)$ where S is a finite non-empty set of states, I and O are input and output alphabets, $\lambda_S \subseteq S \times I \times O \times S$ is the transition relation and Δ_S is the timeout function. We consider the timeout function $\Delta_S : S \to S \times N \bigcup \{\infty\}$ where N is the set of positive integers: for each state this function specifies the maximum time of waiting for an input. If no input is applied until the timeout expires then the system can spontaneously move to another state that is prescribed by the timeout function. The timeout ∞ means that an FSM can stay at a current state forever until an input is applied. Given state s of TFSM S such that $\Delta_S(s) = (s', T)$, if no input is applied before the timeout T expires then the TFSM S moves to state s'. The clock value is set to zero when a TFSM performs a transition prescribed by a timeout or an input.

The notions of a complete (partial), deterministic (non-deterministic) and observable TFSM are introduced similar to classical FSMs and in this work, if the converse is not explicitly stated, we consider complete observable possibly non-deterministic TFSMs. In other words, given a TFSM S, for each pair $(s, i) \in S \times I$, there exists a transition $(s, i, o, s') \in \lambda_S$ or there exist several such transitions but for every two transitions $(s, i, o, s_1), (s, i, o, s_2) \in \lambda_S$ it holds that $s_1 = s_2$. By definition, for each state of the TFSM exactly one timeout is specified.

For each state s of TFSM and delay $t > 0$, a timed transition is defined as $s \xrightarrow{t} s'$ where state s' is the state reached by the TFSM from state s if no input is applied at state s during time t. Note that there can exist several states $s_1, s_2, ..., s_n$ such that $s \xrightarrow{t} s_k$, $0 < k \le n$, since TFSM can have different values of the clock variable when a timed transition is executed. The TFSM has an input/output transition $s \xrightarrow{io} s'$ if $(s, i, o, s') \in \lambda_S$.

For an FSM and its state, a trace defines a path in the flow diagram. In a TFSM, such a path should include timed transitions. Correspondingly, instead of a trace, we define a timed trace for an FSM with timeouts which is a sequence of alternating timed and input/output transitions. Given a timed trace $ttr = s_0 \xrightarrow{t_1} s_0' \xrightarrow{i_1 o_1} s_1 \xrightarrow{t_2} s_1' \xrightarrow{i_2 o_2} \ldots \xrightarrow{t_n} s_{n-1}' \xrightarrow{i_n o_n} s_n \xrightarrow{t_{n+1}-t_n} s_{n+1}$ of TFSM S with the initial state s_0 and the tail state s_{n+1}, state s_{n+1} is a ttr-successor of state s_0. Instead of IO-sequence $\alpha/\gamma = i_1/o_1, i_2/o_2, \ldots, i_n/o_n$ of a trace for an FSM, we define a timed IO-sequence (TIO-sequence) $t_1, i_1/o_1, t_2, i_2/o_2, \ldots t_n, i_n/o_n, t_{n+1}$ for a timed trace ttr of TFSM. A timed input is a pair (i, t) where $i \in I$ and t is a nonnegative real; a timed input (i, t) means that input i is applied to the TFSM at time instance $t \ge 0$ counting from the appropriate initial time instance. A timed input (i, t) is defined at state s if there exists at least one timed trace $s \xrightarrow{t} s' \xrightarrow{io} s''$. A sequence of timed inputs $\alpha = (i_1, t_1) \ldots (i_n, t_n)$, where $t_1 < \ldots < t_n$, is a timed input sequence. For a timed trace ttr of the TFSM S at state s_0, a timed input sequence $\alpha = (i_1, t_1) \ldots (i_n, t_n)$ is said to induce the trace ttr; $\gamma = o_1 \ldots o_n$ is the corresponding output sequence and $\alpha/\gamma = t_1, i_1/o_1, t_2 - t_1, i_2/o_2, \ldots, t_n - t_{n-1}, i_n/o_n, t_{n+1} - t_n$ is the TIO-projection of the ttr. State s_{n+1} is the ttr-successor of state s in TFSM S.

As an example, consider a TFSM in Fig. 1. A timed input sequence $(i_1, 2.4)$, $(i_1, 3.6), (i_2, 3.8)$ induces a timed trace $s_1 \xrightarrow{2.4} s_2 \xrightarrow{i_1 o_1} s_1 \xrightarrow{1.2} s_1 \xrightarrow{i_1 o_2} s_3 \xrightarrow{0.2} s_3 \xrightarrow{i_2 o_1} s_4$ with the TIO-projection $2.4, i_1/o_1, 1.2, i_1/o_2, 0.2, i_2 o_1$.

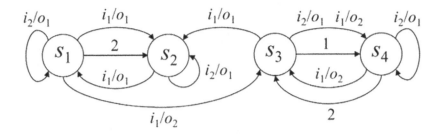

Fig. 1. FSM with timeouts S.

Note that differently from classical FSMs, a timed input sequence α can induce several traces at the same state of a deterministic TFSM, due to timed transitions.

3   Adaptive Homing Sequences for an FSM with Timeouts

A Homing Sequence (HS) is an input sequence that allows to uniquely determine a state of an FSM under investigation after applying this input sequence and observing the produced output sequence. A homing sequence can be preset or adaptive [1,3] and, in this section, we remind the definition of an adaptive HS for a classical complete and observable FSM [22] and then define an adaptive HS for an FSM with timeouts.

3.1   Homing Test Case for an FSM

Given FSM $P = (P, I, O, h_P)$, a test case $C(I, O)$ for P is an initialized partial non-deterministic FSM $C(I, O) = (C, I, O, h_C, c_0)$ with an acyclic transition graph, where for every state at most one input with all outputs is defined; a state without defined inputs is a deadlock state. An initialized FSM (C, I, O, h_C, c_0) starts at the designated initial state c_0 differently from non-initialized FSMs which can start at any state. An initialized FSM with timeouts has the same feature.

A test case $C(I, O)$ for FSM P represents an adaptive input sequence [23] which is applied to a complete FSM P over input and output alphabets I and O using the procedure below until a deadlock state of the test case is reached.

For the first iteration, the current state c of $C(I, O)$ is c_0.

A defined input i at the current state c is applied to FSM P; P produces an output o to i and the test case moves to the next state c', where $c \xrightarrow{io} c'$.

An input/output sequence α/γ is homing for FSM P if for every pair of states $p_1, p_2 \in P$, for which there exist traces tr_1 and tr_2 with the IO-projection α/γ, the tr_1-successor of p_1 and the tr_2-successor of p_2 coincide.

$C(I, O)$ is a homing test case for FSM $P = (P, I, O, h_P)$, i.e., a test case representing an adaptive homing sequence (AHS) for P, if for every trace tr

from the initial state to a deadlock state of $C(I, O)$ the IO-projection of tr is homing in P. In this case, the observation of such IO-sequence allows to uniquely determine the state of an FSM.

The following statement has been proved in [21]. Given a homing FSM P with n states and $|O|$ outputs represented by proper arrays, there exists a homing test case of the height at most n^3 with at most $(n-1)^2 n/2 + n + 1$ states and at most $|O|(n-1)^2 n/2$ transitions; the (time) complexity of deriving this test case is $O(|O|n^5)$.

3.2 Homing Test Case for an FSM with Timeouts

When talking about test cases representing an AHS for FSMs with timeouts, traces and IO-sequences of a test case become timed traces and timed IO-sequences. Thus, for every timed trace of the test case, the observation of the corresponding timed IO-projection has to guarantee that a non-initialized TFSM moves from every state $s \in S$ to the known state s' and, thus, the clock value must be taken into account.

Given an input alphabet I and an output alphabet O, a timed test case is an acyclic FSM with timeouts $Q(I, O) = (Q, I, O, \lambda_Q, \Delta_Q, q_0)$, where for every state either a finite timeout or a single input with all outputs is defined. By default, at each deadlock state the timeout is infinity. We also add a designated deadlock state $Fail$ to the timed test case and for every state q where an input is defined, a timeout transition of value 1 to state $Fail$ is added, i.e. $\Delta_Q(q) = (Fail, 1)$. By definition, a timed test case is a partial TFSM.

A timed test case $Q(I, O)$ is applied to a complete TFSM S using the procedure below until a deadlock state of the test case is reached.

For the first iteration, the current state q of $Q(I, O)$ is q_0.

If q is a non-deadlock current state where no input is defined then wait for time T_q that is a finite timeout value at state q; the test case moves to state q' where $q \xrightarrow{T_q} q'$.

If a current state q is a non-deadlock state where an input i is defined then wait for $\theta, 0 < \theta < 1$, apply input i and observe an output o produced by S; the test case moves to the state q' where $q \xrightarrow{io} q'$ and its next current state is q'.

Thus, the trace $q \xrightarrow{T_q} q' \xrightarrow{io} q''$ of a timed test case induces a timed input $(i, T_q + \theta)$ when the test case moves from q to q''.

Given a timed test case in Fig. 2 for the TFSM in Fig. 1. Since at the initial state finite timeout 2 is defined, we wait for 2 time units. At the next state, an input is defined and thus, we wait for $\theta = 0.5$ and apply i_1. Thus, timed input $(i_1, 2.5)$ is applied first. If the TFSM produces o_2 then the test case moves to state $\{s_3, s_4\}$ where input i_2 is defined; else if o_1 was produced then test case moves to state $\{s_1, s_2\}$ with the finite timeout. Correspondingly, at state $\{s_3, s_4\}$, we wait for $\theta = 0.5$ and apply i_2. Then the test case moves to the deadlock state and, since there is only one $i_2 o_1$-pair at $\{s_3, s_4\}$, we know that the current state of the TFSM in Fig. 1 is s_4.

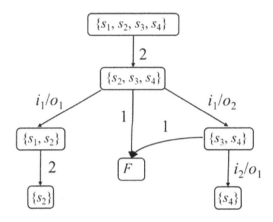

Fig. 2. A homing test case for TFSM S in Fig. 1.

After applying the above AHS in Fig. 2, we can conclude that if the TFSM in Fig. 1 at any initial state executes a trace with TIO-projection $2.5, i_1/o_2, 0.5, i_2/o_1$ then the TFSM reaches state s_4.

The height of a timed test case is the length of the longest (timed) input sequence that can be applied to an FSM (with timeouts) during the adaptive experiment; the latter equals the maximum number of inputs in a path from the initial to a deadlock state.

A TIO-sequence α/γ is *homing* for the TFSM S if for every pair of states $s_1, s_2 \in S$, for which there exist timed traces ttr_1 and ttr_2 with the TIO-projection α/γ, the ttr_1-successor of s_1 and the ttr_2-successor of s_2 coincide.

A timed test case $Q(I, O)$ represents an adaptive homing sequence (AHS) for FSM with timeouts S if for every trace ttr from the initial state q_0 to a deadlock state of $Q(I, O)$ different from state *Fail*, the TIO-projection of ttr is homing in S.

Informally a timed test case $Q(I, O)$ represents an adaptive homing sequence for FSM with timeouts S if for every timed input sequence α from initial to deadlock state of $Q(I, O)$, traces ttr_1 and ttr_2 induced by α at any pair of states s_1 and s_2 (possibly with different values of the clock variable) with different tr-successors have different TIO-projections. Thus, output responses of a homing TIO-projection correspond to the only reached state after an adaptive homing experiment and the current TFSM state can be uniquely determined.

For the TFSM in Fig. 1, a homing timed test case is shown in Fig. 2.

Note that when a homing test case is applied and the current state of the FSM with timeouts is known, the TFSM still can move to another state by timeout transitions. In order to set a TFSM to a state with the infinite timeout additional properties of an adaptive HS are required. In this paper, we do not discuss such test cases.

We also mention that there is a special case when an FSM with timeouts has the empty adaptive homing sequence, i.e. no input is applied for setting the

TFSM into the known state. It is the case when there exists a state that can be reached from every state only via timed transitions after appropriate time t. Thus, a timed test case has only two states, the initial state where a finite timeout is defined and a deadlock state, i.e., here is only one path of length 1 in the timed test case. As an example, if we replace timeout $\Delta_Q(s_3) = (s_4, 1)$ with $\Delta_Q(s_3) = (s_2, 1)$ in the TFSM in Fig. 1, then the modified TFSM moves to state s_2 after three time units independently of an initial state.

4   Homing Test Case Derivation

In this section, we propose an approach for deriving a homing test case based on the FSM abstraction of an FSM with timeouts.

4.1   FSM Abstraction

We first recall the notion of the FSM abstraction for FSMs with timeouts and the correspondence between traces of a TFSM and traces of the corresponding FSM abstraction [14].

Given a non-initialized possibly nondeterministic TFSM $S = (S, I, O, \lambda_S, \Delta_S)$, we derive the FSM abstraction $A_S = (S_A, I_A, O_A, h_{AS})$, where $I_A = I \bigcup \{1\}$, $O_A = O \bigcup \{1\}$ and the input/output 1 is an abstract input/output of the FSM abstraction denoting the time advancing. For each state s of TFSM S where $\Delta_S(s) = (s', T_s)$ and timeout T_s is finite, the set S_A has the states $(s, 0), \ldots,$ $(s, T_s - 1)$. Formally, $S_A = \{(s, x) : (s, x) \in S \times N \wedge x < T_s \wedge \Delta_S(s) = (s', T_s)$ $\wedge T_s < \infty\} \bigcup \{(s, 0) : s \in S\}$. Given state $(s, t_j) \in S_A$ of the FSM A_S and input i, a transition $((s, t_j), i, o, (s', 0))$ is a transition of the FSM abstraction A_S if and only if there exists a transition $(s, i, o, s') \in \lambda_S$. In other words, transitions under input $i \in I$ correspond to transitions under timed inputs (i, t) until the timeout at state s is expired. Transitions under the special abstract input 1 correspond to timeout transitions between states, i.e., to time advancing. Given state s such that $\Delta_S(s) = (s', T_s)$ where $0 < T_s < \infty$, there are transitions $((s, 0), 1, 1, (s, 1)), .., ((s, T_s - 2), 1, 1, (s, T_s - 1)), ((s, T_s - 1), 1, 1, (s', 0))$ in the transition relation h_{AS}. If $\Delta_S(s) = (s, \infty)$ then there is a transition $((s, 0), 1, 1, (s, 0)) \in h_{AS}$. By definition the number of states of the FSM abstraction is the sum of all finite timeouts plus the number of states when the timeout is infinite and thus, does not exceed the number of states of a given FSM with timeouts multiplied the maximum finite timeout at a state. In Fig. 3, there is the FSM abstraction of the TFSM in Fig. 1.

By definition, the FSM abstraction of a complete observable non-deterministic TFSM is a complete observable non-deterministic FSM; the FSM abstraction of a deterministic TFSM is a deterministic FSM.

A timed input sequence $\alpha = (i_1, t_1) \ldots (i_n, t_n)$ of the TFSM S can be transformed into the corresponding input sequence α_{FSM} of the FSM abstraction A_S as follows. Let $t_0 = 0$ and $\lfloor t \rfloor$ is the integer part of t then every timed

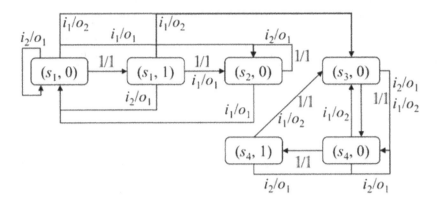

Fig. 3. The FSM abstraction of the TFSM S in Fig. 1.

input (i_k, t_k) is converted into the input sequence $\alpha_k = 1^{\lfloor t_k - t_{k-1} \rfloor} i_k$ where $k = 1, \ldots, n$ and, respectively, $\alpha_{FSM} = \alpha_1.\alpha_2.\ldots.\alpha_n$, where '.' is the concatenation operator. The corresponding output sequence of the FSM abstraction is $\gamma_{FSM} = 1^{\lfloor t_1 \rfloor} o_1.1^{\lfloor t_2 - t_1 \rfloor} o_2.\ldots.1^{\lfloor t_n - t_{n-1} \rfloor} o_n$, where $\gamma = o_1, o_2, \ldots, o_n$ is the output response of TFSM to a timed input sequence $\alpha = (i_1, t_1) \ldots (i_n, t_n)$. An input sequence $\alpha_{FSM} = 1^{T_0}.i_0.1^{T_1}.i_1 \ldots 1^{T_{n-1}}.i_{n-1}.1^{T_n}$ of the FSM abstraction A_S can be converted into a timed input sequence $\alpha = (i_0, t_0)(i_1, t_1) \ldots (i_{n-1}, t_{n-1})$ of the TFSM S where $t_0 = T_0, t_k = t_{k-1} + T_k + \theta$, where $0 < \theta < 1, 0 < k < n$. The corresponding output sequence γ is derived by removing all abstract outputs 1 from γ_{FSM}.

Thus, a timed trace $ttr = s_0 \xrightarrow{t_1} s_0' \xrightarrow{i_1 o_1} s_1 \xrightarrow{t_2} s_1' \xrightarrow{i_2 o_2} \ldots \xrightarrow{t_n} s_{n-1}' \xrightarrow{i_n o_n} s_n \xrightarrow{t_{n+1}} s_{n+1}$ of the TFSM S can be transformed into the corresponding trace $ttr_{FSM} = (s_0, 0) \xrightarrow{11} \ldots \xrightarrow{11} (s_0', x_0) \xrightarrow{i_1 o_1} (s_1, 0) \xrightarrow{11} \ldots \xrightarrow{11} (s_1', x_1) \xrightarrow{i_2 o_2} \ldots \xrightarrow{11} (s_{n-1}', x_{n-1}) \xrightarrow{i_n o_n} (s_n, 0) \xrightarrow{11} \ldots \xrightarrow{11} (s_{n+1}', x_{n+1})$ of the FSM abstraction A_S, where the number of transitions $\xrightarrow{11}$ between $(s_k, 0)$ and (s_k', x_k) is $\lfloor t_{k+1} \rfloor$. In other words, the input/output transition $s_{k-1} \xrightarrow{i_k o_k} s_k$ corresponds to the input/output transition $(s_{k-1}, x_{k-1}) \xrightarrow{i_k o_k} (s_k, 0)$ and the timed transition $s_{k-1} \xrightarrow{t} s_k$ corresponds to the trace $(s_k, 0) \xrightarrow{11} \ldots \xrightarrow{11} (s_k', x_k)$ with the number $\lfloor t \rfloor$ of transitions $\xrightarrow{11}$.

The following statement can be proven based on [14].

Proposition 1. *A timed input sequence $\alpha = (i_1, t_1) \ldots (i_n, t_n)$ of the TFSM S induces a timed trace ttr with the TIO-projection $\alpha/\gamma = t_1, i_1/o_1, t_2 - t_1, i_2/o_2, \ldots, t_n - t_{n-1}, i_n/o_n, t_{n+1} - t_n$ at state s if and only if the input sequence $\alpha_{FSM} = 1^{\lfloor t_1 \rfloor} i_1.1^{\lfloor t_2 - t_1 \rfloor} i_2.\ldots.1^{\lfloor t_n - t_{n-1} \rfloor} i_n.1^{\lfloor t_{n+1} - t_n \rfloor}$ of the FSM abstraction A_S induces a trace ttr_{FSM} with the IO-projection $\alpha_{FSM}/\gamma_{FSM} = (1/1)^{\lfloor t_1 \rfloor} i_1/o_1.(1/1)^{\lfloor t_2 - t_1 \rfloor} i_2/o_2.\ldots.(1/1)^{\lfloor t_n - t_{n-1} \rfloor} i_n/o_n, (1/1)^{\lfloor t_{n+1} - t_n \rfloor}$ at state (s, x).*

Corollary 1. *Given an FSM with timeouts S and its FSM abstraction A_S, state s' is the ttr-successor of state s if and only if state (s', x') is the ttr_{FSM}-successor of state (s, x) in A_S.*

Thus, in order to derive a homing sequence for a TFSM based on its FSM abstraction the following correspondence can be established between homing TIO-sequences of the TFSM and homing IO-sequences for its FSM abstraction.

Corollary 2. *Given an FSM with timeouts S, its FSM abstraction A_S and a TIO-sequence $\alpha/\gamma = t_1, i_1/o_1, t_2 - t_1, i_2/o_2, \ldots, t_n - t_{n-1}, i_n/o_n, t_{n+1} - t_n$, the TIO-sequence α/γ is homing if and only if the IO-sequence $\alpha_{FSM}/\gamma_{FSM} = (1/1)^{\lfloor t_1 \rfloor} i_1/o_1.(1/1)^{\lfloor t_2 - t_1 \rfloor} i_2/o_2. \ldots .(1/1)^{\lfloor t_n - t_{n-1} \rfloor} i_n/o_n.(1/1)^{\lfloor t_{n+1} - t_n \rfloor}$ is homing in A_S.*

4.2 Algorithm for Checking the Existence and Derivation of an Adaptive HS for FSM

Since an adaptive HS for a TFSM with timeouts is derived based on its FSM abstraction, we next recall an approach for deriving a homing test case for a classical FSM [24].

Algorithm 1 for deriving an adaptive HS for an FSM abstraction

Input: A complete non-initialized observable possibly non-deterministic FSM abstraction $A_S = (S_A, I_A, O_A, h_{AS})$

Output: The message 'There is no HS for A_S' or a homing test case $C(I_A, O_A)$ for FSM A_S that represents an adaptive HS

Step 1. Derive the homing FSM $P^L_{home} = (P_H, I_A, O_A, h_{PH}, p_0)$ for A_S where states of P^L_{home} are subsets of S_A with cardinality at least two, initial state $p_0 = S_A$ and special state F. Only states reachable from p_0 are added to P_H while h_{PH} is derived iteratively up to length $|S_A|^3$.

Let $P^0_{home} = (\{p_0, F\}, I_A, O_A, h^0_{PH}, p_0)$ has states p_0 and F and every transition takes P^0_{home} to state F, i.e., $h^0_{PH} = \{(p_0, i, o, F), (F, i, o, F) : i \in I_A, o \in O_A\}$. Initial state p_0 is marked.

Step 2. Homing FSM P^{l+1}_{home} is derived based on P^l_{home}. Let p be a marked state of P^l_{home}; then transitions from this state in h^l_{PH} are replaced with new ones in h^{l+1}_{PH} by the following rules:

1. $(p, i, o, F) \in h^{l+1}_{PH}$ if there exist $o' \in O$, such that the set of states $\left\{ (s', 0) : (s, 0) \xrightarrow{io'} (s', 0) \wedge (s, 0) \in p \right\}$ coincides with set p.

2. if for every $o' \in O$ $p' = \left\{ (s', 0) : (s, 0) \xrightarrow{io'} (s', 0) \wedge (s, 0) \in p \right\}$ do not coincide with set p and has cardinality at least two, then $(p, i, o, p') \in h^{l+1}_{PH}$. If p' is not state of P^l_{home} then a marked state p' is added to the FSM P^{l+1}_{home}, $h^{l+1}_{PH} = h^{l+1}_{PH} \cup \{(p', i, o, F) : i \in I_A, o \in O_A\}$.

3. the transition at state p under input i is undefined if for every o' the set $\left\{ (s', 0) : (s, 0) \xrightarrow{io'} (s', 0) \wedge (s, 0) \in p \right\}$ is a singleton or the empty set.

When transitions for every input at state p are added, p becomes unmarked in P_{home}^{l+1}.

Step 3. If $\mathsf{P}_{home}^{l+1} = \mathsf{P}_{home}^{l}$ then output the message 'There is no HS for $\mathsf{A_S}$' and **END** the algorithm.

Check whether the FSM P_{home}^{l+1} has a complete submachine by iterative deleting states with an undefined input from P_{home}^{l+1}. State p is removed with all incoming transitions if there exists an undefined input i at p. The process of removing states is not terminated until either there are no undefined inputs in P_{home}^{l+1} or the initial state of P_{home}^{l+1} has an undefined input. When removing a state p with undefined inputs, we denote such undefined input by $i(p)$. If the initial state of P_{home}^{l+1} has an undefined input then P_{home}^{l+1} has no complete submachine.

If P_{home}^{l+1} has no complete submachine then **Step 4**, else if $l + 1 = |S_A|^3$ then output the message 'There is no timed adaptive HS for S' else $l = l + 1$ and **Step 2**.

Step 4. Derive a homing test case $\mathsf{C}(I_A, O_A)$ for FSM abstraction $\mathsf{A_S}$ based on stored undefined inputs $i(p)$ of P_{home}^{l+1}. $\mathsf{C}(I_A, O_A) = (C, I_A, O_A, h_\mathsf{C}, c_0)$ where $C \subseteq P_H, c_0 = p_0$ and input $i(p)$ is the only defined input at state $c = p$ in C; $(c, i(p), o, c') \in h_\mathsf{C}$ if $(p, i(p), o, p') \in h_{\mathsf{PH}}^{l+1}$, where $c' = p'$. If for $o \in O_A$ there is no transition $(p, i(p), o, p')$ in h_{PH}^{l+1} then the transition $(c, i(p), o, D)$ is added to h_{PH}^{l+1} where D is a deadlock state.

Here we notice that the upper bound $|S_A|^3$ for deriving a homing FSM is implied by the following statement [20]. If a complete observable FSM with n states has an AHS then the length of a shortest AHS does not exceed n^3. Moreover, in [21], the authors show that the complexity of checking the existence of an AHS for a complete observable possibly nondeterministic FSM with n states and an output alphabet O is $O(|O|n^5)$. A homing test case for the FSM abstraction in Fig. 3 is presented in Fig. 4.

4.3   Algorithm for Checking the Existence and Derivation of a Homing Timed Test Case

In this section, we propose an algorithm for the derivation of a homing timed test case for an FSM with timeouts based on its FSM abstraction.

We first check whether an AHS exists for the FSM abstraction calling Algorithm 1. If there is no AHS for the FSM abstraction then there is no timed AHS for the given FSM with timeouts (Corollary 2). However, when an AHS exists for the FSM abstraction then a corresponding test case has to be converted to a timed test case. The proposed algorithm for transforming an FSM test case to a timed test case is proposed below.

Algorithm 2 Derivation of a timed homing test case based on a homing test case for the FSM abstraction.

Input: A homing test case $\mathsf{C}(I_A, O_A) = (C, I_A, O_A, h_\mathsf{C}, c_0)$ for the FSM abstraction.

Output: A homing timed test case $\mathsf{Q}(I, O) = (Q, I, O, \lambda_\mathsf{Q}, \Delta_\mathsf{Q}, q_0)$.

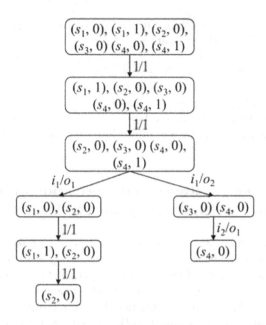

Fig. 4. A homing test case for the FSM abstraction in Fig. 3.

Step 1. The set of states Q of the timed test case $Q(I, O)$ is a subset of the state set C of $C(I_A, O_A)$; states of $Q(I, O)$ are states of $C(I_A, O_A)$ with incoming or outgoing transitions induced by input from I and deadlock states (i.e., $Q(I, O)$ has no abstract input 1). Denote this correspondence as $q = St(c)$.

Step 2. Let state q be a state of $Q(I, O)$ such that $q = St(c)$ and c is a state of $C(I_A, O_A)$:

$\Delta_Q(q) = (q', T)$ if there exists a trace tr at state c such that c' is the tr-successor of c, $(1/1)^T$ is an IO-projection of tr and $q' = St(c')$;

$(q, i, o, q') \in \lambda_Q$ if $(c, i, o, c') \in h_C$, where $i \neq 1$ and $q' = St(c')$.

Step 3. For every state q of $Q(I, O)$ with a defined input $\Delta_Q(q) = (Fail, 1)$; for every deadlock state of $Q(I, O)$ the timeout is the infinity.

Proposition 2. *Let timed test case $Q(I, O)$ be derived by Algorithm 2 for test case $C(I_A, O_A)$. The test case $Q(I, O)$ is homing for FSM with timeouts S if and only if test case $C(I_A, O_A)$ is homing for FSM A_S.*

Proof. Due to Proposition 1, there exists a trace ttr_{FSM} at state (s, x) of FSM abstraction A_S if and only if there exists a timed trace ttr at state s of the FSM with timeouts S. Moreover, the IO-projection $\alpha_{FSM}/\gamma_{FSM}$ of ttr_{FSM} is homing in A_S if and only if the TIO-projection α/γ of ttr is homing in S. Respectively, for trace ttr_{FSM} from the initial state to a deadlock state of $C(I_A, O_A)$, the IO-projection is homing in A_S if and only if the TIO-projection is homing in S for trace ttr from the initial state to a deadlock state of $Q(I, O)$.

Thus, we propose the following procedure of the homing timed test case derivation for an FSM with timeouts S.

1. Derive the FSM abstraction $A_S = (S_A, I_A, O_A, h_{AS})$ for TFSM S and call Algorithm 1 for checking the existence and derivation of a homing test case $C(I_A, O_A) = (C, I_A, O_A, h_C, c_0)$ if such a test case exists. If there is no homing test case for A_S then there is no adaptive HS for S.
2. Call Algorithm 2 for deriving a homing timed test case $Q(I, O)$ from test case $C(I_A, O_A)$.

5   Checking the Existence and Derivation of an Adaptive Synchronizing Sequence for an FSM with Timeouts

Another input sequence allowing to set a system under test into the known state is a so-called synchronizing sequence. Intuitively a homing sequence is a synchronizing sequence (SS) if there exists a special state s such that an FSM under test reaches s after applying this input sequence independently of the initial state and produced output sequence. For an adaptive SS, the designated state is reached after applying an adaptive input sequence where next input depends on the outputs to the previous inputs. We first remind the definition of an adaptive SS (ASS) for a classical complete and observable FSM and then define an adaptive SS for an FSM with timeouts.

Given a state p' of the FSM P, an input/output sequence α/γ is p'-synchronizing if for every state $p \in P$ for which there exists a trace tr with the IO-projection α/γ, the tr-successor of p is p'. Similar to an AHS, an ASS is represented by a corresponding test case. A test case $C(I, O)$ is a p'-synchronizing for FSM $P = (P, I, O, h_P)$, i.e., a test case representing an adaptive p'-synchronizing sequence (ASS), if for every trace tr from the initial state to a deadlock state of $C(I, O)$, the IO-projection of tr is p'-synchronizing in P. In this case, after applying a corresponding input sequence, the FSM under test reaches state p' independently of the initial state.

In [21], it is shown that a non-initialized observable FSM has a homing test case if and only if each pair of states is homing, i.e., FSM can be set to a known state from each pair of states. In the same paper, corresponding necessary and sufficient conditions are established for a synchronizing test case. Given a complete observable non-initialized FSM P, state $p' \in P$ is (adaptively) definitely-reachable (d-reachable) from state $p \in P$ if there exists a test case $D(p, p')$ such that for every trace tr of $D(p, p')$ from the initial state to a deadlock state, the tr'-successor of state p in FSM P is either the empty set or the state p', where tr and tr' have the same IO-projection. We hereafter refer to such a test case as a d-transfer test case. There exists a p'-synchronizing test case for FSM P if and only if the P has a homing test case and a state p' that is d-reachable from any other state.

An efficient method for checking whether a state $p' \in P$ is d-reachable from state p is presented in [21]. In particular, it is proven that state p' is d-reachable from state p if and only if P has a single-input acyclic submachine P′, i.e., a submachine where at most one input is defined at every state and the transition graph has no cycles, with the initial state p and the only deadlock state $p′$ such that for each input defined in some state of P′, this state has all the transitions of P labeled with this input. Note that since any d-transfer test case $D(p, p′)$ is an acyclic submachine of the machine P, then the length of any trace in $D(p, p′)$ does not exceed the number n of states of P. In other words, one needs at most $n - 1$ inputs to adaptively transfer the possibly nondeterministic machine from state p to state $p′$. Therefore, the length of a longest trace in a shortest test case $D(p, p′)$ is polynomial and is at most $n - 1$.

Given a non-initialized complete observable FSM P, if there is no state $p′$ that is d-reachable for any other state then FSM P has no synchronizing test case. On the other hand, if there exists state $p′$ that is d-reachable for any other state then this condition does not guarantee that the FSM has a $p′$-synchronizing test case; the homing test case must also exist for the FSM.

An algorithm for deriving an ASS for non-initialized complete observable FSM P has the following steps.

1. Call Algorithm 1. If there is no AHS for an FSM P, then there is no ASS for this FSM, else a corresponding homing test case $C(I, O)$ is derived.
2. If there is no state $p′$ that is adaptively d-reachable from every state p of P, then there is no ASS for this FSM; else for each deadlock state c of $C(I, O)$ marked by $\{p\}$ add a test case $D(p, p′)$ in order to derive an adaptive $p′$-synchronizing test case.

Given a state $s′$ of TFSM S, a TIO-sequence α/γ is $s′$-synchronizing for S if for every state $s \in S$, for which there exists a timed trace ttr with the TIO-projection α/γ, the ttr-successor of s is $s′$.

A timed test case $Q(I, O)$ represents an adaptive $s′$-synchronizing sequence (AHS) for an FSM with timeouts S if there exists state $s′$ such that for every trace tr from the initial state q_0 to a deadlock state of $Q(I, O)$ different from state *Fail*, the TIO-projection of tr is $s′$-synchronizing in S.

Informally a timed test case $Q(I, O)$ represents an ASS for TFSM S if there exists a state $s′$ such that for every timed input sequence α from the initial to the deadlock state of $Q(I, O)$, a trace tr induced by α at any state s has an $s′$-synchronizing TIO-projection, i.e., the trace is ended at state $s′$.

Based on Proposition 1 the following statement holds.

Proposition 3. *Let timed test case $Q(s, s′)$ be derived by Algorithm 2 for test case $D((s, x), (s′, x))$. The timed test case $Q(s, s′)$ is a d-transfer test case for FSM with timeouts S if and only if the test case $D((s, x), (s′, x))$ is a d-transfer test case for FSM A_S.*

Therefore, a timed an ASS for an FSM with timeouts can be derived using the following steps.

1. If there is no AHS for FSM abstraction A_S of TFSM S, then there is no ASS for S, else derive a corresponding homing test case $C(I_A, O_A)$ for A_S.

2. If there is no state $(s', 0)$ that is d-reachable from every state of A_S, then there is no ASS for this FSM; else for each deadlock state c of $C(I_A, O_A)$ marked by $\{(s, 0)\}$ add a d-transfer test case $D((s, 0), (s', 0))$.
3. Call Algorithm 2 to convert a derived test case to the timed test case.

Proposition 4. *Let timed test case $Q(I, O)$ be derived by Algorithm 2 for test case $C(I_A, O_A)$. The timed test case $Q(I, O)$ is s'-synchronizing for FSM with timeouts S if and only if the test case $C(I_A, O_A)$ is $(s', 0)$-synchronizing for FSM A_S.*

Similar to AHS, the length of a shortest ASS and the time complexity of the ASS derivation can be evaluated based on the number of states of the FSM abstraction [20].

Here we notice that given the maximum value of the finite timeout T_{max} at a state, the length of a shortest AHS and ASS is cubic with respect to $(T_{max}n)$ and in the cases when T_{max} is rather small, two or three, for example, the length of a shortest AHS and ASS is much less than the upper bound for the length of a preset HS for a nondeterministic FSM that can be exponential in this case. However, this advantage disappears in the case when finite timeouts are rather big.

Similar to homing test cases, when a synchronizing test case is applied and the current state of the FSM with timeouts is known, the TFSM still can move to another state by timeout transitions. In order to avoid this, a TFSM has to be set into a state with the infinite timeout.

6   Conclusions

In this paper, we propose the notions of adaptive homing and synchronizing sequences for FSMs with timeouts. For this purpose, we introduce the notion of a timed test case which represents an adaptive timed input sequence. We have also proposed algorithms for deriving such state identification sequences based on the FSM abstraction of a timed FSM. All the statements are proven for complete and observable FSMs with timeouts. However, once there is a corresponding solution for a possibly partial or non-observable FSM, the corresponding procedures can be constructed for a corresponding FSM with timeouts.

As a future work, we are going to consider distinguishing sequences for FSMs with timeouts as well as state identification sequences of a special kind which take an FSM with timeouts to a state where the FSM does not change states without applying an input, i.e., the FSM is taken to a state with the infinite timeout. An interesting question is how to extend the obtained results to FSMs which have both timed guards and timeouts. Another interesting question is how to minimize the number of states of the FSM abstraction preserving its abilities for deriving AHS and ASS. We started this work in [25] but only for FSMs with timed guards.

Another promising avenue is to apply the obtained results for minimizing testing efforts for protocol implementations, since the protocol descriptions often include timeouts.

Acknowledgements. This work is partly supported by the RSF project № 22-29-01189.

References

1. Gill, A.: Introduction to the Theory of Finite-State Machines. McGraw-Hill, New York (1962)
2. Lee, D., Yannakakis, M.: Testing finite state machines: state identification and verification. IEEE Trans. Comput. **43**(3), 306–320 (1994)
3. Hibbard, T.N.: Least upper bounds on minimal terminal state experiments of two classes of sequential machines. J. ACM **8**(4), 601–612 (1961)
4. Kohavi, Z.: Switching and Finite Automata Theory. McGraw-Hill, New York (1978)
5. Wang, H.-E., Tu, K.-H., Jiang, J.-H.R., Kushik, N.: Homing sequence derivation with quantified Boolean satisfiability. In: Yevtushenko, N., Cavalli, A.R., Yenigün, H. (eds.) ICTSS 2017. LNCS, vol. 10533, pp. 230–242. Springer, Cham (2017). https://doi.org/10.1007/978-3-319-67549-7_14
6. Yenigün, H., Yevtushenko, N., Kushik, N., López, J.: The effect of partiality and adaptivity on the complexity of FSM state identification problems. Trudy ISP RAN/Proc. ISP RAS **30**(1), 7–24 (2018)
7. Kushik, N., Yevtushenko, N.: On the length of homing sequences for nondeterministic finite state machines. In: Konstantinidis, S. (ed.) CIAA 2013. LNCS, vol. 7982, pp. 220–231. Springer, Heidelberg (2013). https://doi.org/10.1007/978-3-642-39274-0_20
8. Sandberg, S.: 1 homing and synchronizing sequences. In: Broy, M., Jonsson, B., Katoen, J.-P., Leucker, M., Pretschner, A. (eds.) Model-Based Testing of Reactive Systems. LNCS, vol. 3472, pp. 5–33. Springer, Heidelberg (2005). https://doi.org/10.1007/11498490_2
9. Kushik, N., López, J., Cavalli, A., Yevtushenko, N.: Improving protocol passive testing through "Gedanken" experiments with finite state machines. In: Proceedings of IEEE International Conference on Software Quality, Reliability and Security, Vienna, Austria, 1–3 August, pp. 315–322. IEEE (2016)
10. Hennie, F.C.: Fault detecting experiments for sequential circuits. In: Proceedings of Fifth Annual Symposium on Circuit Theory and Logical Design, Princeton, USA, 11–13 November, pp. 95–110. IEEE (1965)
11. Krichen, M., Tripakis, S.: Conformance testing for real-time systems. Formal Methods Syst. Des. **34**, 238–304 (2009)
12. El-Fakih, K., Yevtushenko, N., Fouchal, H.: Testing timed finite state machines with guaranteed fault coverage. In: Núñez, M., Baker, P., Merayo, M.G. (eds.) FATES/TestCom -2009. LNCS, vol. 5826, pp. 66–80. Springer, Heidelberg (2009). https://doi.org/10.1007/978-3-642-05031-2_5
13. Merayo, M.G., Núñez, M., Rodriguez, I.: Formal testing from timed finite state machines. Comput. Networks **52**(2), 432–460 (2008)
14. Bresolin, D., El-Fakih, K., Villa, T., Yevtushenko, N.: Deterministic timed finite state machines: equivalence checking and expressive power. In: Proceedings of International Conference GANDALF, Verona, Italy, 10–12 September, pp. 203–216 (2014)
15. Gromov, M., El-Fakih, K., Shabaldina, N., Yevtushenko, N.: Distinguing nondeterministic timed finite state machines. In: Lee, D., Lopes, A., Poetzsch-Heffter, A. (eds.) FMOODS/FORTE -2009. LNCS, vol. 5522, pp. 137–151. Springer, Heidelberg (2009). https://doi.org/10.1007/978-3-642-02138-1_9

16. Kushik, N., El-Fakih, K., Yevtushenko, N.: Adaptive homing and distinguishing experiments for nondeterministic finite state machines. In: Yenigün, H., Yilmaz, C., Ulrich, A. (eds.) ICTSS 2013. LNCS, vol. 8254, pp. 33–48. Springer, Heidelberg (2013). https://doi.org/10.1007/978-3-642-41707-8_3

17. Kushik, N., Yenigün, H.: Heuristics for deriving adaptive homing and distinguishing sequences for nondeterministic finite state machines. In: El-Fakih, K., Barlas, G., Yevtushenko, N. (eds.) ICTSS 2015. LNCS, vol. 9447, pp. 243–248. Springer, Cham (2015). https://doi.org/10.1007/978-3-319-25945-1_15

18. Yenigün, H., Yevtushenko, N., Kushik, N.: The complexity of checking the existence and derivation of adaptive synchronizing experiments for deterministic FSMs. Inf. Process. Lett. **127**, 49–53 (2017)

19. Doyen, L., Juhl, L., Larsen, K. G., Markey, N., Shirmohammadi, M.: Synchronizing words for weighted and timed automata. In: 34th International Conference on Foundation of Software Technology and Theoretical Computer Science, New Delhi, 15–17 December. Leibniz International Proceedings in Informatics, vol. 29, pp. 121–132 (2014)

20. Kushik, N., El-Fakih, K., Yevtushenko, N., Cavalli, A.R.: On adaptive experiments for nondeterministic finite state machines. Int. J. Softw. Tools Technol. Transf. **18**(3), 251–264 (2014). https://doi.org/10.1007/s10009-014-0357-7

21. Yevtushenko, N., Kuliamin, V., Kushik, N.: Evaluating the complexity of deriving adaptive homing, synchronizing and distinguishing sequences for nondeterministic FSMs. In: Gaston, C., Kosmatov, N., Le Gall, P. (eds.) ICTSS 2019. LNCS, vol. 11812, pp. 86–103. Springer, Cham (2019). https://doi.org/10.1007/978-3-030-31280-0_6

22. Kushik, N., El-Fakih, K., Yevtushenko, N.: Preset and adaptive homing experiments for nondeterministic finite state machines. In: Bouchou-Markhoff, B., Caron, P., Champarnaud, J.-M., Maurel, D. (eds.) CIAA 2011. LNCS, vol. 6807, pp. 215–224. Springer, Heidelberg (2011). https://doi.org/10.1007/978-3-642-22256-6_20

23. Petrenko, A., Yevtushenko, N.: Conformance tests as checking experiments for partial nondeterministic FSM. In: Grieskamp, W., Weise, C. (eds.) FATES 2005. LNCS, vol. 3997, pp. 118–133. Springer, Heidelberg (2006). https://doi.org/10.1007/11759744_9

24. Kushik, N., Yevtushenko, N.: Adaptive homing is in P. Electron. Proc. Theor. Comput. Sci. **180**, 73–78 (2015)

25. Tvardovskii, A.S., Yevtushenko, N.V.: Deriving homing sequences for finite state machines with timed guards. Aut. Control Comput. Sci. **55**, 738–750 (2021)

Author Index

Alhazov, Artiom   27
Aman, Bogdan   42

Blanc, Manon   58
Bournez, Olivier   58

Cienciala, Luděk   75
Ciencialová, Lucie   75
Csuhaj-Varjú, Erzsébet   75

Demaine, Erik D.   91
Drastík, Jan   158

Formenti, Enrico   1
Freund, Rudolf   27

Hearn, Robert A.   91
Hendrickson, Dylan   91

Ivanov, Sergiu   27

Lynch, Jayson   91

Nagy, Benedek   109

Olejár, Viktor   126
Orellana-Martín, David   143

Pérez-Jiménez, Mario J.   143

Sosík, Petr   158
Szabari, Alexander   126

Truthe, Bianca   12
Tvardovskii, Aleksandr   172

Valencia-Cabrera, Luis   143
Verlan, Sergey   27

Yevtushenko, Nina   172

Printed in the United States
by Baker & Taylor Publisher Services

Printed in the United States
by Baker & Taylor Publisher Services

Printed in the United States
by Baker & Taylor Publisher Services